ARKANA

The Karmic Journey

Judy Hall has been exploring the links between reincarnation and astrology for the past fifteen years. Her astrological training has been long and varied but has principally involved studying and working with Howard Sasportas to explore the links between psychology and astrology. Her psychic 'far memory' training was facilitated by a long and close friendship with the late Christine Hartley. She now works as a Karmic Counsellor and utilizes various healing techniques in her therapeutic work. She runs workshops all over the country and at her beautiful Dorset home to enable participants to explore their own karma.

CONTEMPORARY ASTROLOGY
Series Editor: Howard Sasportas

Judy Hall

THE KARMIC JOURNEY

The Birthchart, Karma and Reincarnation

ARKANA

ARKANA

Published by the Penguin Group
Penguin Books Ltd, 27 Wrights Lane, London w8 5tz, England
Viking Penguin, a division of Penguin Books USA Inc
375 Hudson Street, New York, New York 10014, USA
Penguin Books Australia Ltd, Ringwood, Victoria, Australia
Penguin Books Canada Ltd, 2801 John Street, Markham, Ontario, Canada l3r 1b4
Penguin Books (NZ) Ltd, 182–190 Wairau Road, Auckland 10, New Zealand

Penguin Books Ltd, Registered Offices: Harmondsworth, Middlesex, England

First published 1990
1 3 5 7 9 10 8 6 4 2

Made and printed in Great Britain by
Clays Ltd, St Ives plc

Filmset in Linotron Sabon by
Rowland Phototypesetting Ltd, Bury St Edmunds, Suffolk

For Bayer with love

May your life-path be one of love, joy and fulfilment

You can't kill the Spirit
She is like a mountain
Old but strong, going on and on and on . . .

CONTENTS

ACKNOWLEDGEMENTS 11

INTRODUCTION
THROUGH DEATH TO REBIRTH   13

CHAPTER 1
CHARTING THE JOURNEY   35

*Karmic Dilemmas   Will and Karma   Collective Karma
The Karmic Houses   Planets in the Twelfth House
Karmic Aspects   Karmic Potential*

CHAPTER 2
WHERE ARE WE GOING?   87

*Nodes in Signs and Houses   Reversed Nodal
Placement   Aspects to the Nodes   Murder, Mayhem and
Nodal Conflict   The Nodes in Relationships
Resolution of the Nodal Dilemma*

CHAPTER 3
SIGNPOSTS ALONG THE WAY   135

*The Ascendant   The Moon through the Signs
The Sun through the Signs   Chiron: The Wound of the Soul
Chiron in Aspect and Houses*

CHAPTER 4
BURDENS AND BAGGAGE   180

*The Karma of Health   Planets in the Sixth House   Sexual
Malfunctioning   Gender Difficulties   Aids   Patterns of
'Dis-ease'   The 'Sins' of Omission and Commission
The Elements   Stillbirth and Suicide*

CHAPTER 5
FELLOW TRAVELLERS 236

*Nature Versus Nurture   Facing Up to Incarnation: Ascendant
and First House   Emotional Expectations   Parental Karma
and Family Interaction   Synastry between Charts
The Fourth–Tenth House Axis   Sibling Karma: the Third
House   Ancestral Karma   Relationship Karma in Action*

CHAPTER 6
COMPANIONS ALONG THE WAY 293

*Planets in the Seventh House   Planets in the Eighth
House   Synastry and Karma*

CONCLUSION
JOURNEY'S END? 328

APPENDIX I
CASE STUDY: 'PEOPLE AND PURPOSE' 331

APPENDIX II
CASE STUDY: FAMILY INTERACTION 341

NOTES 349

GLOSSARY 355

CHART SOURCES 358

BIBLIOGRAPHY 359

COPYRIGHT PERMISSIONS 363

INDEX 365

ACKNOWLEDGEMENTS

First of all to Robert Jacobs for the beautiful painting which has been my inspiration and which now forms the cover for this book; and for all his love, support, good food and cups of coffee during the writing of this book, go my love and many thanks. Also to the six small furry secretary-people who gave me so much love and purr therapy when I needed encouragement, I couldn't have done it without you all.

And to my daughter Jeni and her husband Paul, for all their help and for being here and making the world a nicer place, much love.

To Anthony, Earl of Shaftesbury, my heartfelt loving thanks for providing such a beautiful space in which to write.

I must thank my teachers Christine Hartley, Robert Tully, Thelma Reardon and Howard Sasportas for all the wisdom they imparted to me over the years. And to Howard my particular thanks for encouraging me to write this book in the first place. Also, to all those others whose work I have absorbed over many years of study and used without acknowledgement, my apologies and thanks.

To Jacqueline Clare my very special thanks for her beautiful chart drawings so caringly produced.

To Judy Holland my most grateful thanks for her meticulous work and helpful comments on my rough draft; and also to Liz Moore for her friendship and wonderful work on my feet; to Beata Bishop for her insight and humour; and Helen Lowson for facilitating my inward journey during writing.

To Claire Massy especial love and thanks for her openness and courage in sharing her own karmic journey with me for use in this book.

Alan Humphries led me beyond the bounds of karma and into a place of infinite possibilities — my own being.

My article, on which Chapters 5 and 6 are based, together with 'Murder, Mayhem and Nodal Conflict' in Chapter 2, first appeared in the *Astrological Journal*. My thanks to Zach Matthews for allowing the use of these and other articles from the *Journal*.

I am most grateful to John Lahr, Jonathan Cott and the estate of the late Christine Hartley for permission to quote at length from their work, and to publishers CRCS, Element Books, Anodyne, The Aquarian Press and The Women's Press for their assistance.

And to that old wise woman Julie Felix for the words to '*Graduation Day*' and for her continuing love and friendship, *amor y muchas gracias*.

And finally, to all my clients and workshops participants, who have helped me to learn so much about lives and living, my loving wish for happy lives.

Introduction
Through Death to Rebirth . . .

I hold that when a person dies
His soul returns again to earth;
Arrayed in some new flesh-disguise
. . . the old soul takes the road again,
My road shall be the road I made,
All that I gave shall be repaid.

John Masefield, 'A Creed'

Karmic astrology is based on the premise that Man is an eternal, spiritual being who reincarnates into a physical body, meeting karma generated in past lives, and that the pattern of those past lives can be identified in the chart for the moment of birth, as can the structure and purpose of the present incarnation. The motivating basis of life is perceived as one of compensation and expansion, which take place through successive incarnations into physical and spiritual bodies. This is the karmic journey of the soul of Man on its evolutionary journey towards perfection.

In the East the life of man is held to be a pilgrimage, not only from the cradle to the grave, but also through that vast period of time, stretching from the beginning to the end of a period of evolution, and as such he is held to be a spiritual being, the continuity of his existence is unbroken . . . starting from the great ALL, radiating like a spark from the central fire, he gathers experience in all ages, under all rulers, civilisations and customs, ever engaged in a pilgrimage to the shrine from which he came.[1]

It is not, however, necessary to believe in reincarnation in order to utilize an understanding of karmic patterns. Karma is the working of the law of cause and effect, the 'reaping of what has been sown', an activity which has been set in motion *at some point in the past*. The past is whatever has gone before in the particular time-frame one is utilizing. It is therefore possible to read a chart from the karmic perspective without necessarily relating it back to former incarnations.

The potential for moving back into past lives, however, adds another dimension to the birthchart, a deeper level of esoteric meaning, and can explain why natal aspects manifest in different ways according to the previous experience of the incarnating soul. If each baby incarnated with a 'clean slate', it would be logical to expect, particularly from the astrological perspective, its temperament, reaction and approach to the environment into which it is born to be exactly the same as that of another born at the same time, allowing of course for cultural and parental differences. This is manifestly not the case, however. Although sharing some basic characteristics astrological twins, born at the same moment in time, will express themselves differently. Identical twins, born in the same place and into the same family, nevertheless have their own distinct temperament from birth which cannot totally be accounted for, astrologically, by the relatively short time separating entry into the world, or purely by 'pre-existence as a foetus' during the intra-uterine experience. It can be argued that: 'Personality is the creation of the parental and ancestral biological inheritance, and is conditioned by social environment. It is an incidental experiment for the widening experience of the individual soul'[2]. However, in the here and now, the personality is the incarnating soul's way of presenting itself to the world *in this particular lifetime*. The concept that each baby is a soul incarnating with the weight of the past experience of many lifetimes behind it more adequately explains individual difference and the 'inherent' personality. The soul is encountering its karma:

Karma is the principle of universal causality, perpetuated by one's actions. Every thought, word or deed and desire, has a dynamic quality, producing good or bad results. Some simple act of charity may change a life or mould a destiny. Actions give rise to effects, and the sum total of these actions determines the nature, status and circumstances of happiness or misery of a person in his next life, and so on from incarnation to incarnation.[3]

In *The Astrology of Fate* Liz Greene considers why some people experience particularly difficult lifescripts – 'a catalogue of apparently unmerited human vicissitudes'[4]. She comments that she 'cannot talk glibly about karma as many astrologers do, and imply that it was something to do with one's previous incarnations so not to worry, just close your eyes and think of England . . .'[5] For her, the explanation is seemingly a different one:

> As with many people the presence of extreme suffering invokes in me the question of meaning. But for me, the roads of human perversity and catastrophe . . . lead to fate . . . Fate means: It has been written. For something to be written with such immovability by an unseen hand is terrifying . . . and such a vision of fate threatens an experience of real despair, or a chaotic abreaction when the spinal column of the moral and ethical man collapses.[6]

With respect, it would seem that here she is missing the point of reincarnation. Fate may imply, in the traditional Eastern approach, 'an unseen hand' at work. Equally, however, if one includes the concept of free will in reincarnation, the incarnating soul can choose to encounter the result of its own handiwork or to make reparation for the past – no matter how hard a present life that may lead to. It is extremely difficult to evaluate the long-term spiritual effects of traumatic or painful karmic experiences upon the eternal Self; the working of karma is in any case subtle and far from straightforward. In the fatalistic approach the rule is 'an eye for an eye, a tooth for a tooth'. If a man murders, he will become a victim; if he injures, he will be injured. However, there are many ways of making reparation. The murderer may achieve a degree of spiritual enlightenment and choose a life of service. It does not appear to be necessary to make direct repayment to the person who has been injured, although the choice may be made to do so. Once the incarnating soul has found another to whom a debt is

owed, to perform the appropriate task will be sufficient reparation. Neither does it seem to be necessary to fulfil every last duty or
debt. There is a point when enough has been done, understanding
has been reached, and the soul is freed from the karmic round.

Belief in karma and reincarnation does not exclude a belief in
fate, or chance, nor does it imply the fatalistic view that 'what will
be, will be', or that the future is fixed and unmoving, with no
evolution. 'Fate' is capricious and punitive and offers no explanation as to *why* people suffer, other than perhaps the medieval
Christian monastic belief that suffering has merit in its own right.
Karma implies a belief in *continuous* causality, what is experienced now is seen as the result of personal or collective prior
action, *but* what one experiences in the future will be the result of
present action: the exercise of choice and free will is possible.
Therefore, the doctrine of karma adds a dimension of personal
responsibility to 'destiny' and anyone aligned to Western thought
who takes reincarnation seriously is likely to have an attitude of:
'Let's get it right this time', rather than: 'Well, what does it matter
I can always get it right next time'.

In this view of reincarnation, contrary to the fatalistic
approach, there is conscious choice which arises out of attunement to the needs of the Self – which Jung described, under the
name of the soul, as 'the greatest of all cosmic miracles'. The Self is
the holistic, eternal, spiritual monad of Man and it is seeking to
evolve back towards perfection and reintegration into the divine
force. It is, however, a spiritual, not an intellectual concept,
approached through meditation rather than through the rational
processes of the mind: 'Knowledge of the soul cannot be derived
from reason, observation or science.' It would appear that it is the
Self Liz Greene refers to when she says:

From what I have observed . . . there is certainly something
– whether one calls it fate, Providence, natural law, karma
or the unconscious – that retaliates when its boundaries are
transgressed or when it receives no respect or effort at
relationship, and which seems to possess a kind of 'absolute
knowledge' not only of what the individual needs but of
what he is *going* to need for his unfolding in life. It appears

to make arrangements of the most particular and astonishing kind, bringing a person together with another person
or an external situation at precisely the right moment, and it
appears to be as much a part of the inner man as the outer. It
also appears to be both psychic and physical, personal and
collective, 'higher' and 'lower', and can wear the mask of
Mephistopheles as readily as it can present itself as God. I
make no pretence of knowing what it is, but I am unashamedly prepared to call it fate.[7]

Throughout *The Karmic Journey*, this organizing principle is
referred to as the Self and the portion which incarnates into the
physical body as the soul. A difficulty I have consistently encountered whilst writing is that the eternal Self has no gender, but the
incarnating soul takes on the masculine or feminine character
through the physical body. I personally have no problem accepting 'Man' as a generic term for mankind encompassing both
sexes. Aware, however, that many readers, particularly women,
will object to the use of 'Man ' and 'he', and wishing to avoid the
clumsy construction of 'he or she' where possible, I have resorted
to referring to the incarnating soul and to the zodiacal energy to
which it is attuned in the neutral, sexless form of 'it'. To those
readers who object to being referred to as 'it' I can only apologize.

From my experience with running seminars on reincarnation and
karmic astrology, I know that several questions arise as to the
concept of reincarnation, and that there are other possible explanations for the type of experiences which lead people to accept
the reality of an independent, continuous state of Being. I shall
explore these prior to penetrating the depths of astrological
karmic significators and manifestations.

The doctrine of reincarnation is a very ancient one, prevalent
worldwide, particularly in the so-called 'primitive' societies which
have survived with their beliefs intact, and of course throughout
Hindu and Buddhist countries. Stated simply, it is the belief that a
soul, which formerly inhabited a body on earth and died, is reborn
again into a different body. For example, in Bali children are

expected to be the reincarnation of deceased family members and are praised for having the 'good' qualities of those ancestors. Many of the Greek philosophers, including Plato, refer matter-of-factly to reincarnation, and the concept was widely accepted in the Western world prior to the Roman version of Christianity. The Jews are expecting a Messiah who will be the reincarnation of one of the prophets and Jesus implies (Matthew 11:14) that John the Baptist was Elias. There are still traces of the doctrine within the four Gospels and in the other books that make up the New Testament. These particular books were finally selected from over two hundred gospels and other writings in existence in the first few centuries after Christ's birth – and there are many more references in the rejected books. Similarly, in his *Gallic Wars* Julius Caesar mentions the belief in reincarnation in connection with the Celts, a belief which passed into the early Celtic Christian Church.

Many of the early Christian saints expressed the belief that the soul had inhabited other bodies prior to its present life. According to Origen (AD 185–254), every soul comes into this world strengthened by the victories or weakened by the defeats of its previous life. Its place in this world as a vessel appointed to honour or dishonour is determined by its previous merits or demerits. Its work in this world determines its place in the world which is to follow this.[8] St Gregory (AD 257–332), whilst not here specifically mentioning the pre-existence of the soul, insists: 'It is an absolute necessity that the soul should be healed and purified, and if this does not take place during its life on earth it must be accomplished in future lives.'[9] St Augustine (AD 354–430), in his *Confessions*, addressed a question to God concerning his prior existence: 'Say, Lord to me . . . did my infancy succeed another age of mine that died before it? Was it that which I spent within my mother's womb? . . . and what before that life again, O God my joy, was I anywhere or in any body?'[10]

However, in AD 553 a Church Council ratified the anathema of the Emperor Justinian against the doctrine of Origen concerning the pre-existence of the human soul, and by implication reincarnation. From this time onwards the belief in reincarnation officially ceased in the Christian Church, although several Gnostic 'heretical' sects, such as the Cathari, strove to reinstate it and it never completely died out in Western thought.

In the West belief in reincarnation was taken up by the Theosophists and other esoteric and occult organizations at a time of resurgence of interest in the survival and purpose of the human soul, the two concepts being very closely linked. As Dr Ian Stevenson pointed out in his *Twenty Cases Suggestive of Reincarnation*:

> Survival could occur without reincarnation. On the other hand, reincarnation by definition cannot occur without some preceding survival of a physical death. Thus evidence for reincarnation is *ipso facto* evidence for survival while the reverse is certainly not true . . . In mediumistic communication we have the problem of proving that someone clearly dead still lives. In evaluating apparent memories of former incarnations, the problem consists in judging whether someone clearly living once died.[11]

A considerable number of books have been published on the subject of reincarnation, some scholarly and 'scientific', others experiential, and the reader wishing to pursue the matter further is referred to the Bibliography. So far, despite the considerable efforts of researchers like Dr Ian Stevenson, there is no objective 'proof' of the fact of reincarnation. As Benjamin Walker points out: 'The testimony of tradition is in its favour, while scientific evidence is against it.'[12] There are several other possible explanations for so-called reincarnation memories. According to the psychologist and philosopher William James, 'There is a verge of the mind which these things haunt; and whispers therefrom mingle with the operations of our understanding, even as the waters of the infinite ocean send their waves to break among the pebbles that lie upon our shore.'[13]

Many people do not need scientific proof in order to accept the validity of the reincarnation experience. There are subjective states of consciousness which can lead to an acceptance of the survival of the human soul, and thereby to the *a priori* knowledge of reincarnation. One of these altered states of consciousness is hypnosis, during which the person is directed back to the past, an experience which 'convinces' many people of the veracity of former lives.

Another subjective state, but one which often appears to have objective consciousness as well, is the Out of the Body Experience (OOBE). During an OOBE the etheric or astral body, which houses the soul, becomes temporarily separated from the physical body and serves as a vehicle for consciousness. Such separations take place for a short time in sleep or trance states, OOBE, etc., and permanently at death. In a classic book, *The Projection of the Astral Body*, written in 1929, Sylvan Muldoon expressed his certainty of the immortality of man: 'For my part, had a book on immortality never been written, had a lecture on survival never been uttered . . . in fact had no-one else in the whole world ever suspected "life after death" I should still believe implicitly that I am immortal – for I have experienced the projection of the astral body.'[14]

Once someone has had that experience, they 'know' and no amount of psychological explanation or rationalization can remove the knowledge that there is a vehicle for consciousness which can function independently of the physical body. Once in possession of that inner knowing, which is a matter of intuitive apprehension rather than intellectual comprehension, one is truly aware of one's immortality and of the totality of one's being.

Some fifty years after Sylvan Muldoon's experience of OOBEs, Robert Monroe in his book *Journeys Out of the Body*, which is also a classic, sought to differentiate, from his own experience, between the dream state and the OOBE. He cites continuity of conscious awareness and the ability to make and implement decisions in a sequential time-frame as typical of the OOBE. The experience is subtly different from 'lucid' dreaming in which the dreamer knows he or she is dreaming but chooses to go along with the dream, or from dream or imaging work in which the 'dreamer' chooses to explore further or create new scenarios. In the dream state there is very rarely any sense of separation from the physical body, whereas in the OOBE experience there is *always* a feeling of freedom, of having been released from the necessity for physical sentience – although sense and other perceptions continue. Robert Monroe points out that the 'astral' body, which is the vehicle for the OOBE, responds directly to thought which is the 'vital creative energy' and can, for example, translocate instantaneously if required.

Another subjective area which leads many people to believe that they will survive physical death is the Near-Death Experience (NDE) which has been widely documented (see Bibliography). Such an experience occurs when a person is clinically 'dead' or is dying, but consciousness on another level continues and the soul ultimately returns to earthly existence. One of the earliest references to such an experience is found in Plato's *Republic* and, in the seventh century, the Venerable Bede records a wonderful story 'of one among the Northumbrians who rose from the dead and related the things he had seen, some exciting terror and others delight' which has all the classic components of an NDE.

Fig. 1 is the chart of a somewhat unusual National Health Service psychiatrist: he utilizes fairy-tales, myths and Liz Greene's tarot pack in his clinical work with disturbed adolescents. He had an NDE whilst still a medical student. Scorpio intercepted in the sixth house points to a karmic health or career need to penetrate the depths and darkness of the psyche and Chiron in the eighth house indicates a significant life change following an encounter with 'death'. He is the son of a high-ranking army officer and his chart indicates considerable karma involved with power and aggression issues linked to the Pluto–Mars opposition across the MC(Midheaven)/IC, and Mars being the ruler of the karmic twelfth house (see Chapter 1). He has a fascination for military history which may perhaps be an expression of his own past or his inheritance.

In addition to Chiron in the eighth house, which points to the need for an antidote to the 'suffering' he has created, however unconsciously, and endured in the past, the chart also has two Fingers of Fate (utilizing wide karmic orbs for quincunx aspects) involving Pluto, the Nodes, the Sun, Mars and Neptune. Karmically, one would therefore expect him to have been involved in a

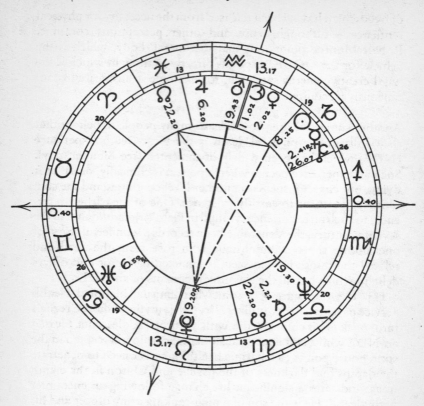

Fig. 1

traumatic event which resulted in the need to integrate these powerful energies that are linked to an understanding of the birth-death-rebirth cycle, and the transformation of his spiritual awareness:

My near-death experience was the most important event in my life so far. I was told by my physician afterwards that I very nearly died. During the days I was most ill I was entirely unaware of my surroundings, and yet the experience itself had a timeless clarity. In the preceding weeks I had been in continual physical agony, but this was a time of complete tranquillity and absence of pain. The recollection of the actual events is hazy, but the inner certainty of their ultimate validity over and above ordinary experience is as overwhelmingly real as ever.

During the weeks leading up to the manifestation of his disease, transiting Mars was opposing natal Saturn and bringing out his underlying pain. As the NDE approached, transiting Mars had moved on after opposing natal Neptune, which induces euphoria and expanded states of consciousness, and transiting Saturn was squaring natal Saturn and opposing Mercury, paving the way for a classic NDE 'life review':

My soul came to be in the presence of a completely benign person who was male, was somehow all around and was entirely good. This person was totally uncritical, calm and loving in an unsentimental way. I felt completely safe and at ease. In his presence I appraised my life so far and found that it had been good and worthwhile. I was satisfied and grateful for what had been given and had no desire for it to carry on, or to finish. He let me know that this wasn't meant to be the end of my life but that I would carry on as I had work to do [a need to express the Fingers of Fate and the eleventh house Pisces North Node out to the world]. I accepted this without question. Interestingly, many years later, my mother consulted a clairvoyant who incidentally told her that sometime before I had almost died, but did not because I had important work to do. After recovery, I identified the person as being most like Jesus Christ. After this my life fundamentally changed. I lost all worldly ambition, which seemed to me to be a ridiculous delusion.

Here he was moving out of the earth-orientated Virgo South Node and into the mystical Pisces North Node and the Finger of Fate focused on it, which embodies the karmic need to integrate the transforming, regenerative energy of Pluto and the spiritual consciousness of Neptune. He was also moving beyond the personal power games and egotistical level of the other Finger of Fate, which includes the Sun, Pluto and Mars as well as the Pisces Node, which produces difficulty in assimilating and eliminating the past, and resulted in his bowel disease and consequent NDE. He began to own his own creative and healing power (the constructive manifestation of the Pluto energy) and to develop his spiritual understanding: 'I was endowed with a strong curiosity in spiritual matters which has remained with me. The progressive uncovering of what life signifies has seemed to me ever since to be the only worthwhile quest.' Uranus in opposition to Mercury, fifth house Neptune and Saturn, the Gemini Ascendant, and Chiron in Sagittarius in his chart indicate attunement to the 'higher mind' energies and a need to understand how the spiritual-mind link functions – he also works with Neuro-Linguistic Programming:

> Since then, deep within me, I have the certainty of acquaint-ance with the transcended reality [the effect of the Sun square Neptune], despite the overlay of my fair share of life's hardships. I regard myself as fortunate in having had this realisation. Having come face to face with my own mortality [exemplified by his earthy Sun in Capricorn and the eighth house Chiron], I have had to come to terms with it, and the vulnerability of my body. Death holds no fear for me.

In an article in the *British Journal of Psychiatry*, Drs Glenn Roberts and John Owen critically review the NDE literature and experience from both the historical and clinical perspective. They base their criticism of the NDE on the fact that death is notori-ously difficult to diagnose and also irreversible and therefore, according to them, no one claiming to have 'died' and returned can have been 'dead'. However, as they point out:

> The process of dying takes a finite time, and if the arrested heart is restarted, the dying process is reversed.
> Non-psychiatric authors have confused phenomenologi-cal reality with ontological reality and equated vivid sincere reports with veridicality . . . Many seem unfamiliar with the

defining characteristics of hallucinations. Consequently, the common features of NDEs are viewed as indicative of a common objective reality and not a common subjective reality.[15]

They found that: 'A frequent, consistent and apparently enduring pattern of changes in attitudes, values, beliefs and conduct have been observed in people who have had an NDE.'[16] They also examined the effects of both cultural expectations, psychopathology, epilepsy, drug experiences, etc., and concluded that 'all the separate elements can occur in non-life-threatening situations and that typical NDEs can be chemically induced . . . it may be that NDEs are common end points of a number of aetiological pathways.'[17] However, the question of the varying impact of the NDE is left unanswered: 'It remains to be explained why some return from a close brush with death with a vivid, extensive and profound experience, and others report nothing. This review has attempted to describe the work done so far; a great deal remains to be explored, described, quantified, tested, understood and applied.'[18] As Roberts and Owen point out, there is a considerable difference between objective and subjective reality, but an acceptance of subjective states is a *cultural* difficulty stemming from the West's insistence on intellectual comprehension rather than intuitive recognition and inner knowing. The East would have no difficulty in accepting the 'evidence' of mystical experience. Healer Matthew Manning's comment on a similar paradox would seem to be appropriate here: 'To those who know, no explanation is required. To those who do not know, no explanation is possible.' And, as Robert Hand pointed out in the *Astrological Journal*, mystical consciousness encompasses astrological cognizance:

> True mysticism is not merely something that is mystifying as scientists would have us believe. It is the belief that all of the apparent diversity of nature and Man is one whole, an interacting oneness. In this sense astrology is applied mysticism because it is a day-to-day manifestation of the Oneness. Humanity and the movement of the planets are parallel

manifestations of the One. In the mystical worldview astrology does not require an explanation. In fact astrology's *not* working would have to be explained.[19]

As part of the concept of 'Oneness', it has been hypothesized that places can hold 'imprints' of past events or of past lives which have taken place there. Although auto-suggestion can of course be an explanation for this, many people have found, on visiting the sites of old battlefields for example, that they are suddenly able to tune in to what has passed there – and some believe that they actually took part in the events: the *déjà vu* experience. This 'imprint' theory is one of the explanations for 'ghosts' who haunt a particular spot, endlessly repeating an action; as opposed to a 'spirit' who may appear and interact with the observer.

A print sales representative I knew, normally the most cynical and sceptical of men, arrived at my office much shaken by an experience he had had. He lived in a new house on the site of an old orchard. In the middle of the night he was awakened by an old man bending over the bed. His immediate reaction was to hit out. His fist went straight through the man, who looked quite amused. The next morning the same old man was standing next to the rep's wife in the kitchen and he blurted out: 'What's that ghost doing here?' 'Don't worry dear,' his wife soothingly replied, 'it's only Fred. He used to work here and likes to pop in for a visit.' She had been communicating with Fred ever since they moved into the house but had not liked to mention it in case her husband thought she had 'gone screwy'. I suggested that Fred might be an earth-bound spirit and that perhaps they could persuade him to move on to other realms. When this was relayed to Fred, he said he would consider it in his own good time!

The *déjà vu* experience is a subjective state which produces a sense of re-entering the past, and in which the subject apparently 'knows' the place without necessarily having ever been there. This is often explained away as a perception difficulty in that the eye perceives some time before the brain acknowledges, or as knowledge acquired as a result of, for example, having seen a picture of the place many years earlier. When my mother had an NDE she suddenly found herself wandering on a high moor-like road on which a signpost said 'Winchcombe'. Having been to that part of the road myself, I know that it is featureless apart from the signposted side road, and is not particularly memorable. Nevertheless she is convinced that she, in some non-physical form, not only travelled to the place – to which she has never been in the present life – but recognized it as somewhere she had been before. A friend's elderly father had exactly the same experience on visiting Dunster for the first time. He could describe exactly what was around the next corner and what the buildings had been in the last century. When a friend and I visited Wells Cathedral and asked the Chancellor about a particular feature we wanted to see, his reply was that it hadn't been like that since the fourteenth century or thereabouts.

A similar, but usually much more detailed, experience is that of spontaneous past-life recall in which the subject appears to relive a prior experience. I have had many of these experiences. Once, when watching Karnak temple on television, I suddenly found myself 'seeing', superimposed on the ruins, a picture of how the temple was when it was first built and drifted into a long 'reliving' of a life there. One of my first actions on visiting the temple in this life was to seek out a particular 'secret' temple which was still exactly as I had seen it all those years ago. As psychologist Dr Frederick Lenz points out: 'Spontaneous past-life memory tends to occur in dreams, during meditation, via *déjà vu* experiences and as waking visions. These waking vision cases are the most characteristic. The experiencer usually feels as though he has been literally transported in time back to his or her past life.'

A client was referred to me by the College of Psychic Studies. A psychotherapist, she had had the unsettling experience of suddenly finding herself trying to commit suicide, but knowing that it was a few centuries ago. She was full of a despair that she could not shake off. During a regression she returned to a life in which she had killed herself. In her present life she had met a person with whom she had been involved in that lifetime, and the meeting had triggered off the memory. Once she recognized it as part of the past and no longer relevant to the present relationship, she was able to let it go.

My own sense of 'knowing' in connection with reincarnation is almost totally subjective and based on an NDE, OOBEs, and on many spontaneous regressions to other lives. Prior to these experiences I thought that reincarnation was an interesting theory. After them, reincarnation became an acknowledged causal factor in my life which made sense of the previously inexplicable and which totally changed my notions of both time and the reason for existence. However, this book is not intended to convince the 'unbeliever'. It puts forward one potential answer to the question: 'Why are we here and what can we learn from our experience?' It shows how karma originating in past experiences, which is mapped in the birthchart, may block the progress of the deeper Self, and how an awareness of the pattern laid down may unlock creative energies and potential which the soul can utilize in order to grow.

In *The Visions Seminars* Jung speaks of 'The Ghosts' who are the ancestors:

> The ghosts are remnants of former lives, what one calls ancestral spirits, and the ancestral spirits psychologically are the units which constitute our psyche. If one splits up the psyche into its original components . . . one part of your psyche comes from the grandfather, another from the great grandmother, and so on: one is a sort of conglomeration of ancestral lives. This of course leads to the idea of reincarnation, that one existed in former ages . . . All those ideas come from the vivid recollection of former lives when one is in a certain condition, namely, when an ancestral life is regenerated in one . . . It is possible that one sets out to live the ancestral life right in the beginning, as most people do who develop in a reasonable and positive way; they grow out of several ancestral lives into all-round individuals . . . But also there are people who have their blossom first . . . an ancestral life breaks through, and they become sort of withered mummies . . . In living the inherited nature, one is thoroughly alive because one lives *for* the ancestors, one makes a new attempt to pay off the debts left by the ancestor generations.[20]

This may be another explanation for 'past-life' experiences, and certainly some of my own past-life regressions may conceivably have been a reliving of my ancestral experience. Within a few short generations I can trace English, Scots, French Huguenot and Romany. But, contemplating the dilution and complexity of the route through which ancestral spirits could have inspired my own vivid 'memories' of three or four thousand years ago, I personally find the reincarnation theory much simpler. And it does appear to explain better the experience of an English participant in a past-life workshop who regressed to about seven or eight, 'fairly recent' Far Eastern incarnations although, as far as he could ascertain, he had no ancestral link. However, it may well be that ancestral memory is a contributory, causal factor in the soul choosing to incarnate into a particular family.

In *Masks of the Soul* Benjamin Walker explores the concept of the psychogene, which would appear to be intimately linked into Jung's concept of the ancestral 'Ghosts' as the carrier of 'memory':

> It has been suggested that just as the biophysical traits are carried by the genes, there may be an inherited mind-and-memory factor, the psychogene, carrying a mental legacy from one generation to the next . . . Some psychologists are of the view that a series of such psychogenes, passed on over the centuries, forge a kind of continuing memory chain, a mental continuum built up into instincts, racial and tribal memories, and all the mind-stuff of the antecedent line. It is obvious that there can be no possible break in the chain of succession that leads back to our remotest progenitors.[21]

I would postulate an 'etheric' rather than 'physical' gene: a memory cell — a personal Akashic Record — located in the spiritual entity that survives physical death and forms the blueprint for the next body. This entity incarnates again only in the sense that it is assimilated into, and can be accessed through, the Self where it is stored. Such an 'etheric memory cell' could be the 'missing link' in Rupert Sheldrake's theory of 'Morphic Resonance':

The central idea of morphogenic fields is that these are invisible fields shaping and moulding developing organisms, giving them their form and structure . . . If living organisms are shaped or moulded by this new kind of field, the fields themselves must have a structure or organisation . . . the structure of these fields is derived from the actual physical structure of similar organisms in the past. It is derived by connection across time and space. Thus the fields represent a kind of cumulative memory of the species – the process of morphic resonance.[22]

In an article in *Astrological Journal*, Alan Jewsbury describes morphic resonance as:

an exciting concept that, if true, makes astrology seem much more understandable; and the apparent weirdness of a natal imprint that remains active for life whilst it interacts with currently transiting planets is no longer so strange . . .

The basic personal and unique field at birth remains in force throughout life; if the planets are significators of the original pattern, then the transiting planets will also resonate with the natal field. It is not unreasonable also to assume that the parents' fields mirroring their emotions, concerns and fears have a strong formative effect on the young child's developing field: which will also be affected by the prevailing cultural field. But this is not a fatalistic doctrine because fields can be modified by learning; although a major influence will always be the 'presence of the past.[23]

When exploring the need for an astrological discipline, Robert Hand makes the supposition that 'planetary arrangements might cause some kind of pulsing or modulation in the magnetic field of the earth such that certain kinds of thoughts or behaviour are induced in the brain.'[24] This would seem to be consistent with the morphic fields theory, as Sheldrake believes that via morphic resonance it is possible to tune in to not only our own memories, but also those of other people, which would in effect be a communication from the past: 'If we tune in to the large number of memories from large numbers of people in the past, what we would get would not be specific memories of their particular lives, but rather a sort of composite or pooled memory of the species . . . The idea of course corresponds very well to Jung's idea of the archetypes in the collective unconscious.'[25]

Jungian theory does, of course, offer another interpretation of past-life recall: the collective unconscious, a Neptunian level of (un)consciousness linking all souls together in the depths of their being:

> During Jung's research into the psyche, he 'uncovered' a bottom layer beneath the personal unconscious where the psychic history of man had been written, as though carved with a knife into a tree . . . It is as if we have part of us that connects to the Infinite . . . The planets Uranus, Neptune and Pluto connect us to energies that are beyond everyday experiences, a sort of divine reservoir.[26]

Attunement to this level of unilateral awareness could well bring to the surface buried memories and karma from 'the past' which is both personal and universal.

Other explanations for reincarnation experiences explored by Benjamin Walker include 'possession' by 'dead spirits' – which presupposes that some form of survival after death is possible. When I first began psychic development classes, every meditation would bring vivid scenes of Egypt, ancient Greece and Renaissance Venice. 'How nice, dear,' the circle leader would say, 'the Guides are showing you where they used to live.' I always wondered why, then, I had such a sense of recognition and intimate knowing of these places. Christine Hartley's book, which fell off the library shelf into my hands, suggested another explanation: reincarnation. That is not to say that as someone who utilizes psychic 'far vision', I am not at times aware of discarnate entities who wish to communicate clairvoyantly, but this has a 'different feel', subjectively, to it from a reading of the record of another incarnate being's past.

Benjamin Walker also suggests as explanations of past-life recall the influence of mental states induced by hysteria, epilepsy, or drugs. He also cites the power of suggestion at work. Yet if suggestion, or wishful thinking, were that powerful then all past-life workshop participants would easily and quickly find their 'previous incarnations', and this unfortunately is not the case. It can, however, account for the number of Cleopatras, for example, one meets. In the course of working in the NHS I did meet several people who were undergoing treatment in psychiatric hospitals for experiences not unlike my own – the difference being that in their case these interfered with their functioning in the everyday world, and subjective and objective experiences were not differentiated.

Walker further suggests that paramnesia – false memory – and cryptomnesia – hidden memory in which, for example, a book or film read or seen many years ago will suddenly float into consciousness, might also be explanations for past-life recall. It is true that in past-life workshops participants have expressed recall as being in the form of 'a film set', and that some past-life readings can be rather like novels. In fact several books, by Joan Grant for example, presented as 'historical novels' were based on the authors' past-life experiences. The inspiration for novels has to come from somewhere and the present-life experiences of many people could be passed off as a 'soap-opera' script! However, with over fifteen years of experience in evaluating the usefulness of past-life recall and regressions, I have reached the conclusion that whatever is 'seen' during a past-life regression or creative visualization session is of value in a symbolic form. Symbols are the language of the psyche through which the Self, or the unconscious, communicates – in exactly the same way, but rather more lucidly, as it would in a dream. It is the *meaning and effect* of the experience which have value and validity, rather than the fact that it can be proved 'true' or 'false' in empirical terms, and this same reasoning is applied to the karmic interpretation of charts. If a past life helps a client to understand, and be released from, or utilize, a part of his or her life hitherto inexplicable or blocked, then it has value and meaning.

*

Once I had come to accept reincarnation as an explanation for my own predispositions, experiences and patterns, two questions became crucial: that of space – the 'where' of inter-incarnation states – and that of time.

I began with the source of the 'new' soul which had never incarnated before. The most convincing answer that I could find was based on the concept of a 'pool' of spiritual essence, the Oneness to which the soul yearns to return, from which an individual Self separates in order to gain experience. As an Indian saying goes, 'God breathed out and Man was created. God breathed in and Man began his journey back to the source.' I then asked where the so-called 'dead' souls who are awaiting reincarnation are. In a channelled communication, a discarnate soul answered: 'All around you. We haven't gone anywhere. Only our vibrations and perceptions are different. Our world interpenetrates yours but because we function at a different level of vibration and consciousness, you are not normally aware of us.' According to Tyrell, 'a change of world is not brought about by spatial travel but by a change in what we are aware of.'[27] I also came to see time as symbolic: chronological, linear time sequences being the means by which the incarnated soul makes sense of the physical world. As Joan Grant points out: 'The concept of successive personalities being threaded by Time like beads on a string is intellectually expedient but misleading.'[28] Once one moves out of physical perception of time into spiritual or mystical apprehension, then time loses its meaning. Jane Roberts expresses this notion of flexible time in a poem:

> *Between each ticking of the clock*
> *Long centuries pass*
> *In universes hidden from our own.*

In order to explain how it is possible to 'tune in' to different lives, it can be postulated that time is circular and that if one stands at its central point, then one can access any point on the circle. However, at a very deep level I have come to believe that there is no such thing as time: no past, present or future: it is all happening Now. And, consequently, there are an infinite number of different realities encompassed within that eternal Now being experienced by the Self.

Astrology is a spatial time-frame reference which allows us to make sense of our experience in the present reality. Karmic astrology adds another dimension to our understanding of the inner processes of life, deepening our spiritual perception and linking us into the greater reality of the expanded, holistic, totally aware Self who is our real Being, and who simply Is.

> *I have circled awhile with the Nine Fathers in each Heaven*
> *For years I have revolved with the stars in their signs.*
> *I was invisible awhile, I was dwelling with Him.*[29]

Chapter 1
CHARTING THE JOURNEY

*The soul chooses a time to be born because the astrological
pattern fits the experiences needed for the present stage of
growth.*

HOWARD SASPORTAS, *THE TWELVE HOUSES*

The natal chart viewed from the perspective of the karmic astrologer delineates both the instinctual behaviour and expectations
carried forward from the past *and* possibilities for the future, as
represented by the interaction of the energies of the planets and
the signs. It reiterates and reinforces major patterns and assump-
tions, blocks and potential, wisdom and weakness built up over
many lifetimes. Areas of imbalance and conflict are mapped, and
those for growth and new learning outlined. The pattern of cause
and effect laid down in previous incarnations is reflected in the
heavens at the moment of birth and the incarnating soul chooses a
time of entry which will offer the conditions most conducive to
growth and development: 'The horoscope shows us the individual's karma – it is the study plan that has become necessary for
his present incarnation . . . The horoscope represents what each of
us has acquired through his or her deeds. One cannot complain
about it.'[1]

What we encounter in our lives now can be seen as the direct
result of what we have enacted, or omitted, over many lifetimes.
In regressions to past lives the 'sins of omission' appear over and
over as a soul incarnates time and again into the same conditions
until it finally confronts what it has come to learn. Similarly many
people 'suffer' the same problems until they recognize that only
they are able to change the pattern and that they do in fact create
their own reality and can move beyond karma. 'Karmic justice' is
not simply a matter of having had a difficult time in one's last life,

and therefore now being eligible to have an easy time. The question which must be addressed is: 'Did the incarnating soul learn the lesson for that life or not?' If it did not, then the soul repeats the lesson as many times as it takes to resolve it – or to recognize that it does not have to go on endlessly repeating a pattern. It has the option of changing the way it interacts, of reorganizing its own reality and moving beyond the constraints of karma. A knowledge of pre-existing patterns and the plan for the present lifetime, as seen through the chart, is thus a very potent tool in understanding, adjusting to, overcoming, and growing through current life circumstances.

It should, however, be borne in mind that if everything is attributed to past causes, in effect living in the past, then the soul misses out on its immediate experience of the life it is currently living. The Self, that eternal part of us which is cosmic and eternal, strives to live in the ever-present Now and to fully experience each moment as it occurs. When it is able to do this, it has reached enlightenment. Enlightenment is not a matter of perpetual bliss, it is entering a state of simple Being; interacting with one's whole experience on the physical, emotional, mental and spiritual levels; recognizing that one is a spiritual Self, and finally getting on with the business of fully living each moment.

Every human being contains within itself a mass of contradictions and conflicts. When these are recognized as stemming from different personas and from experiences throughout many lives the possibility of integrating the dissonant energies unfolds, offering wholeness. Repressions are lifted, blockages freed, and the energies which have been subjugated are released for creative use.

Each incarnation, and natal chart, can therefore be seen as a learning experience set up prior to birth in order that the strengths and wisdom acquired in previous lives be utilized to overcome inherent weaknesses and areas of imbalance. These areas can be identified through the placement and interaction of the planets within the birthchart. Karmic patterns are carried over from former incarnations and the appropriate environment created within the family, and early life experience, for those particular patterns to be recapitulated and intensified. The patterns from childhood will then be carried over into adult life and relationships. In due time, they will be brought up into conscious awareness. Awareness offers the possibility of choice and change, with the consequent release from the karmic pattern and growth into a new way of Being. A philosophical dilemma inherent in the concept of reincarnation is the question of whether an incarnating soul is the victim of its immutable fate, or whether it has the free will to control its own destiny. Once it is recognized that the incarnating soul created the circumstances in which it finds itself and that it has a choice in how to meet those circumstances, a resolution of the fate versus free will dilemma becomes possible. As Pauline Stone points out, 'Our experiences on earth are . . . predestined by virtue of our own past behaviour . . . We have freewill in respect of how we meet our karma.'[2]

The karmic patterns stemming from vastly different lifetimes are mapped as difficult aspects, aspects between unsympathetic planets, planets in incompatible signs, or the Sun and Moon in conflicting elements and signs. These aspects and conflicts indicate areas for synthesis or a shift to a new mode of behaviour. 'Difficult' aspects are the square (90°), opposition (180°), inconjunct/quincunx (150°) and, at times, the conjunction (0°), which in the text is indicated in aspect patterns by an oblique stroke between the planets, e.g. Sun/Moon). It should be borne in mind that supposedly 'easy' aspects such as the trine (120°) or sextile (60°) can prove to be difficult if the energies are not yet integrated or manifesting positively and, therefore, throughout the book **when an aspect is not specified the comments apply to any major combination of planets.** In order to obtain a clear outline of the basic karmic pattern of the incarnating soul, I utilize only the major planetary aspects, and the inconjunct. The quintile aspect (72°) is, however, one of 'fate' or 'destiny' and can indicate an area which the incarnating soul has decided it simply must face up to in this life, it gives itself no choice. I believe it is Alan Oken who refers to this aspect as 'evolutionary potential'. This 'minor' aspect can then become a crucial aspect in attuning to the soul's purpose.

For karmic work it has been found that the more usual orbs of aspect can be extended. Orbs of up to 8° for a square, opposition, conjunction or trine and 6° for the sextile will reveal themselves in obvious ways, which then become more subtle in manifestation as the orb moves through 10° to 12° and onwards. Planets which are in the same sign but technically not within orb represent energies which are difficult to grasp and bring together, although there is an inherent awareness of the need for integration. For the quincunx it has been found that up to an 8° orb may apply despite the fact that this can technically include the bi-quintile (144°) aspect.

A difficulty frequently encountered when interpreting charts is that clients do not know their time of birth. For some souls the moment of physical birth may not in any case necessarily coincide with the soul incarnating into the body and beginning its interaction with the earth environment. Under hypnosis and regression many people report being 'loosely attached' for periods ranging from a few minutes to days, weeks and even, in exceptional cases, years before making the final decision to fully incarnate. This is particularly noticeable in autistic children, for example, but there are also seemingly aware adults who nevertheless display all the signs of 'only visiting this planet' and do not appear to have fully incarnated in the physical body. When a time of birth is not available, the symbolism of the sunrise chart with the Sun on the cusp of the first house has been found to work well and to be preferable to a noon chart. It must be borne in mind, however, that the planetary energies may express themselves in a slightly different sphere of life to that of the symbolic house in which the planet falls in the sunrise chart.

Placidus-house cusps are used throughout this book as the amount of 'space' allocated to a house, and the number of planets which a house thereby incorporates, has been found to be significant for karmic work – despite the difficulties encountered in extreme northern latitudes where the restriction of a particular house may well indicate an area of life which is not relevant to the present incarnation; and the expanded house will indicate an important area to be worked on. It would appear that for some souls part of the karmic experience is connected with finding balance within extreme environmental conditions, the darkness and isolation of the period of perpetual night, and also the effect on the pineal gland (a spiritual linkage point) of being bombarded with constant light during the period of the midnight sun. As a

Finnish commentator said: 'In winter, the darkness creeps into my mind and depresses me. But in March, when light conquers dark, you almost go out of your head with joy.'[3]

This book is not intended as an astrological 'cook-book'. It contains insights into the working of karma distilled from fifteen years of experience with both astrological charts and individuals. Although certain themes and aspects have recurred continuously over the years, others have never arisen. Some planetary aspects or house placements have therefore not been included simple because I do not have the experience or examples to illustrate the underlying karma. To any reader who feels 'cheated' because his or her particular placement or aspect has not been covered, may I suggest that you apply your own astrological knowledge and speculate on possibilities. Also, at times, planets and aspects are dealt with in other than the conventional, accepted, planetary order because this has allowed exploration of dichotomies or contrasting experiences. Some readers may possibly find this confusing or difficult to follow and for this reason a detailed index has been included. Similarly, a glossary is incorporated at the end of the book to aid those who are unfamiliar with astrological or karmic terminology and concepts. It must also be borne in mind that the planets do not 'cause', they represent energies and patterns within the psyche. They do, however, have their own energy and peculiar ways of manifesting that energy which will be reflected outwardly in events and inwardly in personality traits.

Although it is possible, with a good measure of intuition, to see the broad outline of karmic patterns and to some extent speculate on exactly how they came about utilizing the planets, houses and signs; the specific detail of previous lives is not usually available from the chart. Throughout this book a combination of psychic vision and regression to former incarnations has been used to supplement astrology in order to examine the past. I have given examples using these techniques as well as experiences from my own journey to illuminate as fully as possible the many and varied manifestations of karma.

KARMIC DILEMMAS

Conflicting past-life experiences produce specific karmic dilemmas for the incarnating soul, that can be illustrated by the examples of Jupiter–Saturn and Saturn–Neptune contacts. How difficult the dilemma is to deal with will be indicated by the aspect. 'Hard' aspects generally produce more problems with the resolution of the conflicting energies than the 'soft' aspects. The same dilemma can also apply to Jupiter in Capricorn, ruled by Saturn; and Saturn in Sagittarius, ruled by Jupiter; or to Neptune in Virgo (Neptune is then in the opposing sign to the one it rules and is given shape and a boundary by the earth which is its antithesis). It is also represented by Neptune in Capricorn, ruled by Saturn (where once again Neptune finds itself confined by the earth); and by Saturn in Pisces, ruled by Neptune, (where Saturn undergoes the discomfort of the boundless deep of the water energy).

The Mystic/Pragmatist

The 'Mystic/Pragmatist' dilemma represented by the Neptune (the Mystic) and Saturn (the Pragmatist) aspect has appeared in so many chart readings for those drawn to Eastern practices such as Transcendental Meditation that such a chart now produces an instinctive assumption that 'this must be a meditator'. Such an assumption has to be put aside, however, as the person may well be living out the Saturn half of the aspect and resisting the seductive lure of Neptunian bliss. Readings are frequently requested at a crisis or changeover point when it becomes apparent that the – so far – unrealized planetary energy has to be incorporated in order for the incarnating soul to achieve the impetus for new growth and wholeness. Meditators may find that, although their spiritual growth has moved forward, their career, relationship or health problems are subtly holding them back from their goal of enlightenment. Similarly, materialists may come to feel that a dimension of life is missing: 'There must be more to life than this.'

The past lives represented by an aspect between Saturn and Neptune involved on the one hand the mystical Neptunian approach which can range from the highest spirituality and states of consciousness, down through the escapist realms, the spurious ecstasy of drink or drugs; and into fantasy and imagination, madness and disintegration. Saturnine lives on the other hand embody religious experiences of strict discipline and an emphasis on guilt and repression, or materialistic experiences which leave no room for spirituality and are based on security and temporal power. In terms of spiritual development, Neptune is attunement to the immanent God-within, Saturn the emanation of a God who is wholly other.

The fundamental opposition between Neptune – the unbounded urge to merge and be one with the cosmos – and Saturn – the planet of boundaries and separateness – can only be resolved through a recognition that man is an eternal spirit (the Self) clothed in a body, a microcosm who lives on the earth and yet is a part of the macrocosmic universe. To live out only one end of the dichotomy by withdrawing from the world is as unproductive in terms of spiritual growth as is the totally materialistic approach. An integration is required which pays due attention both to the practical matters and lessons concerned with living in a physical body, and to spirituality. The evolved person is able to live in the world but is not weighed down by the cares of earth. The truly enlightened being is a fusion of spirit and matter.

Positive aspects between planets – in particular the conjunction, sextile and trine, although it should be remembered that all aspects have the potential to become positive when the energies they represent are being used constructively – and planets in compatible elements and houses, indicate old skills to draw on, potentials to be explored. For example, a person with a Saturn–Neptune contact who has worked on resolving the Mystic/Pragmatist dilemma in past lives and is now ready to make the shift into integration has the potential to live as a truly enlightened man. President John F. Kennedy had Saturn in late Cancer conjunct Neptune in Leo in the ninth house and in his public life tried to put the strength of Saturn and idealism of Neptune into practice, although privately he seems to have reflected other aspects of the Neptune–Saturn conflict through his extramarital activities. His brother Robert had a fixed Neptune in Leo square to Saturn in Scorpio. It is interesting to speculate on how many of his brother's ideals he would have shared and put into practice had he lived, and also to consider the karma which cut short two such promising lives. In her book *A Case for Reincarnation* Christine Hartley explored the idea of a family group incarnating together life after life:

> Take for instance that amazing family of the Borgias. Hardly anything good is said of them, yet in spite of the viciousness by which we chiefly remember them they were great patrons of the arts . . . and above all they are distinguished for the immensely strong family ties which bound them together at a time when brother was frequently ranged against brother.
>
> Then look further ahead and you will see the same basic characteristics, the same abilities in the great House of Guise at the time of the last of the Valois kings . . . (they) resemble in a marked degree that preceding family of the Borgias even to their violent and untimely ends. Could we look around today and find another family with the same fundamental loyalties, the same tragedies at their heels . . . one has the idea that so strong and vital a group will return again and again in much the same proximity and circumstances until they have perhaps learned the lesson of the futility of worldly power.[4]

Although she did not answer her own question in the book, in several conversations Christine and I explored the possibility of a link to the Kennedy family from the Borgias and Guises, or the Medicis, who were an equally powerful family. It could certainly explain the peculiarly tragic and 'fated' life of this New World family: a repeating pattern of nemesis balancing hubris and illustrating, as Christine points out, 'the futility of worldly power' and the inability of wealth to buy long life and happiness. We were particularly intrigued with the notion of Jacqueline Kennedy as Lucretia Borgia. Daughter of Roderigo Borgia, who was elected Pope and became Alexander VI, Lucretia is reputed to have poisoned her enemies, and possibly one or two 'friends' as well.

She was used as a political pawn by her father, who contracted several powerful marriage alliances for her. On the other hand her father, who was a firm believer in nepotism, handed over control of the Vatican to her on two occasions complete with power to open his correspondence.

This idea certainly throws a new light on the 'suffering' Jacqueline Kennedy Onassis has undergone in this incarnation. She incarnated with a need to explore the 'taboo' areas of life and gain insight from them (Scorpio Ascendant). She has first house Saturn opposing Venus in the seventh house and therefore incarnated with a burden (first house Saturn) and an inner feeling of unlovableness (the opposition) and karma around relationships (seventh house Venus). The Saturn–Venus opposition also indicates her marriage to the much older Onassis. She also has Jupiter in the seventh house of relationships and expects partners to be a source of wealth and expansion for her. Her Pluto in Cancer carries issues around power and manipulation and the placement in the eighth house, together with the Sun and Mercury in Leo, relates to how she shares herself and her power with another. Her twelfth house Scorpio South Node signifies she has experienced considerable drama and trauma in past lives on the collective level (see Chapter 2). In the present incarnation there is a need for her to move into the inner security of the Taurus North Node and away from the emotional games of the South Node. Her chart could well reflect a soul who had been married as a pawn in a power game in the past but who nevertheless held power behind the scenes.

The Optimist/Pessimist

The past-life patterns connected with aspects of Jupiter (the Optimist) and Saturn (the Pessimist) involve the profligate and the miser, the person who lives on hope and the person who lives in fear, over-indulgence versus self-denial, and self expansion against repression; they are exemplified in the extremes of the manic depressive. The Jupiter–Saturn square in particular indicates that the soul has had many opportunities to advance in past lives, but failed to take advantage of them, and must now struggle with adverse 'circumstances'. The karma can be one of greed, which an old Indian wise saying perceives as 'a disease of the heart':

> The miser's money,
> which causes uneasiness, hardship,
> blindness and sleeplessness,
> is not money but a disease of the heart.
> Greed is not stilled with money,
> any more than is thirst with salt water.

Liz Greene describes the Saturn–Jupiter conflict as a 'sharp dichotomy between intuitive perception and practical observation' and one which 'symbolise[s] a choice between the faith which stems from an intuitive recognition of purpose in life, and the fear which stems from identification with and consequent control by the forces of one's environment.'[5] Her book on Saturn, read from the karmic perspective, affords many penetrating insights into the working of karma through this planet – who is after all, as she points out, the Lord of Karma – and into its interaction with the other planets.

The challenge of Jupiter–Saturn aspects is to integrate the intuitive perception of the oneness of life with the personal responsibility and self-discipline which Saturn has to offer, and thereby to find both meaning and inner direction. One of the saddest sights life has to offer is the depressed, purposeless Jupiter–Saturn individual who has taken refuge in over-indulgence in comfort, seeking addiction to food or other substances. One client, a Virgoan who had Jupiter in late Sagittarius in a wide trine to Saturn in Virgo, and a wide opposition from Jupiter to Uranus in Cancer, was 'seen' in the past as an enormously fat man, too huge to move and then, in contrast, as an ascetic indulging in total self denial with the result that he died a lingering death from starvation. The client afterwards commented that he had experienced both extremes already in this life. He had been a gross teenager, stuffed with food by his mother, as a substitute for love. Then, when he had gone to university to study Calvinistic theology, he had become anorexic and almost died. His life was saved when he abandoned his training for the priesthood, discovered the discipline of astrology, and the possibility of joy entered his life. He found a belief which was based on hope, trust and optimism of the future, and abandoned a faith founded upon control, repression and fear.

Other karmic dilemmas such as the head versus heart (Aquarius–Leo), freedom versus constraint (Uranus–Saturn), etc., will be examined later in relation to the karmic pathway.

WILL AND KARMA

Another karmic issue which is clearly outlined in the natal chart, and which can offer the opportunity to capitalize on a past skill or to make a creative use of a previously blocked or undirected energy, is that of Will, and the correlating use of personal power and assertion. The Will may be an unconsciously expressed, inhibiting and controlling force, very much at the mercy of another person's assertive or aggressive power. Or it may be a consciously aligned self-assertive energy which directs life in accordance with the needs of the Self, and which was referred to by Assagioli in *The Act of Will*[6] as the Skilful Will. There are many different types of Will and ways of using it, as can be seen from a few of the dictionary definitions: 'faculty by which person decides or conceives himself as deciding upon and initiating action, power of deciding upon one's action independently of causation, control exercised by deliberate purpose over impulse, self-control, what one ordains, affecting one's intention or dominating other persons'. The outer planets in aspect to Mars indicate how the incarnating soul will have experienced the Will in the past, how it will function in the present incarnation, and the changes it needs to make in order to develop its positive use of the Will energy.

Jupiter in Aspect to Mars

Jupiter in aspect to Mars has an inner urge to expand which may manifest through a well-directed Will or, as with all Jupiter aspects, it may indicate that the soul is out of control and may go 'over the top' in its need to assert itself. It does, however, have the potential to harness the Will and to utilize its assertive power in order to achieve its aims and objectives. The Jupiter–Mars Will has the capacity to bring into being whatever it conceives. It has the quality of a courageous Will, it acts with integrity from the heart and is able to go forward in the face of fear because it has a basic trust in its power and purpose through its link to the cosmos.

Saturn in Aspect to Mars

Although in conventional astrology Saturn–Mars contacts indicate a strong Will, in karmic terms this is a potential strength to be developed in the present incarnation and the aspect denotes a blocked Will, an inner feeling of powerlessness and helplessness which stems from a previous experience of being at the mercy of someone else's Will or aggression, or of having had one's own Will systematically broken. How far one has progressed in dealing with this is represented by the type of aspect concerned: hard aspects indicating a struggle in the present life, soft aspects that it will be a little easier this time. In a television interview some years ago ex-nun Karen Armstrong, now a writer on religious matters and TV presenter, described her experience when she entered a convent in this life. She was put to work treadling an empty sewing-machine for days on end, so that she 'would learn obedience to God's Will'. This handing over of the personal Will to an external, controlling God who demanded nothing less than total obedience was a feature of the Christian monastic/convent experience into which many people incarnated for spiritual evolution and to learn about inner discipline. However, as Stephen Lawhead said: 'True religion ennobles, it never debases.' And at times 'spiritual discipline' was taken to pointless extremes and merely inculcated a deep sense of powerlessness which was carried over into future lives. Similarly, slaves, servants or some employees, experienced a negation of their own Will as their master had total power and control. People with Saturn–Mars aspects need to learn how to use the Will, to find their own, considerable, inner strength and discipline in order to direct their life.

Uranus in Aspect to Mars

Uranus in aspect to Mars has issues around extreme wilfulness and the need to learn the 'right' use of force and vibrations. I met a man who 'remembered' blowing himself up not once but twice. He had Uranus square Sun/Mars in Cancer. The first time he blew himself up experimenting with kundalini power, against orders, when he was a magician in ancient Egypt. The second time he was a Victorian music-hall artist who used gunpowder in his act and thought he knew how to handle it. In the present life he was utilizing the healing power inherent within the aspect as an

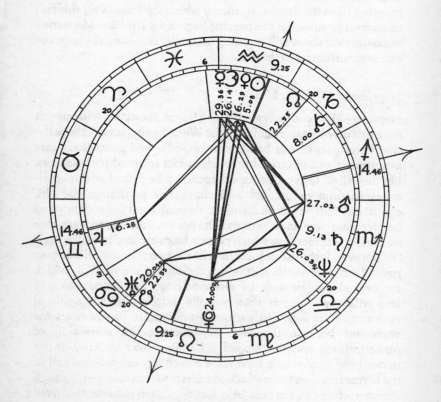

Fig. 2

osteopath, although still exerting 'force' in order to realign the body.

The chart pattern (fig. 2) shown here is for a woman who 'remembers' being present when places blew up, another facet of Uranus–Mars contacts. The first time was Atlantis when she refused to heed warnings to leave in time, believing that she was invincible and could control the situation through the use of crystal power. The second time, on Thera – ancient Santorini – she was a little wiser in recognizing that nothing could prevent the natural forces manifesting. The issue of power is graphically displayed in the chart, there is the full force of that Pluto energy erupting from the depths, an energy which she found very difficult to control or direct in the present life; and a Uranus–Mars trine indicates that she is still working on finally resolving the issues of extreme wilfulness in this life.

Neptune in Aspect to Mars

Neptune–Mars contacts also offer a lesson about the Will but this time this involves spiritualizing the Will, aligning it with the Self – that inner part of our being who is God – and using that inner attunement and intuitive knowledge of its spiritual pathway as a life direction. Often this aspect seems to be linked with experiences of drug or alcohol addiction. It is as though the old, egotistical Will has to be dissolved through total dependency and helplessness over one's actions. The person then has to learn that addiction is something which cannot be overcome by willpower. 'Willpower' is the use of force in order to exert control, either over oneself or over another. It is not the skilful use of Will, which involves alignment with the direction one's Self chooses to take and willingly – rather than wilfully – following the spiritual pathway of the Self. The various 'Anonymous' programmes are successful because the first step includes an admission of powerlessness and the second a handing over to 'God as we understand him' which involves a surrender, not submission, to the divine force – a force which manifests within each one through the attunement to the Self. 'Alcoholics . . . are individuals driven to the point of deciding to live or to die. At this point in the life of any individual, sudden insight and vision are possible. If this experience eludes most of us it may be because we are not sufficiently motivated to surrender our ego into the hands of a spiritual force'.[7]

Other steps for both the alcoholic and the Mars–Neptune contact include a deep, introspective examination of oneself; seeking forgiveness, and making reparation for the past – steps on the spiritual pathway towards the 'perfection' which the Self is seeking. One of the most important karmic lessons for the soul with Neptune–Mars includes learning how to forgive oneself for the past, in order to release from it, finding a spiritual path of self-transformation to which one can dedicate one's life.

The Neptune–Mars aspect has also been linked to a 'disguised lust for conquest' and to the 'missionary' lifestyle. With Neptune there is little violence in the 'conversion'. The 'truth' as the missionary sees it, is taught by example and emanation in true Neptunian style. However, the 'gentleness' of Neptune can be deceptive – thousands of people have been killed in 'holy' wars fought in the name of a man who taught Love.

Pluto in Aspect to Mars

The influence of Pluto in 'conversion' is rather different to that of Neptune as Pluto, although it can be equally devious, is rather more forceful. A client with Jupiter/Saturn square Mars/Pluto regressed to a life in which he had been a fanatical (Pluto) Jesuit priest who was involved in forcibly converting a country and then teaching the children, through the use of harsh discipline, the 'true' religion: it is a Jesuit who is reputed to have said 'Give me the boy up to the age of seven and I will have the man.' 'Coincidentally', a woman to whom this client had a compulsive, and mutual, unlikely attraction (her Sun/Pluto conjunction conjoined his Mars/Pluto conjunction) did not know of this regression. When she regressed she went back to the same incarnation and was terrified of his 'cold eyes'. She commented afterwards that she would not have thought him capable of the fanaticism he displayed at that time. It did, however, explain why, on her first meeting with him in this life, although she was inexplicably pulled to him, she also felt a deep fear. However, in that first meeting he totally turned her life around and helped her to find a new, spiritual, pathway. His way of making reparation for that Jesuit life was to go out to Africa on voluntary service, following a past-life confession and absolution from a priest who believed in reincarnation. In the process he absolved his karma around power – and forcible conversion – represented by his Sun conjuncting Mercury and Pluto in Cancer.

Pluto–Saturn–Mars

A Dominican monk (Saturn opposing Pluto/Mars), who had left his order, called it blasphemy when I suggested he should take back the projection of his Will from God and learn to take control of his own life through utilizing the very strong Will energy indicated by the Pluto/Mars conjunction. The problem he had approached me about was intimately connected with his (Saturn opposing Mars) feeling of helplessness and fatedness and with his projection on to another of that powerful Pluto/Mars Will. He had gone into a monastery for many reasons, not the least of which was to escape from his sexual feelings. On his first night he was brutally raped by another member of the community with whom he had a strong past-life connection, of which he was intuitively aware. The savage, sado-masochistic sexuality and power struggles of the Pluto–Saturn–Mars combination were projected on to and unleashed by another person who acted out his inner conflict for him, enabling him to disown the dark (Plutonian), shadow (Saturn) sexually aggressive (Mars) part of himself. The subsequent violent homosexual affair lasted for seven years and after he left the monastery he still felt that this man had power over him. He could not control his life in any way and he had completely lost the ability to do even simple things like travelling on a train and ensuring that he had sufficient money for the journey. Gradually he began to learn to live in the world again, but was paralysed by his lack of Will and his inability to assert himself. He did not know what he wanted to do, or where he wanted to be. He kept praying to God, but received no answer. He was offered a job running a venereal disease clinic (Pluto and

Mars are connected to the sexual organs), which he very much enjoyed as it brought him into contact with people again and also gave him the opportunity to organize a small department. Ultimately he did learn to use his Will, not to control but to direct his life, and just as importantly, he learnt not to hand his power over to someone else who would then control him. He had learnt the karmic lessons of Pluto and Saturn aspecting Mars.

Will–Love–Power

The chart for a karmic Will–love–power dilemma is shown here (fig.3). The Saturn/Mars conjunction in Scorpio in the eleventh house forms a Grand Trine in the Water element with Pluto and Uranus; squares Neptune, sextiles Jupiter conjunct the South Node, and inconjuncts Chiron. Venus in Aquarius is unaspected: indicating that love is not integrated and that it has been experienced as separate from Will and power. This is the child of missionary doctor parents (the ninth house 'belief system' of Neptune squaring Mars in the eleventh house linking to the medical missionary lifestyle), born into a long line of missionaries. She said of her Chiron in the fourth house, which represents her experience of 'home': 'As a child there was no home. My parents were always there for other people, never there for me. We always had nannies. At seven, having been sent to boarding school, I never went 'home' again. And as an adult one doesn't know how to make a home because one has never experienced a home.'

As a child of four her father explained to her, while teaching her the Lord's Prayer, that she 'actually had two fathers, *one* of whom loved her and she must love Him. HE was an extremely stern, authoritarian, all-powerful God who could see her every move' (a manifestation of her Capricorn South Node energies, see Chapter 2). She was not at all comfortable about this, especially as her own father was strongly Capricornian and lacking in emotional empathy with her.

At about this time I was told the story of Abraham and Isaac (by my father). I identified very much with Isaac and I was the first born – so God became a rather frightening figure as

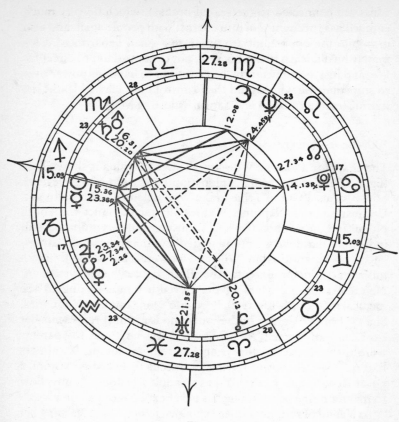

Fig. 3

at any time He might request that I be sacrificed so that God should know that my father loved HIM above everyone else. He (my father) would have to do this (and with hindsight, knowing my luck there would be no ram conveniently caught in the thicket!!).

She grew up literally fearing the love-power of God and the control He had over her (Saturn/Mars). All she could do was obey this external locus of control.

At the age of seven she was sent to boarding school in England and farmed out to an uncaring Aunt for the holidays (Venus in Aquarius incarnates with the expectation of cold and unemotional 'relationships'), seeing her parents once a year when they came home on leave. She felt totally abandoned, rejected and powerless. Later she married a Capricorn army doctor and carried this pattern over into her marriage, living in married quarters wherever he happened to be posted or being left behind in England when it was 'too dangerous' to accompany him. At the age of fifty her husband left her for another woman. She divorced him, taking up her old career and becoming a paediatric physiotherapist (a Neptune–Mars 'rescuer') quickly rising to the top of her profession, advancing to a position of authority (the Pluto–Mars contact representing 'power'). Inwardly, however, she still felt helpless and powerless, at the mercy of 'fate' (Saturn/Mars). At the age of sixty she danced over a long-dead, sun-dried goat in Greece, symbolically laying to rest her Capricorn. At the age of sixty-two, in an unknowing preparation for the conjunction of transiting Pluto to her natal Mars activating the Grand Trine, she began training in psychosynthesis – having been told she would live to be ninety-seven she decided to 'prepare for a useful old age'.

She is still exploring her Will-power issues and has identified a pattern of victim-persecutor-rescuer within her present life which directly related to a regression she underwent several years earlier to an Italian life. In that life, she was the brother of a rather simple-minded boy who was taken off by the local lord for a minor infraction of the law. (S)he followed and tried to argue for his freedom (an action represented by the aggressive Mars energy in contact with the liberating Uranus) but was also imprisoned. Subsequently they were both sent to the war galleys as slaves (Saturn/Mars indicating constraint and powerlessness). (S)he was intelligent and quickly rose to be the slave master, a position which (s)he abused (the power of Pluto–Mars) by demanding homosexual (another Uranus–Mars manifestation) relationships with the slaves for sensual self-gratification (Jupiter–Mars). Crisis point was reached when (s)he demanded intercourse with her own brother (third house Uranus signifying somewhat unusual sibling karma). (S)he committed a murder, possibly of the brother but this was not clear, and was imprisoned again. Before the trial the town was razed by a volcanic eruption (Uranus and Pluto energy) and fire. (S)he escaped from prison and went around the town rescuing women and children and putting them in boats. (S)he sacrificed her own life in a truly Neptune–Mars action, and died in the fire.

In a regression to a later life, linked to her fourth house Chiron, she was in colonial America as a sickly, 'Anne of Green Gables type child' and died at the age of eleven rather than taking on the issue of owning her own power. As she went through her death she 'skirted round a cloud instead of passing through it' – she found it impossible to meet death head on as represented in the present-life chart by the wounded Chiron inconjunct the grim-reaper, Saturn. Prior to her birth into the present incarnation she decided to face the issue of her Will and her power. However, this was delayed until the action of Pluto transiting Scorpio propelled her into her own depths and activated the potential of the Grand Trine for the power to bring about transformation. Her dilemma will nevertheless be unresolved until she is able to integrate the power of love, represented by the very wide conjunction of Venus to Jupiter, into her expression of Will.

COLLECTIVE KARMA

A whole generation is now being born with Pluto in Scorpio and the potential to penetrate the darkness of disease, death and destruction and bring healing to the earth. In the first draft of this book a 'typing error' converted destruction to 'instruction'; this is passed on for what it says about how we educate our young. Many of these souls will also have the conjunction of Saturn to Uranus in either Sagittarius or Capricorn indicating a need to change the existing structure of beliefs or society. The opportunity is being offered to these souls to reverse the collective karma of past generations and to give birth to the New Man of the Aquarian Age who will care for and conserve the planet earth and all who live on her. The parents and grandparents of this new generation may well have Pluto in Leo, signifying the need to explore the meaning and utilization of power, many of whom were born during, and immediately following the major confrontation of the Second World War. They will, hopefully, pass on to their children and grandchildren the knowledge of the consequences of abuse and misuse of power in any form, together with an awareness of man's capacity for self-destruction.

The chart for one of these New-Age children is shown here (fig. 4) with her mother's planets in the outer ring. In a past-life reading a year before the child was born, her powerful, creative, Sun/Pluto in Leo mother was told of an Indian incarnation where she

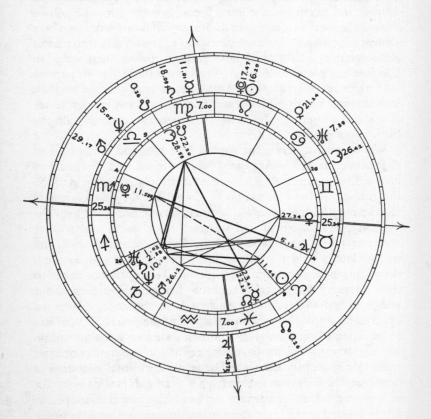

Fig. 4

had voluntarily given up her child to the temple to keep a vow made when she was childless. She was told that this child was waiting to return to her. She was also shown a South Sea-island incarnation where she was a willing sacrificial 'victim' to the sea. On the night she painted her 'memory' of that scene she conceived, and the child was born under water. The mother's South Node is on the child's Moon/South Node conjunction in Virgo opposing Mercury/North Node in Pisces: This was an old connection. The child's chart has a Kite formation and includes the Uranus/Saturn conjunction in Capricorn widely squaring the Nodes, and twelfth house Pluto inconjunct the Sun. She will be brought up both in a village in the interior of Bali (Saturn) – where reincarnation and the interpenetration of spirituality into matter is accepted as a fact of life and crime is non-existent – and in California, a centre for New-Age awareness (Uranus) – by parents who are attuned to a spiritual and artistic way of life. One look into her five-month-old wise and ancient eyes was enough to see that she is a highly evolved soul here to assist mankind with the birth into a new way of Being.

We are now entering the Age of Aquarius and at the time of changeover to a New Age many 'old souls' incarnate in order to help with the transition. The level of spiritual development of the incarnating soul will affect how the energies of the planets are able to manifest. A highly evolved soul will have more inner, growth-inducing, psychological and spiritual, experiences and will be aware that these are necessary for the development of the Self. The less evolved soul will feel it is 'fate' operating through external events impinging on itself. There is a spiral of experience linked to each planetary energy which begins by being event-orientated but which, when the lesson is mastered on the outer planes of experience, moves into the inner world of the psyche. It then has to be repeated on this level, and then tested on yet more subtle spiritual levels which are beyond the conscious awareness of most souls in physical incarnation. The level of spiritual evolution is extremely difficult to ascertain from a chart as it is not a question of 'easy' or 'hard', 'rewarding' or 'punishing' aspects. Indeed, it can be argued that a high degree of evolution is required in order to deal successfully with a difficult chart and that such a chart is therefore a 'reward' for having evolved thus far. As Richard Bach writes in *Illusions*: 'Here is a test to see if your mission on earth is finished. If you're alive, it isn't.'[8]

The more intuitive astrologer can get a feel for the level of evolution when tuning into the chart but such supposition can at best only be tentative and at worst hampering to correct interpretation if the level is wrongly assessed. The working of karma is subtle and things are not always what they seem. This brings to mind the, true, story of a disc-jockey who went out to India. He was told, by a spiritual teacher, that he would meet only one Master during his stay and that it was part of his test to recognize that master. On his return he reported that he had sat at the feet of many gurus and heard much teaching but could not determine which was the true Master. He was asked if he had met anyone else who had made an impression on him. 'Well,' he said, 'I did meet a beggar on a beach. He was different. He didn't ask for money and when I offered him some he told me that he had been blessed with all he needed in life. At the time I didn't understand but I guess now I have my answer. He was the true Master.'

Collective karma, concerned with the nature and utilization of power and control, is also indicated in Uranus–Saturn and Pluto–Mars–Saturn contacts. As Liz Greene has pointed out[9], many people with Pluto–Mars–Saturn aspects, particularly the conjunction, 'remember' on one level or another having been part of persecutory events such as the Holocaust or the Inquisition, either as victim or perpetrator. Many of them seem to have incarnated again within an apparently short time, although it must be remembered that spiritual time is relative. A twelfth house Node, explored in Chapter 2, is also indicative of collective karma.

THE KARMIC HOUSES

When examining the birthchart in the light of karma, certain houses have karmic implications and point to particular areas to be worked on during the present life; other houses indicate skills and abilities that are karmic, or relationships that stem from an old interaction or which will bring up old issues. Aspects to the rulers of these houses can further illuminate the nature of the karma.

The First House

The first house, explored in greater depth in Chapter 5, and the planets located in this house, indicate how the incarnating soul will face the world in which it finds itself. Mercury is enquiring and communicative. Mars is assertive, hasty and impatient and can have an underlying, deep-rooted anger. Venus on the other hand is concerned with creating a beautiful environment and harmonious relationships. Saturn brings with it a burden, a sense of responsibility which the soul meets when very young. Neptune brings with it a veil of illusion which can be difficult to penetrate, a longing to be back in the spiritual realms and no sense of itself as a separate, unique individual. The Sun is very aware of its own individuality, but the Moon is reflective of the feelings of those around it. Pluto is intense and secretive, whereas Jupiter is expansive and naturally expects the world to provide for its needs.

The Second House

The second house indicates resources and abilities which have been brought back to help in dealing with the present incarnation. The Sun in this house indicates that the inner Self has been developed in the past. The Moon in this house signifies that the soul has good experience around mothering and nurturing, although this may be offset by difficult aspects which indicate areas still to be worked on. It has worked on the emotions and feelings and often has psychic abilities that can be employed in empathizing with other souls. Mercury has developed the mind and the innate intelligence and this can be utilized in understanding the world, and other souls, around itself. Venus has worked on relationships and the creative energy in the past, and Mars has developed Will, courage and assertiveness.

Jupiter is at its best in the second house; it indicates an old skill in visualization and in manifesting that which is needed to sustain life. It is the old priest/ess who has a philosophy of inherent goodness of life and knows that the cosmos will provide. In the past it has learnt the laws of creative manifestation and now whenever there is a need it appears, when the energy is being used unconsciously, that a beneficent 'fate' provides. When the utilization of energy is conscious the pattern of putting out the request and receiving the answer is understood, as is the maxim 'as we think, so we are'. This understanding can then be passed on to others. My own experience is perhaps the best example I can give of this. When I was ready to begin working full-time on karmic counselling and to write this book, a friend said, 'I've got an old cottage that would be perfect for you'. It was exactly what I had always 'dreamt' of even down to the walled garden and inglenook fireplace. And it had room for seminars and workshops together with a wonderful healing earth energy just waiting to be plugged into. Exactly what I needed in order to proceed with my work — which includes teaching creative visualization and reconnection to the past.

Saturn in the second house shows wisdom and the inner self-discipline and integration which is the gift of a Saturn whose limitations and difficulties have been overcome. Uranus is creative thought, with a marvellous understanding of vibrational forces and a natural affinity to change and transformation. Neptune in this house offers the gift of imagination and spirituality, and Pluto that of a very deep understanding of the natural cycles of life, healing and regeneration which arise out of experiences with the old mystery/fertility religions and the wisdom of the Mother Goddess.

The Third House

The third house indicates karma with siblings: both the planet and the sign need to be examined in order to understand fully the manifestations of this karma which are explored further in Chapter 5. If the Sun or Moon are located in the third house, then in a past life the father or mother was a sibling. Mars or Pluto often indicates quite a violent karma with a sibling and issues of sibling rivalry and power struggles are also common. Neptune in this house has the effect of making the incarnating soul feel that it must have been adopted because it is so alien to the rest of the family. A third house Neptune is frequently misunderstood and miserable because of a lack of recognition of uniqueness and separateness by the rest of the family. The karma may perhaps result from having been too close to the family in the past, now the implications of the wider 'family of man' have to be recognized. This placement has also been seen in the charts of people who, under regression, have felt themselves to be 'aliens' from another galaxy who have now incarnated into the earth environment for a limited number of lives and their specific purpose is not only to learn their own karmic lessons but also help in the evolution of mankind.

The third house also indicates karma around communication and with Saturn in this house the soul frequently finds that it does not fulfil its intellectual potential until the mid-thirties owing to a fundamental block on learning or communicating what it knows or who it is. Such a block is at times linked to perceptual and conceptual differences, to speech or hearing defects coming forward from the past, or to an inability to fit into the conventional education system as the child simply does not see the world in the same way. On the other hand, the child may have been forced by parental pressure into specific academic pursuits and may develop a different mode of communication when it matures.

The Fourth and Tenth Houses

The fourth and tenth houses indicate parental karma and are dealt with in detail in Chapter 5 within the context of the family.

The Fifth House

The fifth house can indicate both karma with children or creative karma, and that with love affairs. The Sun, Mercury, Venus, Mars and Jupiter in the fifth house are naturally attuned to the creative energy which will flow with ease and manifest through the energy of the sign on the cusp, unless there are difficult aspects to be overcome. For example, with the Sun in Cancer the incarnating soul will naturally produce children, in Gemini it will produce words but if that Sun, or Mercury, is aspecting Saturn then finding a publisher may be difficult or it may lack the confidence to try.

Saturn in this house often experiences a delay or difficulty around physically producing a child or with creating *things*. It arises from not, in the past, having taken advantage of the opportunities afforded to be creative or in not having valued the products of creation/creativity. The result in the present life is that the struggle offers the opportunity to develop a sense of value concerning the ability to create on any level. The fifth house Uranus is naturally inventive and capable of extremely original thought although it may find it difficult to have its 'creations' accepted as 'art', for example because they are considered to be 'too way out', too far ahead of its time. Neptune in this house offers a creative imagination which is the manifestation of previous work in developing and utilizing this ability. Neptune may, however, need some constructive, earthing aspects in order for the potential to manifest as otherwise it may produce someone who is the eternal dreamer, not the doer.

The Sixth House

The sixth house offers pointers to both bodily karma (dealt with in Chapter 4) and career possibilities as it shows the area of work through which an energy may – or may not – manifest. Saturn in this house often brings a need to confront the energy behind chronic illness and to understand psychosomatic dis-ease. This may be dealt with in the body into which the soul is incarnated or it may be dealt with through professions such as nursing, osteopathy, social work, etc.

Uranus may manifest through subtle disruptions of bodily rhythms, causing dis-ease or leading into careers concerned with realigning the energies. It may indicate a karma with technology, sometimes going back as far as Atlantis, the present life being the first opportunity since that time for the soul to reconnect to the same level of technology. A client (Sun in Taurus with Uranus in Cancer in the sixth) had both health and technological karma. She had been the subject of medical experiments in Atlantis, including transplants and replacement of vital organs by synthetic ones. She ended up as a head controlling a body which was mostly a machine. Her experience included:

> A most unpleasant replacement of most of the digestive system with clear, plastic like, tubes and the abdominal cavity being left open so that its working could be viewed by the scientists. As they 'progressed' more and more of the organs were replaced including the reproductive system. A foetus was introduced into the artificial uterus, fed by recycled blood. This produced violent rejection symptoms. The brain was intact and conscious during this time, although it had electrodes and monitoring equipment implanted.

The client had expressed her problem as 'extraordinary health problems'. As a result of that previous life, and of an initiation experience which went wrong, the neural connections within her present body were seen to be misaligned between the etheric and physical body causing a malfunction manifesting as allergies and colitis, and as an 'astral travelling' situation which did not allow for recharging of the physical body during sleep. The client later commented that her bowel condition had been so bad that a colostomy had been proposed, which was why she had requested the reading. She had also experienced migraine and menstrual problems from a very early age. 'Alternative' medicine and aromatherapy were recommended in view of the karmic carry-over and this cleared the imbalances. Her experience with the Uranian energies from that life, and the fact that she had five planets in Fire, led her into a present-life career in psychological and physiological research into the condition known as 'burn-out'.

The soul with the technological karma symbolized by Uranus in the sixth now has the opportunity to make ethical choices connected with how it will utilize its abilities and knowledge in careers such as electronics, computers, alternative medicine, etc.

The Seventh, Eighth and Eleventh Houses

The seventh, eighth and eleventh houses are indicators of relationship karma. The seventh and eighth will be dealt with in Chapter 6. The eleventh house centres on karma connected with both friends and groups, in the widest sense of the word. If Pluto is in this house then there is karma around dominance, manipulation and other power issues, and power struggles are likely to manifest within group situations. Saturn and Uranus both have karma with authority figures and control versus freedom, and may in the past have been too attached to dogma and ideas, whether conventional (Saturn) or revolutionary (Uranus), rather than to the underlying wisdom or understanding. In the present life both Saturn and Uranus must come to accept that each incarnating soul is entitled to maintain its own views on life, without judgement or challenge. For example, many souls still need the guidance of a conventional religion, others have moved into an understanding of karma, and yet others have moved on to create their own reality. To each his own, without interference from Saturn or Uranus manifesting through another soul — although Uranus has the potential to act as a catalyst for another soul *when appropriate*. Saturn has to learn to let go of the past and allow change to occur naturally. Uranus has to develop evolution and not revolution, and the soul with this placement must learn to preserve the best of the past and incorporate it into the future. The tendency is to 'throw out the baby with the bathwater' by jettisoning everything from the past and undergoing radical change. Uranus is a planet of transformation but the choice is between change through chaos or orderly evolution.

Again a personal example may best serve to illustrate how Saturn and Uranus in the eleventh house work. I have both these planets in Gemini. My teacher, Christine Hartley, told me that I had long suffered both trying to fit into conventional society in some lives (Saturn), and in others trying to bring in new ideas and new ways (Uranus). She 'saw' me, amongst other confrontations with the establishment and 'authority', as being burnt as a witch and suffering at the hands of the Inquisition – an experience which several million souls share as the Inquisition and the witch-finders were active for several centuries. Amongst my first reincarnation memories to surface were those of the Cathari and the Egyptian Court of Akhenaton. My chiropractor is convinced that I was hung for insubordination in a previous life.

In this life, as a mature student at college I rarely said anything during a class (the inhibition of Saturn). However, as part of my religious studies course I insisted (Uranus) on doing a thesis on Spiritualism – which did not go down at all well with the college: my Mars sits between Uranus and Saturn and occasionally manifests conflict in order to teach me to stand up for myself and to highlight my need to explore different beliefs. After three years of Saturn being in the ascendancy and me biting my tongue, Uranus broke free. One of the tutors, a United Reform Church minister, said in answer to a question concerning healing, 'I don't think it has any value. I don't know anyone who has been healed'. I asked him since when had his ignorance been the criteria for judgement. I had used his tutorial room for spiritual healing sessions all the time I was at college (the subversive activities of Uranus). The room happened on that day to contain several of my patients and they all leapt to the defence of healing. I was undergoing teacher training at the time and my college record card stated 'Has very peculiar ideas and should not be allowed near children'. I fought long and hard for that comment to be removed (Uranus/Mars/Saturn) although I had no intention whatsoever of actually teaching – it was later pointed out to me by Howard Sasportas that there are many ways of teaching.

Although I have never seen a clear connection from that tutor to myself and did not feel there was personal karma between us, I always instinctively felt that his bigotry and narrow-mindedness stemmed from a life as an Inquisitor. Several years later this particular tutor pulled up at a bus-stop where I was standing in the rain. He told me he owed me an apology, he had become a healer. He then got back in his car and drove off, leaving me still standing in the rain!

The Twelfth House

The twelfth house is the main house of karma and planets in this house always have heavy karmic connotations. Many people ask: 'I have an empty twelfth house, does this mean I have no karma?' The answer is that there is no such thing as an empty house. If there is no planet located in the twelfth, or in any other house, then the sign on the cusp of that house, the placement of its ruler and its aspects, will give indications of the karmic pattern.

PLANETS IN THE TWELFTH HOUSE

The Sun

The Sun in the twelfth house indicates a soul who has been an important, prominent person in a past life, or lives, and may now have to work behind the scenes rather than be in the public eye, and have to content itself with less recognition than it deserves. This was clearly demonstrated in the chart of an opera singer (Sun conjunct Pluto in the twelfth close to the Cancer Ascendant, opposing Jupiter and trining Saturn in Aries) who had not found the fame which her voice merited. Somehow she always seemed to miss 'the big chance' through a series of mishaps. One day she opened a Russian book about a nineteenth-century singer and found that she was looking at a picture of herself. In that life she had received considerable acclaim and adulation. In the chart for the old incarnation, she also has the Sun in Cancer conjunct the Ascendant, but this time in the first house, squaring Jupiter/ Saturn in Aries and trining Pluto on the MC. She also recognized her present-life family as part of that old interaction. In her present life she had tried to 'persuade' her son to be a violinist, but he insisted on becoming a singer (his Pluto/Mars conjunction had a strong Will). In the past life her son had been a violinist and her present-life husband had been a devoted friend, who never married and had, it appears, suffered from unrequited love (twelfth house Neptune inconjunct seventh house Venus). In the present life she has Venus conjunct the South Node in Gemini, indicating the possibility that she may marry an old friend or lover, and her husband's twelfth house Neptune inconjunct seventh house Venus indicated an old idealization, or soulmate contact, with karma returning through a relationship.

The delay, or lack of recognition, can be a hard lesson to learn, particularly if in the past the soul has demanded everything immediately, the 'I want it now' syndrome (often linked to the Fire or Cardinal signs), or who had taken identity from a public role (Libra and the Mutable signs) and now has to learn who it really is. The karma can also be one of pride or egoism (particularly for Leo, Aries, and Capricorn), ruthless ambition (Cancer) or cruelty (Scorpio) and the lesson for the present life that of leadership without arrogance or false humility. The soul with this placement must learn to do the job not for the sake of reward and adulation, but for the sake of 'a job well done'. This applies not only to the working environment but to any sphere of life.

With this placement, there may also be karma with the father and aspects to the Sun and the sign on the cusp will indicate the past pattern. For example, a man with Aries on the cusp and an aspect from the Sun to Pluto was, in the present life, very subordinate to his ageing father who ran the company they both worked in. When he regressed to a past life, he found that the positions had been reversed and his father had then been his son, whom he had held back and who had ultimately fought him, winning control of the country in which they were then living.

The Moon

The Moon in the twelfth house has karma with the mother and around mothering and being mothered. It can have been over-protective and smothering (Moon in Cancer, for example), or too withdrawn and detached (Aquarius). Equally there may be karma around too much sensitivity (Pisces, Cancer and Neptune aspects) and feeling, out-of-control emotions and erratic swings of mood (Uranus aspects). The sign in which the Moon is placed (see Chapter 3), and aspects to the Moon, will further clarify the past pattern. A client with a twelfth house Moon in Leo went back in regression to a time when her mother was her slave. She later commented that she was still treating her mother exactly like a slave. Many people with the Moon in the twelfth house find that they have been through a whole series of incarnations which involve their mother and a repeating pattern which is carried over into the present life. Another client was aware of being very much disliked by her mother in the present life. In regression she explored three other such incarnations but was able to let them go and to begin the process of mothering herself, releasing herself from the chains of the past.

Mercury

The karma attached to the twelfth house Mercury relates to how the mind, tongue, or intellect have been used in the past. The pattern can vary from simple gossip (Gemini), sarcasm (Sagittarius), slander and destruction of a reputation (Scorpio), forcing one's own ideas on to others (often linked to a Pluto aspect), or being coerced into a particular way of thinking by outside pressure. It can indicate a refusal to use innate intelligence (aspects to Saturn), or a rigidity of ideas (Taurus or Capricorn), or too much analysis or criticism (Virgo). In the present life the soul is tested as to how it uses its mind and ability to communicate. Actual blocks on communication stemming from past lives, such as deafness or speech defects, may manifest through this house or the third and sixth houses, particularly if the chart includes difficult aspects to Mercury from Saturn, or Gemini on the cusp of the house and/or aspects to Capricorn planets.

Venus

Relationship karma appertains to Venus in the twelfth. The sign in which Venus appears is a key to the type of old karmic interaction. Aquarius indicates too much detachment. Cancer too much attachment, Capricorn a restriction around relating, and Scorpio old passions, intrigues and jealousies. The dual signs, Gemini, Sagittarius and Pisces, can have a problem with commitment and faithfulness, or promiscuous behaviour. Venus now has to deal with the consequences of these old actions and may experience considerable difficulty in finding the 'right' partner whilst these old issues are being balanced out. Relationships can change dramatically once the karmic implications are understood, particularly when a more appropriate choice of partner is made rather than old patterns and consequent disappointments being endlessly repeated.

Venus in the twelfth may also indicate that the soul has had strong incarnations as a woman, or close past-life links with the women with whom it has relationships in the present life. In the latter case, there may be difficulties as a relationship that feels so 'right' on one level is in fact founded on the past: a great deal of adjustment may be necessary as often the new personality is not so compatible as the old and this may cause friction. On the other hand, if the old pattern was one of discord, it may be necessary to adjust to the fact that the new persona is more agreeable: the old animosity can then be overcome and the past forgiven, thereby opening the way for both souls to grow through the relationship.

Mars

Mars has karmic issues around Will, aggression, assertion, violence and war. It should, however, be borne in mind that a war which one undertakes out of duty to one's country, and in which no hatred of the enemy is felt by the participant, will produce different karma from, for example, a crusade entered upon with burning zeal or a war entered upon for ideological reasons. Mars in the twelfth often involves having been a soldier in at least one incarnation, usually several, and may be indicative of positive qualities of leadership, discipline and self-reliance. Alternatively, Mars may have been drawn back endlessly into violent confrontation, instead of developing the Will and assertive qualities. There may be karmic issues of cowardice and courage – the soul may have to learn that discretion can be the better part of valour and that it can sometimes be foolhardy to continue to attack when a strategic withdrawal would enable the fight to continue another day. The twelfth house Mars placement may also indicate that the soul has had strong male incarnations and that it needs to integrate the masculine energy into balance, particularly if Mars is in the twelfth house of a soul incarnating into a female body in the present life, or if its previous incarnation was a 'macho' male. It now has the opportunity to learn the qualities of gentleness and sensitivity. When war and confrontation have been the old pattern, the present-life lesson may involve developing the other, softer, and more artistic side of the self.

A soldier with twelfth house Mars in Cancer became a major at a very early age, following the family tradition, but was increasingly unfulfilled and disillusioned with his life. He had always been interested in photography and he decided to take the risk of abandoning his 'safe', if somewhat dangerous, lifestyle in order to start again as a photographer. He had learnt his assertive lesson well and was able to put a great deal of drive into promoting himself and his career. He utilized his past experience and contacts by specializing in military subjects, but branched out into his other interests of people, places and words through travel books.

Jupiter

Jupiter in the twelfth can indicate karma centred around over-indulgence and expansion, or mistakes in the handling of assets, particularly when coupled with Saturn, Taurus or Capricorn. A woman with Jupiter conjunct Saturn in the twelfth house had a seven-year battle with her ex-husband over control of her family business after they divorced. Her past background had been to squander her inheritance, and in the present life she had to work hard to save it.

Jupiter can, on the other hand, have a close connection with the priest/ess and the temple and indicate a soul who has a long association with Egypt. There is then a karmic need to put that old knowledge to work, utilizing all the inherent wisdom and skills in order to alleviate the karmic suffering of mankind.

Saturn

Saturn, the Lord of Karma, is very much at home in the twelfth house when there are easy aspects, but rarely displays his wisdom and gifts before middle age is reached. Prior to this the emphasis is on releasing the burdens carried over from the past – which may involve past feelings of separateness and isolation – and on confronting the fears and restrictions imposed on oneself by those burdens. A Saturnian past-life blockage can only be released through following the injunction: Know thyself. When the past has been confronted and the soul has been released from bondage to old inadequacies and karma, twelfth house Saturn offers up its gifts of self-reliance, confidence, discipline and strength.

Uranus

With Uranus in the twelfth the soul often has strong memories of past lives which surface through dreams or *déjà vu*. Such memories involve natural cataclysm and catastrophe, as in the case of a girl with twelfth house Uranus who had always had a recurring nightmare about being buried alive and unexpectedly found its source when she visited the Pompeii exhibition in London. Uranus also has links with man-made revolution and chaos as in the case of the Aquarian with the Sun square to Saturn/Uranus in the twelfth house who uncovered, during a regression, a life as a Puritan in the Roundhead–Cavalier conflict, and then another life as a peasant during the French Revolution who became a leader of the people, Similarly, a workshop participant who had Uranus exactly on the Ascendant had a scar across her throat from ear to ear, and a terrible recurring nightmare of which she could only say: 'It's the Terror'. During regression she too went back to a life in the French Revolution, but as an aristocrat who lost his life to Madame La Guillotine. In the regression (s)he was pulled from bed in the middle of the night, summarily tried and executed at first light.

The twelfth house Uranus also indicates that the soul has links going back to Atlantis and now has to deal with technological karma stemming from the use, and misuse, of science and technological knowledge at that time, the present age being the first time since Atlantis when the technological advances present the same type of opportunities and dilemmas. With this placement the soul knows instinctively what it took science hundreds of years to rediscover, that this seemingly solid and stable earth and everything on it is a mass of vibrations open to manipulation and change, and liable from time to time to follow an erratic course with chaos ensuing, particularly when man has intervened in the natural processes. However, Uranus has the ability to synchronize vibration and to set the pattern back into harmonious functioning. The twelfth house Uranus also has very old insights, through its Atlantean experience, into crystal energies and is naturally attracted to astrology, music therapy, massage, pulsing, acupuncture, polarity therapy, etc., all of which utilize the underlying subtle energies linked to Uranus.

Neptune

Neptune in the twelfth is one of the most problematical karmic placements. It has been variously described as 'divine homesickness' and 'a leaky aura'. It indicates the soul's longing to return to the more celestial realms. The following quote is, I believe, from fiction but it sums up the peculiarly Neptunian ambivalence to life on earth: 'I came back because I wanted to, of my own free will. No one forced me to return. But now that I am here I want to take flight, to hide again in obscurity, to put this vast ocean between myself and this place. It bodes me no good.'

The lesson to be learnt from Neptune is one of surrender, rather than submission, to the divine, of at-one-ment not atonement. The challenge is to develop unconditional love. In the past the soul may have failed to face up to suffering constructively in a realistic, practical way, a pattern frequently accompanied by escapism whether it be into religion, mysticism, drink, drugs, meditation, or an institution. Alternatively, the soul may have an old pattern of endlessly sacrificing itself without thought or analysis of the consequences and may be the archetypal martyr, victim, scapegoat or saviour. It has no boundaries, does not recognize itself as separate and therefore takes on the pain of others by a process of osmosis, often unable to distinguish between its own emotion and pain and that of others. It needs to establish its boundaries and strengthen its protective aura, delineating its own space, whilst maintaining the ability, *when appropriate*, to merge with another or the cosmos.

A middle-aged woman (Neptune in Libra) had a Near-Death Experience induced by a massive, inadvertent overdose of cocaine with which she experimented 'in order to get closer to God', although 'he had told me that I would never get closer than I was already'. Prior to the experience she had felt very loving and very connected to the cosmos, but not earthed, and had a pattern of compulsively giving away all she owned. After a three-day coma she felt totally alienated and overwhelmed by the pains of the world, having to withdraw inside herself. It took two years for her to regain her equilibrium and to begin to restructure her life. She decided to utilize her channelling abilities and began what she described as 'a life of service to suffering humanity', although she still found it difficult to commit herself and displayed an unfortunate, unconscious Neptunian tendency to 'use' people and then move on without taking responsibility for her actions.

Compare the experience above with that of another client who wrote:

> I am aware of an unconscious skill needing to be brought out and used, and I think it is connected with 'seeing' but more, perhaps, 'far sight'. Certainly seeing past and future. I look at Moon inconjunct Neptune in the twelfth, mutual reception Mercury, sextile Jupiter and trine Uranus in the eighth. I feel that when I've learned to handle the exact Saturn opposition Moon, I'll be able to use that sensitivity more effectively. Someone described me as a psychic sponge: and indeed, I've had to learn to examine myself, when strong emotions overtake me. Is it me? Or is it someone else's? And of course had to learn about cleansing.

In a workshop guided meditation she had experienced, when asked to go back to a pleasant, happy life, a 'time of joy and harmony, a sort of Garden of Eden'. Her description beautifully conveys the sense of Neptune in harmony with Being:

> I go through the door and find myself in a simple robe with woven sandals on my feet. I'm in a steeply mountainous country. Although we are in the Tropics it is pleasant since we are at seven or eight thousand feet. The mountains go

much higher and I'm aware that the highest is a pinnacle, like a beacon, shining with crystal or perhaps ice.

I find myself going down a path, and am met by a boy and a girl. There is joy and happiness in meeting them: we jump and hug. Perhaps I am their older sister. We continue down the path and come to a low graceful stone house from a verandah outside. There is an astonishing feeling of no anxiety, no responsibility. A sort of unthinking innocence of being, as though I've never had to face a dilemma or a moral problem. Happiness and a feeling of at-oneness with my surroundings and the people I meet seems to be the normal state. Life feels as if cut from one piece: not the complex problem of reconciling opposites and disparate sub-personalities I experience now. The surrounds are always simple and harmonious too. I think 'what about relations with men?' and a man appears, and picks me up with great love and a sense of fun. My father? I think I must be somewhere between 14 and 16.

A woman comes. It is time. We are dressed in simple white garments. We go from the house down another path and are joined on our way by other women. We come to a round 'temple' building. The atmosphere is calm and everyday. Inside there is a pool of water in the centre of the building. I dip my hand in this and touch my forehead. It is a sort of cleansing. With my scribe, the person who writes down what I say, I go to one of many separate alcoves. I am a seer [the Neptune–Moon–Uranus configuration has psychic abilities]. This is very matter-of-fact [the pragmatic Saturn–Moon], it's like being part of the Civil Service. I have an area of country which I know well by 'seeing'. Every day, like this, I look in my silvered mirror and report what I see. I'm looking for the condition of the crops; the state of the roads, the occurrence of pests, etc. My perception and ability to look at things in the normal way is slightly different. As well as normal seeing I see what is like swiftly moving coloured mist around everything. The colours of the mist indicate the process through which an apparently solid object is moving – how it is changing. As I see, I speak: and

73

my scribe writes everything down. Afterwards all the scribes report back to the 'priestess' in charge, and the seers listen to make sure the report is correct.

Pluto

The soul incarnating with Pluto in the twelfth house has to face the archetypal, evolutionary forces hidden deep within the darkness of the human psyche. Pluto in the twelfth, or on the angles of the chart, can also be a key to obsessions, compulsions and phobias stemming from past lives. Saturn may also be implicated, as a phobia is really fear of the fear one feels on encountering the phobic object.

A client came for a consultation about a relationship problem but mentioned, in passing, that she had a phobia (Pluto in Leo in the twelfth house square Moon in Scorpio). She could not bear to be in a crowd of people because of her overwhelming fear that she would loose control and would either pass out or throw up. She also had great fear of other people vomiting. Part of her fear went back to a past life when she had been in contact with typhoid and had been locked away with the sufferers for several weeks. The dead bodies were not removed and she had a great fear of passing out because as soon as anyone did they were thrown on to the heap of dead and decaying bodies. It appeared that one or two of the survivors resorted to cannibalism and, therefore, staying in control was vital for self-preservation. She did not contract typhoid and lived for many years with the nightmarish memory of her ordeal. The stench in the room had been unbelievable, there was no fresh air and no water and she had had to listen to the typhoid sufferers literally retching their life away. As Pluto is very deep and devious, however, this was not the only root of the phobia and it has still not been released, although it was eased to the extent that she is now able to open herself up sufficiently to take part in meditation groups, which would have been unthinkable prior to reconnecting to that past experience.

The twelfth house Pluto also represents karma connected with using, abusing, and being misused by, power. The soul has to deal with control and manipulation issues and has a deep fear of letting go. When in contact with Mars and Saturn it links into the karma of collective power and many people with these aspects 'remember' being involved in events like the Holocaust. A client (Leo Pluto/Saturn/Mars in the twelfth) regressed to a concentration camp. Although she survived the camp, she later committed suicide as a result of her guilt at surviving. She felt at that time that she 'could not live in a world which had allowed such a thing to happen'. She was very aware of the collective karma of mankind and of the Jewish 'scapegoat' karma in particular as she was born, in the present life, into a Jewish family. The idea of a 'chosen people' who 'suffer' through the capricious acts of an authoritarian God demonstrates clearly the effect of 'as we think, so we are'. In other words, when a people expect to suffer, they are wide open to abuse by those exerting power as they are not 'programmed' by their belief system to resist. On the other hand, those who believe they are 'chosen' in the sense of favoured, for example in their divine right to rule, are much more likely to strongly defend their position when it is threatened and not to allow that abuse of power.

Pluto in the twelfth is also connected to healing power and it is frequently seen in the charts of those who become doctors, nurses or therapists out of some kind of compulsive necessity, the unconscious repetition of an old pattern, rather than out of the conscious choice to heal. The ability to heal is real, however, as is the ability for trance mediumship and clairvoyance, which also has links with the Pluto twelfth house placement, particularly when Pluto is in Cancer or has links to the Moon. The placement represents an old skill coming forward and can become an asset when consciously utilized.

In his book *Pluto, the Evolutionary Journey of the Soul*[10] Jeff Green explores at length the twelfth house Plutonian need to let go of egocentric control and surrender to the universe, and this book is recommended for further study of the placements of Pluto. Howard Sasportas in *The Twelve Houses*[11] gives an in-depth exposition of all the planets in the twelfth and other houses, and includes a karmic perspective.

KARMIC ASPECTS

Aspect patterns indicate how constructively or otherwise the planetary energies will be used by the incarnating soul when dealing with the karma attached to the planetary configuration. On the whole, flowing aspects manifest more easily and hard aspects indicate a struggle to regain and value the planetary principle. Nevertheless, that struggle may be of value if it is required in order to overcome the problem. Without the impetus of the discomfort of a hard aspect the delaying tactic of procrastination can recur.

Fixed Squares

Squares which are in Fixed signs or houses point to long-term karma which has built up over many lifetimes. The Fixed square between Pluto in Leo and the Moon in Taurus or Scorpio, for example, indicate mothering difficulties experienced throughout many incarnations, and associated traumatic emotional experiences such as rejection, abandonment, guilt and resentment (see Chapter 5). Similarly a Fixed square of Uranus to Mars will indicate issues of wilfulness displayed throughout many lifetimes.

Cardinal and Mutable Squares

Cardinal squares indicate karma which became 'fixed' in the last incarnation and which can either be dealt with in this incarnation or become an ongoing difficulty in future incarnations. Mutable squares represent karma in the making, patterns which are becoming 'fixed' in the present life and which can be used positively or negatively. For example, a soul with a Neptune–Mars square may choose to face the challenge of spiritualizing the Will, moving beyond the personal ego into alignment with the eternal Self; conversely it may fall into the trap of self-destruction, drink or drugs as a way of disintegration.

The Grand Cross

Squares can come together to form a Grand Cross, an aspect with powerful karmic connotations and a deep need to integrate the warring factions of the psyche which are represented by the planetary energies involved. Kenneth Halliwell (fig. 5), who murdered playwright Joe Orton (see Chapter 2), had a Fixed Grand Cross (Venus in Taurus square Neptune in Leo square Moon/Saturn in Scorpio square Jupiter in Aquarius). Jacqueline Clare, the sensitive Piscean who drew the charts for this book, described him, through her attunement to his energies, as a 'frustrated soul in torment'. The Orton diaries portray a man wrestling with out-of-control, unconscious, conflicting emotions; depression and elation; self-aggrandizement and deep inadequacy. The emotional separation from his parents was epitomized when his mother, whom he loved obsessively, choked to death when he was a young teenager. Sometime later his father committed suicide. Halliwell appears to have been a man who found it impossible to be happy. His answer to his increasing disintegration and separation from Orton was to kill him, and then himself.

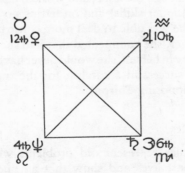

Fig. 5: The Grand Cross

Many charts with a Grand Cross convey a sense of destiny, the incarnating soul choosing to face several old patterns which lock in together. The example shown here (fig. 6) belongs to an alternative medicine practitioner and past-life therapist who had

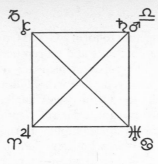

Fig. 6

problems with her endocrine system and intractable, recurrent back pain. Despite years of chiropractic, osteopathic, healing and regression sessions, she had not been able to reach the pain or the imbalance (her sixth house Pluto/Moon conjunction indicates that the cause of dis-ease is subtle and the roots go deep). Her chart showed issues around the use of the Will (Saturn/Mars) and her Chiron placement indicated that she was still attached to past suffering through her body (the Earth element). When she stopped trying to force through the issue, and worked instead on visualization (utilizing Jupiter skills) and on letting go of the pain and past suffering, she was able to deal more constructively with the problem. However, she commented that had she not had to deal with this difficulty in herself, she would never have studied so hard and become so successful a catalyst for the transformation of others (Uranus opposing Chiron).

Trines and Sextiles

Trines and sextiles represent old problems which have been worked on in past lives and show that an understanding has emerged towards the end of life or in the period between lives. In the present incarnation the soul with these aspects needs to strengthen the integration of the energies and put them to work constructively. The difficulty can be that these aspects are 'lazy' and take time to flow properly, often requiring the trigger of a major transit to start them off. Stephen Arroyo points out:

There is some evidence that trine aspects correspond with wasteful or problematical conditions in far more cases than traditional teachings about the 'beneficial' effects of trines would indicate. For example, the trine of Neptune is often found in charts of people who exhibit rather negative Neptunian tendencies: drug problems [etc.] ... or simply the inability to deal effectively with the material world ... Uranus trines are almost as common as the more dynamic Uranus aspects in the charts of people who are particularly self centered, unable to cooperate ... Jupiter trines often seem to indicate little more than a tendency towards lazy self-indulgence and a preference for relying on anything other than one's own hard work.[12]

A client described sextiles as 'the quickest road to hell because they are so smooth and easy, you don't realize how quickly you are getting there'. Her chart comprised 'disjointed sextiles, which didn't quite connect to each other'. She had problems with making choices and decisions, 'things just seem to happen to me regardless of what I want'. It was only when she began to be conscious that her Sun sextile Pluto gave her the potential to handle her own power, and Saturn sextile Mars the potential to use her Will to direct her life, that she began to make progress.

The Grand Trine and the Kite

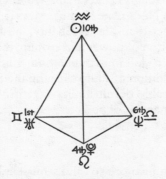

Fig. 7: The Kite

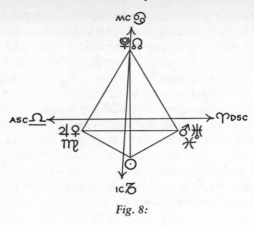

Fig. 8:

The Grand Trine is formed by three trines connecting to each other in the form of a triangle, usually but not always in the same element. A Kite formation (fig. 7) incorporates a third planet which is opposed to one of the planets in the trine, and sextiles the other two. The Grand Trine has enormous potential and the element in which it is placed can indicate the area through which the energies will manifest: Fire through the intuition and initiation, Water through feelings and contact with others, Earth through the senses and environment, and Air through communication and the mind processes.

Metaphysician Douglas Baker had a Water Grand Trine (fig. 8) Pluto/MC/North Node trine Uranus/Mars trine Jupiter/Venus. A formidable, larger-than-life personality, the university he set up teaches the utilization of power and esoteric thought. The Grand Trine shows an old skill in manipulation, vibration and healing forces, and the addition of Pluto forming the Kite configuration indicates considerable occult ability together with karma concerning the use, or abuse, of power.

The Inconjunct

Inconjuncts (the quincunx 150° and semi-sextile 30° aspects) are powerful karmic aspects indicating conflicting energies or experiences from the past which need to be synthesized and balanced in the present incarnation. The planetary energies involved are a major challenge in life and anyone with more than one inconjunct in the chart has a deep need to question the purpose behind incarnation. The inconjunct aspects will provide an answer and a pathway foreward. Alan Epstein[13] sees this as an aspect which requires 'the balancing of the desired against the practicable, the ideal against the real'. He sees one side of the inconjunct as 'what is desired' and the other as 'the price that must be paid to attain it'. Although people may endeavour to live out only one end of an inconjunct, as with any aspect, ultimately there has to be an integration of the basic principles, a creative compromise which offers both a resolution and an expansion of the energies involved.

The quincunx (150°) relates to personal experience of the planetary energies, whilst the semi-sextile (30°) aspect frequently indicates the soul who lives out the problem by attracting a partner who has the same planets in hard aspect. A client asked why he always seemed to attract Scorpionic/Plutonian women. He had the Moon semi-sextile Pluto in his chart and on examining the charts of his last three relationships, all the women had hard Pluto–Moon aspects. His own interest and karma lay in what he described as 'the rape of Mother Earth' (Moon in Virgo) and how mankind could best utilize and conserve the limited resources available whilst still advancing through technology (twelfth house Uranus). The company he ran was concerned with alternative technology and he was planning to write a book on this subject.

Certain inconjuncts run as a karmic theme in charts. With the Sun inconjunct Uranus the soul is seeking its own individuality and self-expression; the Moon inconjunct Saturn is seeking to overcome a fundamental lack of self-worth and a block on the expression of feelings; Mercury inconjunct Saturn has a long-standing block on communication; Venus inconjunct Pluto is dealing with an inner 'black hole' which is insatiable for emotional nourishment and never feels loved enough; Mars inconjunct Uranus is suffering the effects of old wilfulness and unpredictability, whilst Mars inconjunct Saturn is restricted by a sense of powerlessness and helplessness, a blocked Will. The Sun, or Mars, inconjunct Pluto is dealing with old power issues and learning how to handle its own power rather than use it to force and coerce, either as victim or perpetrator. Neptune inconjunct the Moon or Venus is working on spiritualizing relationships in a realistic way through unconditional love, rather than through the old pattern of idealization and illusion.

The Finger of Fate

When two inconjuncts radiate out from a central planet (fig. 9) to two other planets sextile each other, the result is a Finger of Fate which indicates karmic energies which the soul must integrate into itself through the present-life experience. As its name suggests, the Finger of Fate is indicative of a 'fated' life script and the soul will repeatedly meet the energies represented by the planets until it achieves wholeness. Integration and release of the energies is facilitated by the opposition of a planet to the central point, as this can act as an outlet. Configurations without the outlet need to utilize the energy of the opposing sign and house to form a point of release. The Case Study contained in Appendix I has two Fingers of Fate and a Grand Trine which are discussed in detail.

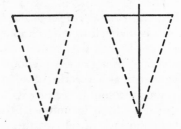

Fig. 9: The Finger of Fate

KARMIC POTENTIAL

Conjunctions, trines and sextiles can be seen as indicators of karmic potential, as can planets in compatible signs and houses.

Some planets 'fit' more naturally into particular elements. Mercury, for example, is at ease in the Air and Fire signs. Such a placement will point to a natural talent for communication, analysis or interpretation – unless hampered by Saturn aspects, in which case there is a struggle to manifest the positive side. It can also indicate an inherent intelligence which is nothing to do with being intellectual or passing examinations. The dictionary definition of intelligence is 'quickness of understanding' and it is this alertness and ability to make intuitive leaps, in order to synthesize information and come up with new ideas, which can be so helpful in dealing with challenging situations. Similarly Mars in the Fire signs can indicate a natural courage and assertiveness when confronted with a challenge. Venus is a changeling planet, taking on the quality of the element and sign in its relationships. In Libra it is naturally 'nice', getting along with everyone, and it has the ability to provide a harmonious atmosphere in which everyone can flourish. In Scorpio, Venus is more suspicious, but loyal, intense and passionate when it learns to trust; in Sagittarius that trust is a natural feature of relating.

Saturn in Capricorn can illustrate the difference between a positive and negative manifestation of the planetary energy. When operating negatively, Saturn in Capricorn can indicate a soul who is particularly fearful, repressed and drawn to very conventional religious practices or ways of organizing society. It will be a pillar of the Establishment, consistently refusing to move forward to learn new lessons. However, when Saturn in Capricorn has worked in previous lives on developing inner discipline, resilience and authority, it has the potential to utilize these skills in business, government, social administration, teaching or counselling others – not in an authoritarian, rule-imposing manner, which is the negative function of Saturn, but rather in a way which draws out the potential in others for self-reliance and self-discipline. It offers the possibility of moving from an external locus of control – a controlling voice from somewhere outside oneself which imposes rules and regulations through 'oughts' and 'shoulds' and is often confused with a judgemental God – to the inner locus of control which is an interior voice which directs in accordance with what is best for the Self and its spiritual purpose.

Saturn in Capricorn thereby attains inner authority and status which reflects *who*, not *what*, it really is.

Neptune Aspecting Venus, Mercury and/or the Moon

Neptune contacts with Venus, Mercury and the Moon can indicate an artistic, musical, visionary or psychic-intuitive potential which is carried forward from past lives. At times, as with all karmic contacts, such potential is indicated through extremely wide orbs of aspect. Claude Debussy (fig. 10) had Sun/Mercury

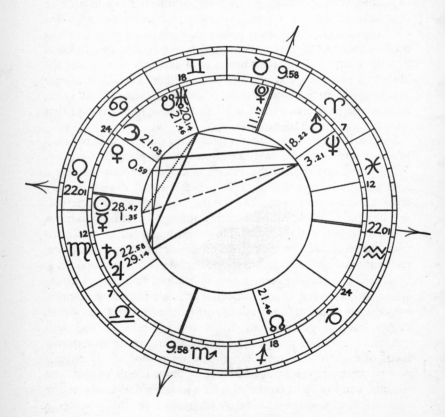

Fig. 10: Claude Debussy

inconjunct Neptune, and Neptune trine Venus, and was something of an infant prodigy, with considerable talent as a pianist.
His father believed him to be a second Mozart (who had Neptune
opposing fifth house Mercury) and had plans for him to give
concerts around Europe at a very young age. His bullying tactics,
however, destroyed Debussy's talent for playing but he went on to
compose music which was revolutionary for its time, and controversial in both form and content: his Uranus/South Node
conjunction in Gemini, square Saturn, indicates old karma
around the revolutionary ideas of the airy Uranus coming into
conflict with the established convention and form of the existing
Saturnine structure. Throughout his life he alternated periods of
intense creativity with stormy love affairs and the deepest despair.
He has a wide Jupiter/Saturn conjunction opposing Neptune,
Saturn squares the Nodes and Uranus conjuncts the South Node,
indicative of the manic depression and genius which would pull
him apart unless he could reconcile the warring energies within his
psyche. Using conventional orbs and the major aspects his chart is
'split' into two parts linked by the wide Saturn conjunction
to Jupiter, plus an unaspected Pluto. One involves Saturn–
Moon–Uranus–Mars (issues around the feelings, and use of
the Will). The other involves Jupiter–Venus–Sun–Mercury–
Neptune (his creative potential and issues around 'love'). One of
Debussy's most contentious pieces, *The Afternoon of a Faun*,
based on a poem about a faun who spies a nymph asleep on the
grass and makes love to her, was composed in the reverie which
followed Debussy's own love-making. The two parts are linked by
a quintile from Mercury to Uranus, indicating the evolutionary
potential of his original and inventive powers of creation, but also
his inability to live in the everyday world.

Debussy was the stereotype of an artist of genius who somehow
cannot live the ordinary life. He was born into a family which he
felt was alien to him, and was 'rescued' by his aunt who was
described as 'totally besotted with him from the first meeting and
determined to make him the child she had never had'. Debussy has
Moon in Cancer inconjunct the North Node in Sagittarius, an
aspect indicative of stress and destiny connected with unconventional mothering (the Saturn–Uranus–Moon part of the chart)

and of the need to find a new way of nurturing, and of being, himself. His aunt educated him to a standard far above that possible for his parents and encouraged his early musical talent. However, she died of cancer when he was young, after his father had forcibly taken him back to his 'family' in order to capitalize on that talent. Debussy's talent only flourished when he left his 'family' and went to study abroad, but he always experienced great difficulty with the discipline required for music. He lived out the extremes of the Jupiter/Saturn and Neptune energies and was constantly in debt, dependent on other people for support, having to 'prostitute' his art by becoming a teacher of piano and writing songs to pay off his creditors. He died from cancer and loss of hope at the age of forty-six.

Singer/songwriter Julie Felix, who has never had a music lesson in her life and cannot read music, but to whom it just came, and Bob Dylan, her contemporary and fellow-protester, have Uranus inconjunct Neptune/North Node, and Neptune/North Node square Mercury. They set out not only to communicate with the world through their music (Mercury in Gemini) but also to change it (Uranus) by pointing out its injustices and failings and, in Julie Felix's case, by taking a very active part in marches and demonstrations for peace and developing an interest in the healing power of music, thereby incorporating the subtle awareness of vibration which Uranus offers to Mercury in aspect to Neptune.

Neptune contacts to Mercury, the Moon or Venus can also indicate the potential for attuning to, and focusing, spiritual vision. The soul with such aspects has a sensitivity which reaches beyond the vibrations of earth and is capable of raising its level of consciousness to the level of the eternal, cosmic Self, thereby receiving guidance and wisdom. It is also one of the indicators of psychic potential and healing power, Pluto contacts with the Moon being another, and of clairvoyance – which is contact with those who inhabit other levels of being. Such aspects are indicative of training received in the ancient temples in esoteric work such as OOBEs, sleep healing, dream interpretation, trance, prophecy and telepathy. These ancient arts are finding a new acceptance and application as the Age of Aquarius dawns in the evolution of human consciousness.

Chapter 2

WHERE ARE WE GOING?

Our life purpose is our own personal path of evolution.

TRACY MARKS, *THE ASTROLOGY OF SELF DISCOVERY*

The karmic purpose of incarnation can be seen in the lunar Nodes. The South Node of the Moon indicates that which has been learned in previous incarnations and carried over, the North Node of the Moon that which is to be developed in the present incarnation. The South Node represents behaviour which is instinctual, unconscious and compulsive. It operates from a very deep survival level, overriding intellect and logic. It is a paradigm constructed from all that has gone before, an endless cycle of repetition and reaction to emotional and environmental stimuli. It is as it is because it has always been that way: fixed, rigid and unyielding. That which has been found to work in the past is relied upon, even though it may no longer be appropriate or relevant to the life plan. The result can be the negative manifestation of energies which were once positive.

A client in her mid-thirties complained that she was always being offered – and accepting – top-level, high-powered management jobs which entailed jetting around the world and taking ruthless decisions (South Node in Aries in the eleventh house), when all she really wanted to do was settle down, preferably within a relationship, and devote her considerable but unexploited artistic talents to the development of a mystical tarot pack (North Node in Libra conjunct Neptune in the fifth house). The aggressively assertive quality of her South Node in Aries, which she had carried over from previous male lives, had been helpful to her in reaching the top of her profession. However, the constant repetition of the South Node pattern was stultifying her growth and interfering with the development of her Libra North Node potential for harmony, beauty and creative relationships.

When challenged by circumstances which demand change, the incarnating soul's initial reaction is to retreat into what is known and familiar: the South Node. However, the relentless inner pressure of the North Node towards growth into new behaviour modes insists upon modification of the old in-built pattern. The predisposition towards instinctive behaviour eventually comes to be recognized as a block on progress, and the potential for change is acknowledged. It is at this point that the energies of the North Node can begin to manifest, awkwardly at first, but gaining in competence as attunement to the karmic purpose progresses and old fears and inhibitions are left behind. The relapses which may occur from time to time are not necessarily detrimental to progress; a falling back into old patterns may, initially, feel comfortable and give temporary respite from the struggle. The impetus towards transformation is renewed when the old patterns are suddenly experienced as confining and suffocating. The resultant surge of growth heralds a new stage of evolution with all its attendant possibilities.

Change is of course never easy, but those who follow willingly find the way smoother than those who resist every step of the way. It must be remembered that the nodal axis is an exact opposition and that, as with all oppositions, there are several approaches to working with the opposing nodal energies. One is to allow the conflicting pull from each end to indiscriminately tear the structure of life apart, swinging wildly from one extreme to the other as each Node has its brief, transit-induced moment of power, or, slightly less destructive, living out each end in totally unconnected compartments of life. The second approach is a variation on the same theme, living out one end, usually the South Node, and rigidly excluding and repressing the other. In both these approaches the flaw is in experiencing the 'ends' as disparate, and having no connection or flow other than conflict between the two points. The tension embodied in an opposition aspect is dynamic, and the possibility of action, compromise and resolution is inherent within it. If the ancient Chinese perception of the Nodes as a dragon is utilized, the North Node representing the head and the South Node the tail, then another possibility emerges, that of synthesis and integration. The positive skills and energies incorporated in the South Node can be harnessed to the growth and development of the North Node potential. And the dragon's tail can perform its function of eliminating that which is outgrown and ready to be discarded.

In the example given above, the client was aged thirty-six and her second nodal return was imminent: the time was ripe to harness the courage and action of her Aries South Node to find a positive outlet for her creative energies. She located a publisher who was interested in a new tarot pack, resigned her job, moved out of a destructive relationship into a supportive one, and gave herself the time for contemplation and reflection which formed the basis of her spiritually orientated designs for the new pack.

Moving into the North Node mode and attuning to the karmic purpose brings about a profound change in orientation, a major shift having been made from unconscious response to conscious choice. The soul no longer feels helpless, powerless, at the mercy of external forces. Awareness brings change. Change is empowering and creates new possibilities. The choice to respond to life in accordance with the karmic purpose provides inner fulfilment and a sense of integration and harmony.

There are many levels of meaning and experience within the lunar Nodes and the house and sign placements must be synthesized to reach the core. The sign in which a Node is placed will indicate *how* the energies will operate, and the house *where* the energies will operate. For example, the energy embodied in a Cancer North Node is one of nurturing. In the fourth house that energy will manifest in the home and with children. In the twelfth house, however, it will manifest on the collective level, perhaps through working in some kind of institution. All the different levels are a valid way of experiencing karma and can be perceived as a spiral leading from the superficial to the profound. During the course of a life, or a series of lives, it is possible to move between the levels many times whilst travelling to the core. Even those who are fortunate enough to attune to their ultimate purpose early in an incarnation will explore the multi-layered Node in all its manifestations.

The following is intended as a brief guide to the behaviour patterns, both inherent and potential, of the lunar axis. House and sign placements need to be integrated in order to reach the deepest understanding of the karmic purpose:

THE NODES IN SIGNS AND HOUSES

North Node: Aries / First House
South Node: Libra / Seventh House

Karmic purpose: to develop the Self unselfishly.

The primary aim for the Aries and/or first house North Node is to develop the Self and its own unique individuality, projecting this out through the sign on the Ascendant and/or the house and sign in which it is placed. The danger is that the new behaviour pattern may be egocentric and wilful, aware only of the needs of 'Me'.

The past pattern indicated by the Libra and/or seventh house South Node is too much adjustment and compromise in meeting the needs of others, the incarnating soul always putting itself aside in relationships and being too easily influenced by what 'they' want. It lacks the confidence to accept its own fundamental need and right to develop as an individual, receiving validation from its interaction with another rather than from its own internal source of power (the Self). The Libra South Node believes that to 'be good' is preferable to being true to itself.

The pattern of compromise and adjustment begins very early in life and is particularly expressed through the parental relationship. One client reported that her first house North Node had tried to manifest early and that, as a small child, her constant cry had been 'I onts' ('I want'). Needless to say, she did not get what she wanted. Any aspirations to individuality and independence were firmly quashed by a mother who 'knew best' 'for her own good'. Her seventh house South Node pattern quickly came to the fore: 'Whatever you want, I'll be a good girl', she whimpered. It took her another forty years to accept that she had her own rights, and several more before she felt comfortable about asserting her needs — a period which corresponded to the transiting North Node conjuncting her South Node and stimulating the integration of the nodal axis.

The development of the Aries and/or first house North Node may entail facing difficulties within a relationship as the partner or parent is thwarted by the unexpected refusal to gratify every whim. The demands tend to be increased as the partner meets opposition and believes that, if enough pressure is applied, the newly emerging autonomous being will cave in and the compliant status quo will be restored. All the Aries Will, energy and courage are called for at this point. Self-assertion classes, martial arts or other means of channelling the Aries or Mars energy can be helpful and supportive. The incarnating soul at this time seeks constant reassurance that it really is 'OK' for it to assert itself and that it is now time for others to adapt to the changes taking place. In this situation group therapy or a self-help group can provide the support family or friends could be unwilling or unable to provide owing to an unacknowledged conflict of interest.

The Libra South Node ability to find balance and harmonize with others can be utilized to smoothe the way to an expression of personal competence and power.

North Node: Libra/Seventh House
South Node: Aries/First House

Karmic purpose: to relate harmoniously.

The karmic purpose of the Libra and/or seventh house North Node is to develop the ability to relate to others and to adapt as appropriate to external needs, rather than slavishly follow its own internal demands to the exclusion of all others. In other words, it is to learn the art of creative compromise.

Work will be needed to overcome the inherent wilfulness and self-centredness of the Aries South Node, and to see beyond the confines of individual needs. For this Node the demands of 'Me' have been of paramount importance, the individual believing that he or she alone is right and has the answers. An unconscious Aries South Node is arrogant and bombastic, its most used word 'I'. An aspiring politician (Ascendant conjunct Sun and South Node in Aries) said: 'Of course I will be elected', 'I know what they need', 'I've told them . . .', 'I can give them . . .', 'When I'm elected I'm going to . . .', etc., etc. He never stopped to listen to his prospective voters, and only ever told them what he could do for them. He was most surprised when he failed to get elected.

Learning to listen to others is the first step in becoming more open to the Libra North Node. Gradually an acceptance of wider needs and aspirations will develop, together with the ability to cooperate within a group to achieve common aims.

The aspiring politician, following his initial defeat, went to talk to a sixth-form college. After his carefully scripted opening remarks, even he could not fail to notice a certain restlessness among his young audience. He had the courage (Aries) to stop and ask them what was wrong. He was told: 'You are just like everyone else, talking at us. You don't care what we think or even what we want to know about.' He threw away his speech and opened up to questions. He learnt a lot from that confrontation and changed his approach, knocking on doors and asking: 'What can I do for you?' He was not elected the next time around, but it was a close run. He continued to work for his prospective constituents, moving more and more into his Libra North Node and channelling all the courage and drive of the Aries South Node into fighting the local council on their behalf on a number of controversial issues.

It is within the field of personal relationships that the Aries South Node takes its worst toll, and the Libra North Node offers its greatest rewards. An understanding of 'Us' brings a closeness and companionship which the ivory tower of the Aries South Node has never before known.

For the seventh house Node (North or South) in particular, the soul may find that personal relationships are also the place for meeting old karmic associates and for striving to balance out what has gone before. With the South Node relationships may frequently be a 're-run' and it may take an extreme effort of Will and determination to move out of an old, self-immolating pattern of relating. North Nodal relationships will be a particular focus for growth based not only on retribution or reparation for old 'wrongs' but also on the development of loving harmony with another person as the North Node learns that two individual entities can come together to make a third whole – a relationship. Individuality is not sacrificed or repressed, it is brought into the relationship and offered, together with love and respect for the individual it is meeting. Two come together in integration and cooperation to form a harmonious partnership which allows for individual and joint growth.

North Node: Taurus / Second House
South Node: Scorpio / Eighth House

Karmic purpose: to find inner security.

The North Node in Taurus and/or the second house indicates that the soul must develop the ability to live within the body, utilizing its own resources to develop inner security rather than relying on others, possessions or the past to provide roots.

There is a need to move away from the manipulative, power-based emotional games of the Scorpio South Node and to free itself from the jealousies and possessiveness that arise out of insecurity. The past for the Scorpio South Node is full of resentment, trauma and upheaval and the resultant suspicion and caution when it is faced with something new can make growth a time of drama and crisis. The Taurus North Node needs to experience the safety of feeling itself unfolding in tune with its own inner, in-built rhythm of evolution. It must learn that steady progress based on the slow accumulation of intangible resources such as stability and patience can lead to growth.

Taurus is an earth-based, practical sign and as such the North Node also needs to deal in tangible assets. The incarnating soul has to utilize the senses when interacting with the environment, in contrast to the Scorpio South Node which feeds on emotional interaction. It needs to experience the unity between body and Self, to take pleasure in sensual rather than sexual contact, and to be self-sufficient on all levels.

One client, who had a flourishing professional practice, was nevertheless 'terrified that her marriage was over' despite the fact that she had hardly seen her husband for many years. Indeed, the setting up of her practice, and the satisfaction of her Taurean North Node demands for self-sufficiency, had meant that they had to live in separate countries most of the time. With the Scorpio South Node, however, she found it very difficult to let go of the apparent, and illusory security of 'the marriage'. Moreover, she felt that as a divorced woman, she would not have the same status and assets she enjoyed as a married woman, despite the fact that, on a purely materialistic level, she was well able to provide for herself. She also discovered that she had secretly rather enjoyed the Scorpionic games they had played with each other – lovers, fights, reconciliations, etc. As actress Sheila Steafel put it: 'Alone you miss the adrenalin of a bad relationship – there's nothing to complain about.'

Taurus, however, is rooted in survival, and that Scorpio South Node knows from way way back that it has been down into the pit not once but many times – and survived. From there it has brought back insights and endurance available to very few people – resources which the Taurus North Node can apply to growing and everyday living.

North Node: Scorpio / Eighth House
South Node: Taurus / Second House

Karmic purpose: to regenerate.

The Scorpio and/or eighth house North Node soul learns to share its own unique insights and resources with others. This is not a nodal placement that can be taken superficially, it goes where others fear to tread.

Scorpio can penetrate into depths of blackness and taboo areas no one else can reach to bring back insights. This nodal placement explores the 'dark' side of the eighth house 'birth, death and rebirth' cycle. It is usual for the eighth house North Node to undergo several significant 'deaths' and new beginnings during the course of a lifetime as the quest for regeneration continues. The sensuality of the Taurus South Node can be utilized as a way of communing and sharing emotionally with another, leading the way into the intensity of the Scorpio North Node relationship.

Many power issues will be raised and must be worked through before the regenerative energies can be freed. There is a need to overcome material possessiveness and to move beyond obtaining emotional security from possessions (Taurus South Node) in order to learn to share oneself fully with another.

A uniquely honest, penetrating and loving relationship is possible for the Scorpio North Node brave enough to open its heart to another. However, few souls with a Taurus or eighth house Node, whether North or South, can resist the temptation to look back longingly to the past and what might have been, or forward to the future and what might be, and yet such a behaviour pattern does not express any dissatisfaction: Scorpio likes a little fantasy to add spice to life but will be genuinely bewildered if its partner expresses jealousy as a result.

This tendency to cling to what might have been is illustrated by a North Node in Aries in the eighth house. A man, then in his early thirties, met a woman on the tube whom he had known briefly years before. They went for a drink: 'I caught hold of her hand to help her cross the road and that was it, I just never let go again. There was an electric current between us.' His North Node conjuncted her Sun and his Libra South Node conjuncted her Neptune. The 'affair' was never consummated despite the fact that he 'could hardly keep his hands off her'. He was unable to move from the sensuality of the South Node into the sexuality of the Aries eighth house North Node. Both were married to other people, and both had sexual problems within the marriage. They discussed living together and eventually, after four years, he left his wife: 'Someone had to make the first move.' (Aries Node beginning to manifest.) However, she never left her husband and the 'affair' finally ended after another four years and much vacillation on both parts. In the meantime every new relationship he started ended as soon as it began to be sexual. He explained that it wasn't fair to the new woman, as his lady friend might decide to come to him. The beautiful illusion of the Neptune conjunct the South Node lasted longer than most, reinforced by the attraction of the Sun conjunct the North Node but he never managed to manifest the potential for a 'real' relationship.

The eighth house North Node has far deeper and older links

with the creative cycle than may appear on the surface. This is also the house of levels of consciousness and awareness, and there is a corresponding – balancing – ability to go 'higher' than anyone else as well as 'lower'. There is a correlation with the old fertility religions and their deep understanding of the underlying cycles, seasons and forces of creativity. The North Node in the eighth house often denotes the artist, medium or mystic with access to different 'higher' levels of consciousness, and sexual encounters can also lead to expanded levels of awareness.

The eighth house Node (North or South) can also lead to karmic sexual encounters. A man (eighth house North Node, Sun in Scorpio) met a woman (seventh house South Node) on a Greek island. He stood holding her beneath an olive tree, that age-old symbol of fertility, by an ancient church. 'A spontaneous cosmic super-orgasm was the result. Two beings fused together on all levels and reaching a point where past, present and future held no meaning. It was all Now, total awareness, total expansion. We were the cosmos.' His Libra conjunction of Neptune/Mercury/South Node was conjunct her Venus. They had worked the old Mysteries together many times before.

North Node: Gemini / Third House
South Node: Sagittarius / Ninth House

Karmic purpose: to communicate.

The Gemini and/or third house North Node desires to develop the ability to communicate what it is, rather than what it believes in. The Sagittarian South Node has, in the past, developed a set of principles or ideals to live by and has available a wider vision which could be utilized to process information, to see beyond 'the facts' and to develop the intellect and mental abilities as a way of perceiving the world. However, the 'ideals' of the Sagittarius South Node may be of the 'blind faith' persuasion, and the Gemini North Node needs to use the intellect to re-examine whether the precepts by which it now lives are really meaningful and in accord with what it has experienced. In the past Sagittarius has acquired knowledge, now Gemini must *live* it by *Being*.

There is a duality about both the Sagittarius and Gemini Nodes which can lead to a 'double' life based on the nodal contradictions. A very old and experienced occultist had the North Node in Gemini in the third house. Outwardly she led a very respectable, upper-class life; inwardly she was a high priestess. She wrote popular fiction under a pseudonym, serious works under her own name. Her non-fiction work on occult and mystical matters betrayed the very deep knowledge which came from years of magical working. And yet she would not allow the autobiographical account of her occult life to be published while she was alive, or for several years after her death 'for fear of upsetting my very conventional family'. She privately complained that she did not receive the public recognition to which her work entitled her, but what she did not recognize was that her own ambiguity and inherent contradiction, evident in the half-public, half-hidden airing of her knowledge, prevented acknowledgement of her contribution to modern occult understanding.

Another facet of the Gemini and/or third house Node is that karma may be confronted through, or with, a sibling. The position of Mercury and its aspects in the chart will provide a clue as to the area of life in which this will manifest. For example, a Mars/Mercury conjunction in the fourth house, with an opposition to Saturn and an inconjunct (quincunx) to the third house North Node, indicated a long-standing rivalry between souls who had been born in this incarnation as twin boys. It manifested in the present life as a constant battle for their mother's attention and an inability to concentrate in school, with consequent disruptive behaviour. Separate schools proved helpful in allowing each of the boys to express himself as a separate personality and eventually they learnt to live in harmony with each other.

North Node: Sagittarius/Ninth House
South Node: Gemini/Third House

Karmic purpose: to seek meaning.

The Sagittarius and/or ninth house North Node seeks principles to live by and asks the ultimate questions of life: 'Why are we here?', 'Who am I?', 'What does this mean?'. It synthesizes information and makes great leaps of intuition to give meaning and purpose to life.

The ninth house and/or Sagittarius North Node indicates the natural philosopher of the zodiac and the soul with this placement is drawn towards the religious, spiritual and metaphysical areas of life. It frequently travels long distances, both physically and mentally, in its search for truth and meaning. Rarely is anything taken at face value, knowledge is esteemed, as are morals and principles, not just for its own sake, but because it gives under-lying structure and pattern to life. Life itself is often intuited as a giant mandala.

Edgar Cayce, the 'sleeping prophet' who gave thousands of past-life readings had his North Node in Taurus in the ninth house. In a reading on himself, quoted by Alan Oken, he reported:

This body [Taurus] is controlled in its work through the psychical [Scorpio], or the mystical and spiritual [ninth house]. It is governed by the life that is led by the person who is guiding the subconscious when in this state [i.e. Cayce himself]. As the ideas given the subconscious to obtain its information are good, the body becomes better. The body should keep in close touch with the spiritual side of life if he is to be successful mentally, physically and financially.[1]

In his work Cayce utilized the ability of his Scorpio South Node to penetrate the past and communicate (third house) insights to aid those who could not venture into the hidden realm for themselves.

The South Node in Gemini can retreat into superficiality, busily gathering information and facts, rather than face the implications of the knowledge they impart. Knowledge brings responsibility and the need to live it, not just to believe. The Gemini South Node soul is not always ready to take the enormous evolutionary step forward into being what it believes. One becomes truly what one is when moving into the Sagittarius North Node.

There may be karma to overcome with the ninth house North Node from having preached in the past rather than teaching by example – through *Being* – or from having been over zealous in carrying out religious duty, rather than attending to the meaning behind it. St Paul places 'faith', defined in the dictionary as 'spiritual apprehension of divine truth apart from proof', above 'works' in the hierarchy of desirable spiritual qualities. The Sagittarian North Node has to bring out in-built faith based on knowing rather than belief. A Benedictine monk, a fervent convert to the Catholic faith (ninth house North Node) was sent out of the monastery and back into the world by his fellow brothers 'in order that he could round himself out as a person by experience of living'. For him, blind faith was not enough.

North Node: Cancer / Fourth House
South Node: Capricorn / Tenth House

Karmic purpose: to nurture.

The development of the nurturing capacity and emotional give-and-take is vital for the Cancer and/or fourth house North Node. The Capricorn South Node has an ingrained, restrictive, 'tight-fisted' attitude to emotional giving, and a judgemental attitude based on an external locus of control: 'somebody out there' provides the authority, not the Self. With this placement, the soul is extremely uncomfortable with emotion and has not learnt how to provide sustenance on the feeling level, although it will prob-ably be most proficient at providing the physical/materialistic necessities. When threatened, the Capricorn South Node can retreat into a strict, authoritarian 'Thou Shalt/Shalt Not' type of response, and allow no opposition or interference. A father (Saturn/Sun conjunct South Node in Capricorn) took out a court injunction against his sixteen-year-old son (fourth house Capri-corn Chiron/North Node opposing tenth house Uranus/South Node in Cancer) to have him removed from the family home. His submission was that as the boy refused to remain a strict veg-etarian, in accordance with the father's rules, he was no longer part of the family.

The disciplinary skills which the Capricorn South Node has developed in the past can be harnessed in a constructive way to the soul developing the ability to take a caring responsibility for itself and its family. 'Rules' could become a code of conduct which is based on an internal locus of control, the inward voice of the Self providing guidance and direction. And the inner strengths of Capricorn which include self-discipline, self-reliance and authority could be utilized towards the development of the Self and the expression of its loving energies.

With the Cancer North Node the soul has the potential to learn not only to mother, the traditional Cancer role, but also to move beyond this into nurturing both itself and a family in the widest sense of the word, supplying food and nourishment for the Self as well as the body. This arises out of an intake and outpouring of love which is supportive and growth-inducing, not smothering as Cancer love can so often be in its all-embracing relentless grip. It is rather like breathing, spiritual nourishment is taken in from the cosmos, and breathed out as a gently nurturing cloud to fall wherever it is needed. Elisabeth Kubler-Ross has the North Node in Cancer (fifth house). No one who has listened to her can doubt that she lives and breathes disciplined love. Her fifth house Node provides a very creative outlet for her unique nurturing qualities through her patients, books, tapes and workshops. In *Death, the Final Stage of Growth* she provides a perfect example of the synthesis of the Capricorn – Cancer, fifth–eleventh house Nodes:

> Humankind will survive only through the commitment and involvement of individuals in their own and others' growth and development as human beings. This means development of loving and caring relationships . . . You can become a channel and a source of great inner strength. [You must give up] all that is not truly you, all that you have chosen without choosing and value without evaluating, accepting because of someone else's extrinsic judgment, rather than your own . . . [You will gain] your own, true self; a self who is at peace, who is able to truly love and be loved, and who understands who and what (s)he is meant for.[2]

Karma may be experienced by the Cancer and/or fourth house Node through the family. It can be seen in placements where there

WHERE ARE WE GOING?

is a difficult family relationship or family stress, or where there is a handicapped child to be cared for. Planets, and aspects to those planets, in the fourth house will further delineate the karmic patterns involved.

The wife of the Capricorn father mentioned above had Saturn conjunct South Node in Libra (fourth house), closely conjunct her son's Neptune/Mars conjunction. She saw her role as keeping the family together at all costs and providing a buffer between her children and her husband. She could not move out of her Libra South Node. Many years later she was able to obtain a divorce, but was unable to adapt to the situation as she felt she had no role in life. She feels very strongly that the karmic tensions in the family situation have not been worked out because of her husband's refusal to grow or change in any way. It would appear that her fears may well be justified and there may be a need for the family to continue to try to work out the old patterns embodied in the interaction in another incarnation. However, it will also be necessary for her to move into her Aries North Node in order that her own growth may proceed.

North Node: Capricorn / Tenth House
South Node: Cancer / Fourth House

Karmic purpose: to gain authority.

The karmic lesson for the Capricorn North Node is to learn to control the excessive emotionality and possessiveness of the Cancer South Node in order to develop self-discipline and a corresponding authority in the outer world.

Cancer and the fourth house are concerned with the inner world of dependency and vulnerable emotions, Capricorn and the tenth house with the outer world of achievement and self-sufficiency.

The Capricorn North Node seeks success through a career: from a secure material foundation an inner spiritual strength develops. Capricorn has to find within itself self-reliance, self-control, and its own autonomous Being. It can then contain and channel the nurturing capacity of the Cancer South Node and express this to the world in an ordered, disciplined flow. As a part of this process the Capricorn Node may take on the role of the 'scapegoat', one who suffers for, or on whom fall, the 'ills of the world'. This may be a part of the process of alleviating the collective karma of mankind, but it is approached in a less 'unthinkingly sacrificial' way than that of the Pisces and/or twelfth house Node. There is always the sense, with Capricorn, of deliberation before action, of weighing up all that is involved prior to incarnation, and then acting with commitment to the course decided upon. This was particularly noticeable in a client who had contracted Aids and felt that he was thereby partaking in a cleansing of the planetary energy, a choice that he took seriously and that he believed he had made prior to incarnation. He spoke of himself as a scapegoat, not in self-pity, but as a positive force for good.

On a deeper level the Cancer–Capricorn, or fourth–tenth house nodal axis is concerned with the integration of the male and female cosmic energies. The Earth Mother, boundless in her giving, has to unite with the stern Father-God to soften his heart with love so that together they will find an outlet for the universal love energy: just enough control and just enough free will to provide optimum conditions for growth. To reach this goal may involve exploration of the inner world of the psyche, of the archetypal energies invoked by the words 'Father', 'Mother', 'God', and of the anima-animus principles, whose energies need to be recovered into consciousness and reintegrated into the Self in order to achieve wholeness. Psychoanalysis can be undertaken for many years in order to penetrate the core meaning to the Self of these archetypes and to attune to the energies they invoke. However, the language of the sub-conscious mind – the temporary abode of these energies whilst the soul is in incarnation – is symbolic and it is possible to remove 'negative conditioning' and replace it with a powerful attunement to these energies through the use of symbolism, imaging and affirmations. Phyllis Krystal, in her book and tape *Cutting the Ties that Bind*, provides useful exercises for attuning to the cosmic parents and experiencing the balancing of these energies on the inner levels, and for nurturing the inner child – who may be a remnant of the Cancer South

Node. She points out that 'unless the subconscious mind is impressed, no changes can be made in a person's life, no matter how much he may consciously desire to change and evolve'. A way through to the resolution of the Cancer–Capricorn nodal axis is offered:

> A major part of our work involves cutting the cords or ties connecting us to anything or anyone in whom we place our trust and which therefore become gods for us. Because these lesser gods are impermanent and can be taken from us, they are unreliable as a source of security. It is not important whether these bonds were forged by love, need, pity, fear, hate or any other emotion [Cancer South Node]. What is important is that they have the power to keep us dependent on the things to which they attach us instead of on the high C (Higher Consciousness) ... When a human being is willing to reach up in consciousness to make contact with the indwelling source of wisdom and healing, his work [Capricorn North Node], whatever its nature, is necessarily refined and strengthened as it is raised beyond the domination of the ego.[3]

The integration of the male-female nodal energies takes the traveller a very long step on the evolutionary pathway towards wholeness and enlightenment.

North Node: Leo / Fifth House
South Node: Aquarius / Eleventh House

Karmic purpose: to be self-enabling.

The impetus for the Leo and/or fifth house North Node is towards using its own power creatively, rather than operating through collective power (Aquarian South Node), and thereby to solve the head–heart dilemma.

The soul with the South Node in Aquarius sees power as belonging to the group or collective. It purports to have the detached perspective of love and power without emotion, operating from the head. Yet Aquarius can be one of the most emotionally motivated signs – although it is frequently cut off from awareness of that motivation, particularly when exhibiting an unconscious South Node reaction. Aquarius is prone to living in the head rather than using it, as it can inhabit a world of fancifulness. Greta Garbo is perhaps as well known for wanting to be alone as for her acting ability. Her Aquarian South Node is in the tenth house, representing her interaction with the outer world. She is quoted as saying: 'Even when I was a tiny girl, I preferred being alone . . . I could give my imagination free reign and live in a world of lovely dreams.'[4] And yet, through her Leo North Node, she was capable of portraying deep emotions so vividly that her audience were caught up and carried along with her, totally believing in the make-believe reality (Aquarian South Node) she was creating.

Aquarian detachment is frequently not-in-touchness rather than impartiality. One of the dictionary definitions of detachment is 'selfish isolation' and this is a useful interpretation of the space inhabited by the unconscious Aquarian South Node. The conscious Aquarian South Node has a deep, universal love for humanity in the abstract, but the incarnating soul may find it difficult to apply this feeling in a one-to-one interaction. It may be too involved in solving the wider world issues to deal with the problem on its own doorstep. The Leo North Node can draw on this universal love and wider awareness, and refine and channel it to one pointedness.

Leo is connected with the heart, and the Leo North Node is impelled towards communicating itself through the heart energy. Recognition of the link between love and power, and taking back the projection of power from outside itself, is necessary in order to own its power: until power has been retrieved from the external object on to which it has been projected, it cannot be internalized as one's own.

Power is an emotive word, wrongly associated with ego, manipulation and exploitation. And it can easily become this if we are not in touch with the higher purpose of power. True power is true inner authority, clarity, and total freedom. To be in touch with power we have to be 'centred', a state when all of our being is aligned in balance . . . The state of being centred is one of being connected to the universal forces and is essential for true power to manifest. To be centred is to be powerful . . .[5]

The Leo–Aquarius nodal axis encompasses one of the most difficult dilemmas to resolve, that of the head versus the heart: 'Do I do what I think is right (Aquarius) or what I feel is right (Leo)?', 'Do I follow the conventions of logic, upbringing and society, or do I act in accordance with my instincts?', 'How do I move from an involuntary emotional response to one which I know will promote my growth and well-being?', 'How do I operate from a base of love without falling into the trap of mushy sentimentality?'.

The answer is found in the integration of the collective with the personal, the Nodes becoming the focal point for universal love directed through the individual. St Augustine taught 'Love God, and do as you will'. When Will, power and love are aligned to the personal expression of the cosmic Self, the dilemma is resolved. Head and heart become one.

North Node: Aquarius / Eleventh House
South Node: Leo / Fifth House

Karmic purpose: to channel collective power.

The soul with the Aquarius and/or eleventh house North Node must give of itself freely to humanity, working with the collective rather than exercising personal power. The Leo South Node has already become competent in the exercise of its own power and now that power must be aligned to the generic purpose. There is a need to work through interaction with others for the common good.

An unconscious Leo South Node may become involved in domination and power struggles, trying to take egocentric control of the group with which it is working, and may share the Orwellian *1984* view of 'real power' as 'power over men', and perhaps extending as far as the Pluto–Mercury–Mars–Saturn destructive power impulse: 'Power is in inflicting pain and humiliation. Power is in tearing human minds to pieces and putting them together again in new shapes of your own choosing.' In the past the Leo South Node has been the leader, 'the king'. 'Come to me' is now its innate response to life. It tends towards individualism and needs to learn that interdependence is not weakness, that cooperation is not debilitating, that accord is not impotence. It will still lead as that antipodal Aquarian energy is always one step ahead, but when the Leo South Node energies are consciously utilized, benign autocracy is transformed into democracy.

The Aquarian North Node progresses towards a comprehension of equality and coexistence founded on each member of the group contributing according to his abilities and potential. Equality in this context does not mean uniformity, there is an acceptance and appreciation of individual difference which allows each one to develop and grow in accordance with one's own unique pathway. It is not, however, an insular passage, progress is aligned to the group ideals and purpose. Coexistence is based on an appreciation of the parity of mutual essence – humanity. The whole of mankind is the extended family of the Aquarian North Node and its concern is for the progress and well-being of all. With the Leo South Node the soul is its own unique creation, the time has now arrived to offer that creation up as a part of the greater whole.

The Trappist monk and mystic Thomas Merton had the North Node in Aquarius in the fifth house (conjunct Mercury and Jupiter) and the South Node in Leo in the eleventh house (a reversed nodal placement). The conjunction of Mercury/Jupiter to the North Node in the fifth house demanded to be heard and, despite his vow of silence, he became a writer on mysticism and monasticism and, towards the end of his life, became concerned with Aquarian issues such as 'racial discrimination, the threat of nuclear war, the "God-is-dead Movement" and with Catholic renewal.'[6] Suzanne Lilley-Harvey, in an article on Merton, summed up the man:

Thomas Merton ... was a man whose life was a living parable of [the] attempt to awaken and to find his purpose which was both individual and universal. He was a man who ... was attempting to achieve self-mastery over the lower desires and to give birth to the divine principle within himself ... During the latter part of his life he became known for his ecumenical views on religion and his active cultivation of universal tolerance for and interest in the truth in all religions makes him in many ways a kind of harbinger of the Aquarian Age ... his gaze out towards the world again but centred in a new and illumined identity, whereas earlier he ran from the world and its intoxicating ways, he now embraced suffering mankind and the problems of the world. This is characteristic of the 'evolved' Aquarian who derives his sense of ego from an identification with the collective ... Throughout Thomas Merton's life and work the theme of unity winds its way to a resounding chorus: the unity of man with God and of man with man. And the interior resolution of the freedom versus responsibility dilemma [a Leo–Aquarius nodal dichotomy] was his most urgent need and goal.[7]

Merton himself wrote: 'God leaves us free to be whatever we like. We can be ourselves or not, as we please. We are at liberty to be real, or to be unreal ... But we cannot make these choices with impunity. Causes have effects.'[8]

North Node: Virgo / Sixth House
South Node: Pisces / Twelfth House

Karmic purpose: to serve with love.

The Virgo and/or sixth house North Node calls for discriminating service to humanity as a way of expressing an inner attunement to 'divine' love. The soul with this placement does whatever is required of it, because it loves unconditionally. 'It's not how much you do, but how much love you put in the doing' (Mother Teresa, Sun in Virgo)[9].

All too often the Virgo Node, North and South, gets mired in a rut of servitude and obsequiousness, stuck with the 'dirty jobs' of life. This can manifest on many levels, Virgo can function as the hatchet man just as often as the janitor. One client summed up her nursing job as 'dirty, degrading and disgusting. We are the shit-shovellers of Daffodil ward'. She felt no connection with those she 'served', no pity or compassion for their pain, no instinct towards brightening their day. By contrast another client (Virgo North Node, tenth house), matron of an old people's home said: 'Everything we do is an expression of our love, nothing is distasteful, we have fun and laughter, we are a family.' She had developed the compassion and empathy which her Pisces South Node had brought forward from the past, together with a very real connection to 'divine love', and expressed this through her Virgo North Node as service which was an inner state of being.

The unconscious Pisces South Node has many negative patterns. It can express sympathy but tends to wallow in another's suffering or pain, lacking the detachment of compassion which creates space for objective help. It is capable of great self-sacrifice but all too easily falls into the victim-martyr-saviour pattern. Its most oft-repeated cry from the heart is: 'I did it all for you.' It sees virtue in vicarious suffering and self-immolation, but never verifies whether the sacrifice is appropriate or growth-inducing. Indeed, such 'sacrifices' can be very inhibiting for the development of the recipient, who can become the victim as guilt is a common by-product of the Pisces South Node oblation. Piscean guilt is often all-pervasive, and those self-effacing individuals who feel they have no right to be alive are a good illustration of it. They perform constant acts of reparation under the name of 'service' in order to validate their very existence. True altruism is a rare commodity but it is the positive expression of a well-developed Virgo North Node.

One of the most common manifestations of the unconscious Pisces South Node and its connection with 'family karma' is the mother who 'gives up everything for the sake of her children', and then tries to live out her own unfulfilled dreams through subtle manipulation of those children. An obsessively religious mother (twelfth house Cancer South Node), married late in life, gave up her much loved nursing career to care for three children and an alcoholic husband who quickly developed throat cancer. Her husband died when the children were young and she had to integrate her Cancer—Capricorn nodal energies by taking on the role of mother and father, and supporting the family. However, her unconscious sixth—twelfth house nodal axis pervaded and influenced the family. 'After all I've done for you' was her constant theme. Her eldest son (second house Libra South Node) became a doctor, against the advice of his school who said he was manifestly unsuitable as he disliked people; her daughter (fourth house Pisces North Node) became a nurse and felt 'called by God' (or Mother?) to devote herself to the under privileged; her other son (twelfth house Capricorn North Node) lived with his mother and worked at home, but felt a pull to the priesthood.

The sixth house North Node may also have to face karma through health and work. Bodily karma is indicated in the sixth house and may be a manifestation of psychosomatic causes, or a misuse or abuse of the body, carried over from previous lives. One of the lessons for the Virgo and/or sixth house North Node is to develop an understanding of the interaction of mind-body-emotions-spirit and the dis-ease that results from any disharmony. A client had the reversed nodal connection of North Node/Jupiter/Uranus in Pisces in the sixth house opposing Saturn/South Node in the twelfth. Past-life experiences with skeletal manipulation and healing had led him, unconsciously, into osteopathy where he was able to utilize these skills, but was held back by arthritis in his hands — a sign of locked-in anger, helplessness and frustration. He also presented problems of: 'herpes, over-eating, weight loss, mood changes and flatulence . . . obviously I am working out a lot of karma via my body . . . how can I shift my karmic workload into modes of expression which are not so patently self-destructive?' Among the past-life conditions which surfaced were torture, rage, unexpressed grief at the loss of a twin, religious conflict, fasting to produce hallucinations and visions, emotional frustration and a self-chosen wasting disease.

Clearly much work was needed to unlock his inner inhibitions and guilt. He had had a difficult, emotionally conflicting and traumatic childhood and part of his problem was centred on the psychosomatic effects of a disharmony of the mind and emotions on the body which manifested as disease. Another factor was the blocked, non-flowing nature of the Pisces (and afflicted Neptune) energies within the chart, and of course within himself, which needed to be freed and expressed. His work was in a sense a reparation for that which had gone before, and he needed to move into being of true service. Liz Greene was quoted to him:

> Service, rather than 'good works' is an innate quality of the inner man. It is a state of consciousness rather than a planned act. Service of this kind is the result of inner integration, for once the body, feelings and mind of a man are in balance, then he can begin to become aware, intuitively, of the purpose and nature of his inner psyche. He is no longer occupied in reconciling the battling components of his nature, but through an inner attunement . . . he can listen to his real direction . . . Service which is the result of inner balance is the potential of Saturn in Virgo when he is expressing in a conscious way and this placement is common among physicians, surgeons and those who tend the mental and emotional ills of others because it is a fulfilment of the inner needs of the group.[10]

An equally appropriate and apt exposition for the sixth house North Node and the Pisces–Virgo nodal axis.

North Node: Pisces / Twelfth House
South Node: Virgo / Sixth House

Karmic purpose: to attain enlightenment.

The Pisces and/or twelfth house North Node explores the karmic lessons of the past on both the collective and the personal levels to attain enlightenment. It has the potential to move beyond the wheel of rebirth, to attain release into the 'divine whole'.

The Virgo South Node can fall back into an over-analytical, critical, judgemental mode of behaviour which restricts and inhibits the free-flowing, mystical and visionary, expression of the Pisces Node. It therefore needs to develop detached, accepting, compassionate and unconditional love for all. However, the Pisces North Node has to utilize the constructive discrimination of the Virgo South Node, as otherwise it may give, or act, without thought, evaluation or restraint.

The exploration and expression of the collective karma of mankind may involve taking on an archetypal 'victim', 'saviour' or 'fantasy' role. Film star Marilyn Monroe, whose portrayal of woman was the archetypal essence of the feminine and who was revered by many as a goddess, had a twelfth house Cancer North Node. Pop star Bob Geldof, who initiated Band Aid to feed the starving millions of Africa, has a Pisces North Node in the second house. He identified the collective need, putting aside his own career (Pisces sacrificing itself) to raise money for practical aid (second house). However, when the famine crisis was repeated the next year, the scheme faced criticism and Geldof flew out to Africa to see for himself what had gone wrong. The answer to the crisis could perhaps have involved a little more practical Virgoan organization and follow-through to aid the visionary idealism of Pisces. Band Aid became more successful in the years following as it broadened its base of operations.

The investigation into personal karma may entail an enquiry into the hidden, darker side of life, and into the karma of the family into which it is born: this is the Node of hidden ancestral skeletons surfacing into the light of conscious awareness. A friend (twelfth house Sun in Scorpio conjunct North Node) was surprised when one day, having idly turned on the television, he was faced with a programme investigating the disappearance of his great-grandfather from a non-stopping train between Scotland and London. The research had been meticulous and many details, previously unknown to the family, were brought to light.

For some twelfth house and/or Pisces North Nodes the descent into the darkness of mankind has to be faced in a very intense way. It would seem that, in order to have the prospect of release from the cycle of rebirth, some souls take on the daunting task of dealing with a 'huge chunk' of karma all at once. Much suffering may be involved, including experience of institutions and other traditionally twelfth house areas of life. For many souls this includes descent into chaos, breakdown and disintegration of the old self in order to move beyond its confines towards a more esoteric level of incarnation and manifestation of the Self. For others, it may entail working with those who are undergoing the descent into madness and alienation, guiding their journey towards a new wholeness. Some evolved souls offer themselves in order that others may learn their lessons from caring for the, seemingly, disadvantaged and handicapped.

One brain-damaged child (reversed nodal placement, twelfth house North Node in Virgo and the sixth house South Node conjunct Sun and Mercury in Pisces) brought about a profound growth both in herself and in her parents. She unfailingly displayed love, patience and perseverance to overcome her handicap, no matter how difficult and painful her life became. Her mother (tenth house Taurus North Node) developed her own healing talents through the Metamorphic Technique, applying it first to her daughter and then to a wide circle of handicapped children. Mother and child became channels for unconditional love.

It is the pathway of unconditional love and the transmutation of atonement into at-one-ment with the divine which offers the Pisces North Node the opportunity to move beyond the endless round of birth, death and rebirth into a spiritual state of grace. 'Grace' is the point of karmic balance, all debts and obligations cleared, through forgiveness or reparation. Evolution on this incarnational level is complete, all possibilities are open.

REVERSED NODAL PLACEMENT

The reverse nodal placement occurs when the sign of the Node falls in the opposite house to its natural zodiacal placement. For example, Virgo is the natural sixth house, the reverse nodal placement is a twelfth house Virgo North Node opposing a sixth house Pisces South Node.

This placement indicates that the soul has already worked on both of the opposing nodal energies in the past. The purpose of incarnation now embraces a deeper integration and focused expression of the positive energies. The twelfth house Virgo North Node has, for example, to deepen its attunement with the divine (Pisces) and focus this through practical service (Virgo) to the collective. The sixth house Pisces North Node draws on its ability to channel the divine energies from the collective level and express this in everyday life and work.

A client who had the sixth–twelfth house Virgo–Pisces axis strongly emphasized in her chart, tried to live in a drifting, dreamy Piscean way but kept meeting the Virgoan need to pay the rent. She had Venus conjunct the North Node in Pisces, opposed to Saturn conjunct the South Node in Virgo and kept finding herself 'somehow drawn back again and again into prostitution, actual and metaphorical'. However, she spent more time counselling her men about their problems than engaging in sexual intercourse. Eventually she made the transition to counsellor without the need for the intermediate stage. The unconditional love of her Pisces Node became expressed and earthed through the Virgo Node, which offered practical solutions based on a deep understanding of the psychological and spiritual *malaise* suffered by her clients.

ASPECTS TO THE NODES

Planets conjuncting the South Node are continually pulled back into old patterns and may be the source of powerful sub-personalities or dissociated complexes operating from deep within the sub-conscious. It is as though a facet of a previous personality had been transported whole and unchanged from another incarnation and located deep within the instinctual functioning of the present personality. From its firmly entrenched position it makes forays into consciousness, disrupting and sabotaging attempts by the developing Self to express itself more constructively through the North Node or occasionally offering a tantalizing glimpse of a buried skill or asset. Saturn, for example, can indicate a very fearful, dependent and depressive sub-personality, constantly inhibiting growth through its needs for safety, defensiveness and limits; there may also be a powerful inner critic or saboteur figure who wrecks any possibility of growth through its undermining internal comments and doubts. Mars may indicate a very angry sub-personality who lashes out from time to time, or a very courageous one which surfaces in times of extreme crisis only to disappear from view again when things calm down.

Mars conjunct the South Node may also be anger which is disowned and projected out into the world. A client with a first house Libra South Node/Mars conjunction was jilted by her fiancé. During counselling she denied being angry about this and said she understood the cultural pressures which had led to his decision (Libra South Node bending over backwards to be 'fair' and adaptable) – he was of a different race and religion. As she said this, a very large angry wasp buzzed in through the window and circled around her head. It then got stuck in the double glazing and its loud buzzing punctuated her further denials of anger. When she went back to her bedroom, it had been invaded by a swarm of wild bees which were clearly demonstrating both her anger and her feeling of trapped helplessness within the situation.

South Node conjunctions need reworking in order that the trapped energies can be released into consciousness and used constructively. That Saturn/South Node conjunction has reserves of inner strength, discipline and resilience – once the fear is released – which can be harnessed to the North Node to consolidate and structure its development. The Mars energy can be channelled into active growth, drawing on its assertiveness and courage to make changes aligned to the spiritual Will.

A client with Pluto/Mars/Moon conjunct the South Node in Cancer was regressed back to a former life in which he experienced being 'abandoned' by the death of his mother. He commented afterwards that for many years he had been aware of an 'angry child' sub-personality who needed constant reassurance. During the regression he was able to accept the child, incorporating it into his present being. After several years the very powerful healing energies contained within the conjunction were released when he healed himself of cancer. He developed his ability further and became a successful healer, thereby satisfying and incorporating his Capricorn North Node.

An alcoholic had a Mercury/Neptune conjunction to his Libra South Node. He was seen as a sadhu in a past life, one who had totally withdrawn from everyday life into a permanent, drug-induced haze of disassociation and ecstasy. The escapist traits had been carried over into the present life. As a child he was two people: one bright and intelligent, the other sensitive and withdrawn. He was sent to a very conventional public school where the emphasis was on academic achievement. He then 'chose' a very pressured career (Aries North Node). Whenever the pressures of 'living' became too much he escaped into his 'other self', at first into mental withdrawal, then into meditation, soft drugs and drink, finally into breakdown and benders. As part of his recovery programme in Alcoholics Anonymous he was introduced to computers and was able to lose himself in fantasy games. Later he rediscovered his artistic talent and channelled his energies into painting bouts instead of alcoholic benders. However, he had not yet found the inner motivation to bring about an integration of the nodal axis which would have harnessed the positive, visionary qualities of Mercury/Neptune to the Aries North Node. He said that he could not face becoming that which he knew he could be. 'The alcoholic has many, many "good reasons" for his drinking, and all of them are solidly based in Neptune. He drinks, finally, because he wants to drink, because he has to drink. And, finally, he must reach his own moment of truth, and want *not* to drink.'[11]

Conjunctions to the North Node propel the incarnating soul forward into a new way of being, emphasis being placed on the planetary energies – which may be overwhelming as they manifest. A Pluto conjunction to the eighth house Leo North Node brought one client close to death on several occasions, each time bringing out her latent psychic abilities more forcefully. She found it extremely difficult to cope with her very vivid psychic experiences and the pressure was such that she had to develop her ability as a medium as otherwise she 'would go mad'. As soon as she began to utilize the psychic energy the intensity of her experiences diminished and the power came under her control. Another client, with Uranus conjunct the North Node in twelfth house Libra, left England and went to live in an Israeli kibbutz 'to regain my heritage and, hopefully, to find a mate – English men are much too tame and ordinary for me'. She had, as a teenager, expressed her Uranian Node by distributing underground Jewish literature in

Russia whilst masquerading as a tourist. She dismissed any hazard to herself with a shrug of the shoulders: 'It is something I have to do.'

Planets squaring the nodal axis indicate the potential for synthesis of the past and future, but the soul may experience pressure from both ends of the axis and may find this destructive. Uranus, for example, may offer a creative and humanitarian resolution of the nodal dilemma, or it may be disturbed and anti-social, acting out all the archaic energies inherent within the opposing forces. Trines and sextiles to the Nodes may help with the integration of the energies, but the soul will often tend towards vacillation back to the old ways.

A transit may be the trigger required to bring in a more harmonious functioning of planets and Nodes, particularly where the aspect is a close one, as the transiting energy can mediate in the natal conflict. At times, such triggers may, however, act as a brutal catalyst to resolve the seemingly unresolvable, literally propelling the soul into a new way of being through the inner dynamics of the irreconcilable opposites.

MURDER, MAYHEM AND NODAL CONFLICT

Playwright Joe Orton was murdered by his lover, Kenneth Halliwell, who then committed suicide. It was the culmination of a fifteen-year relationship which 'transformed Orton from a provincial nobody to one of the most talented, comic playwrights since Oscar Wilde'[12], and which totally destroyed Halliwell. Throughout the troubled month leading up to the brutal killing, Orton had transiting Pluto conjunct his natal Mars. On the day he died, transiting Mars exactly sextiled his South Node/Neptune conjunction. Although birth times are not available for Orton or Halliwell and the charts shown are for sunrise, the effect of the Nodes is clearly visible. The relationship between the two men illustrates the complex interweaving and shifting power balance of the nodal axis in the individual charts and in the synastry between the two.

Orton (fig. 11) had the North Node conjunct the Moon in

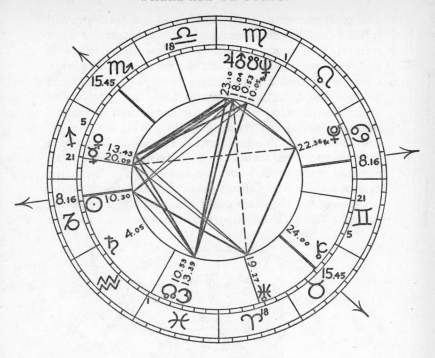

Fig. 11: Joe Orton

Pisces, opposing a Neptune/South Node/Mars/Jupiter conjunction in Virgo, squared by Venus/Mercury. The conjunction of Mars and Neptune to the South Node indicate both an old Will dilemma, and the potential for Orton having had past-life experiences in which he retreated into drink or drugs as an 'escape' from a reality which he found unbearable. In the present life Orton utilized this aspect more constructively in his writing, but nevertheless drugs and sex played a major part in his life. Orton's biographer, John Lahr, repeatedly points out both Orton's loyalty to Halliwell (fig. 12) and his promiscuity (nodal axis square Venus in Sagittarius). Orton's Neptune/South Node/Mars conjunction is constantly illustrated in his diaries, quoted by Lahr, who comments:

The combination of sex, hashish and sun [in Morocco] fulfilled the Dionysian intention behind his comedies. They celebrate instinct and gratification and aspire to corrupt his audience into pleasure ... like the votaries of Dionysius, Orton was hounded by his passion. In his plays, Orton faced his rage and exorcised it with his lethal wit [Mercury in Sagittarius inconjunct Pluto] ... Morocco slaked the tension that was always erupting in Orton's life between his emotional needs [Moon conjunct North Node in Pisces] and society's social and sexual taboos [Virgo South Node and a virtually unaspected Saturn in Aquarius] ... the battle against society was difficult [Mars conjunct South Node] ... in England the strain could create a painful confusing rage ... When Orton discovered the theatre, he found a

Fig. 12: Kenneth Halliwell

focus for his energy and an answer to his needs [an outlet for
the nodal axis] . . . Theatre consolidated Orton's fascina-
tions — literature, music and make believe [Venus square
Neptune] and made them legitimate labour [Virgo] . . . You
can't be a rationalist [Virgo] in an irrational world [Pisces].
It isn't rational . . . Orton wrote: 'I'm a great believer in the
absolute logic of Alice in Wonderland' [Pisces incorporates
Virgo].[13]

Orton met Halliwell at RADA. Lahr's biography and the
Orton diaries chronicle their obsessive, claustrophobic, destructive relationship and its seemingly inevitable resolution through
violence — in synastry each Mars trines the other Saturn and
Saturn opposes Mars in the composite chart. Halliwell, a literate
man with a facility for language, was in the ascendancy when they
met. He had money and owned a small bedsitter into which Orton
moved. According to Lawrence Griffin: 'he, Orton, would do
anything Kenneth [Halliwell] wanted him to'. 'Halliwell was like
a Svengali to John [Orton]. He took John over.'[14] Halliwell's
nodal axis dominated the interchange at that time. 'Halliwell
asserted almost complete control [Capricorn South Node] over
the relationship. Halliwell cooked and provided the food [Cancer
North Node].'[15] Halliwell initially nurtured Orton's talent
[Cancer], but in the end his possessiveness and emotional
instability alienated Orton who escaped whenever possible
[Pisces]. 'Once, hallucinating on hashish, Orton saw himself as a
little boy being beaten by a teacher. The teacher was Halliwell
[Halliwell's Capricorn South Node].'[16]
There are strong Mercury contacts between the charts: 'It was
Orton's mind, the gorgeous wicked fun it poked at the world
which made him irresistible and obsessed Halliwell.'[17] Halliwell's
Mercury conjuncts Orton's Pluto which is inconjunct Mercury.
Mercury–Pluto aspects appear frequently in the charts of 'black'
comedy writers, for example practically the entire Monty Python
team. In synastry Mercury forms an exact inconjunct (quincunx)
to Mercury. Orton and Halliwell were jailed for what Lahr
describes as 'mischievous literary vandalism. Books . . . were
appearing on the [library] shelves with photographs and book

jackets humorously altered . . . most perturbing to the court was not the abuse of private property but the care and intelligence with which Orton and Halliwell tampered with the books.'[18] The synastry between the charts also includes a trine from Orton's North Node/Moon conjunction to Halliwell's Pluto, which opposes Orton's Sun; Halliwell's North Node sextiles Orton's Mars and Halliwell's Venus sextiles Orton's Pluto. Orton's Chiron conjuncts Halliwell's Venus and indicates an old wound in the relationship between them. Jealousy, anger, envy, resentment and revenge were the Plutonian undercurrents which pervaded the seemingly harmonious relationship, and which broke through the claustrophobic relationship with tragic consequences.

Halliwell's chart has Mercury and Pluto conjunct the North Node in Cancer, with a Scorpio Saturn trine to the Node. It is a depressive, emotionally unstable chart (Sun in Cancer square Uranus/Mars in Pisces, Grand Cross of Moon conjunct Saturn in Scorpio opposing Venus squaring Neptune opposing Jupiter, and Chiron inconjunct the Moon). The Capricorn South Node, the Chiron–Moon inconjunct and the Saturn/Moon conjunction indicate an old, painful constriction around emotion which is evident in a RADA assessment of Halliwell as 'stiff and rigid'. 'Seems to be unconvinced that acting is the expression of emotion. The result is that his approach is all mental [Mercury conjunct North Node in Cancer]'.[19] In Lahr's words:

Halliwell's instinct was always to retreat, rejecting the source of the pain before it could reject him [Pluto conjunct North Node] . . . Halliwell was no stranger to horrific death. When he was 11 his doting mother had been stung in the mouth by a wasp and within minutes had choked to death before his eyes. Twelve years later, Halliwell came downstairs to breakfast to discover his father with his head in the oven, dead from asphyxiation . . . The pain of failure, the waste of talent and the sense of betrayal the orphan feels towards those who have left him bred in Halliwell a festering and terrifying hostility towards the world. Halliwell had no reason to trust life [Pluto/North Node/Mercury conjunction in Cancer].[20]

Orton found fame and notoriety as a playwright. Halliwell, who had literary aspirations of his own, found only failure. He progressed backwards from placing his name above Orton's on their early, joint, manuscripts, to being Orton's 'literary editor', and finally to signing himself 'Secretary to Joe Orton'. Orton was moving towards the integration of his nodal axis through his work: 'The liberties Orton took with language and plot were built on a disciplined vision [Virgo–Pisces].'[21] At the same time, however, Halliwell moved into crisis and disintegration:

> Orton's almost magical resilience inevitably sank Halliwell into deeper depression. Unable to compete, Halliwell instinctively tried to punish and control Orton [Capricorn South Node] . . . In his sickness Halliwell, who needed love and said so [Cancer North Node demanding to be heard], became increasingly unlovable. His panic to make people draw closer only pushed them away and he broadcast his pleas for attention in his complaints about Orton's 'trolling', his demands on Orton's allegiance and his psychosomatic illness. [Orton was here offered the opportunity to fully comprehend this peculiarly Virgoan condition, but he declined.] Orton's sensual rapacity was a threatening reminder of Halliwell's emotional dependence.[22]

Halliwell left a suicide note: 'If you read his diary all will be explained.' The diary chronicles a deteriorating relationship as the balance of power inexorably shifted from Halliwell to Orton.

> The diaries offer a rare, if unwitting glimpse of the punishing dynamics of a celebrity's self-aggrandisement . . . The diaries are not just a chronicle of the drama between them, but a prop in it . . . Halliwell could – and did – read their punishing contents. Everything about the diaries was provocative, a symbol of Orton's retreat into himself and away from Halliwell . . . Orton was the centre of Halliwell's life; but, as he could read, Halliwell was an increasingly minor – and frequently irritating – extra in the drama of Orton's eventful life.[23]

The relationship with Halliwell epitomized Orton's own nodal conflicts: 'The struggle between licence [Pisces] and control [Virgo], between identity and invisibility, between consciousness and "self-consciousness" [was] the mirror image of Orton's own struggles with Halliwell's neurotic problems.'[24] Actor Kenneth Williams insists that Orton had 'heart': 'If we're talking about compassion and sympathy, I'd say Joe had it. He showed tremendous loyalty to Halliwell. He showed it to me . . . He was the most marvellous counsellor.'[25] However, when faced with the challenge of his Pisces North Node for empathy in the shape of the demanding and suicidally depressed Halliwell, Orton could only retreat into his Virgoan Neptune/South Node conjunction, denying what was happening. Actor Simon Ward was 'puzzled by Orton's indifference to Halliwell's pain . . . no one could be as insensitive as that if you really cared about the person'.[26]

Within days Orton and Halliwell were dead. 'Halliwell's final fillip was nine hammer blows to Orton's head.'[27] Their ashes were intermingled and scattered. 'Through murder Halliwell achieved the public association with Joe Orton's career he had been denied in life.'[28] In his plays Joe Orton articulated many of the dilemmas inherent within his own and Halliwell's charts. 'The joke at the heart of Orton's farce mayhem is that people state their needs, but the other characters, in their spectacular self-absorption, don't listen [the incompatible demands of the Cancer–Capricorn and Pisces–Virgo nodal axes].'[29]

THE NODES IN RELATIONSHIPS

In the synastry between charts, contacts from the Nodes or planets can indicate an old soulmate relationship, and lessons and possibilities for growth through the new interaction. Unfortunately this does not always indicate, as so many people feel a soulmate should, loving harmony in the relationship. Although on a deeper spiritual level there is the feeling that here is a soul who truly loves and who offers an opportunity to grow beyond the confines of an old way of being, the circumstances in which that growth can take place may be extremely difficult. The lessons learnt from such a contact are often impossible to understand from the perspective of the earth plane. They can occur in the context of different types of 'relationship', which may or may not include sexual interaction.

Planetary contacts from the partner's chart to the South Node pull the soul back into an old way of being and relating, which may initially feel very comfortable and familiar. However, if progress is to be made into the North Node new way of being with a constructive expression of the planetary energies, sooner or later conflict will emerge particularly if the other party is not expressing the energies of the Node or planet positively. Ultimately, unless the expression of energy shifts into a different mode, it may be necessary to move out of the relationship to be free to express that energy constructively. The difficulties and frustrations of trying to deal with a South Node conjunction may finally push some souls into breaking through to their North Node or to a positive functioning of the planet. For other souls, however, this lesson may take a long time to learn and it may therefore be repeated through many incarnations.

A client had her Scorpio South Node conjuncted by her husband's Venus/Saturn. She described him as a 'wounded animal'. 'He lives alone, but with us, sleeps alone, thinks alone.' His Saturn/Venus conjunction showed that he perceived himself as inherently unlovable, and that he had difficulty in relating. His behaviour pulled her back into the emotional pain and trauma of her Scorpio South Node. When she had had enough of that pain, she realized that she could not help him and decided to 'move on to expressing her own purpose and becoming a better human being'.

I was asked to look at the synastry for a client and a mysterious 'Mr X' with whom she afterwards revealed she had always felt she had had an old 'illegal' relationship. They shared, in this life, 'memories of love-making in the past which coincided exactly'. Mr X's Libra North Node conjuncted her Neptune, his South Node her Jupiter. His Venus and Mars trined her Aquarian North Node, Mercury and Jupiter sextiled it. Her Moon was inconjunct his North Node, and Mars sextiled it.

In the past-life part of the reading I 'saw' her as a lady of high rank and temple office. He was a slave. They had had a passionate relationship, but one which had ended violently when he was discovered in her bed and killed. Later relationships had continued the theme of dangerous liaisons and secrecy (not always as lovers). In the present life he was married and they were unable to be open about the very deep love they had rediscovered for each other, they were still playing furtive South Node–Neptune games. His North Node indicated that he needed a relationship which met both his own needs and those of another. Her Neptune conjunction to his North Node helped him to identify those needs and taught him about unconditional love. It also gave them a telepathic contact and accounted for the shared memories which arose spontaneously between them. However, the Neptunian tendency to not have things out in the open was being continued and her Jupiter conjunction to his Aries South Node pulled him back into the old pattern of selfishly indulging sensual needs – and her Jupiter in Aries was very headstrong.

There was a danger of repeating the pattern of disaster and violence indicated in the Mars sextiles to the North Nodes. As a way of moving out of the difficult situation and away from the emotional games of the Leo South Node, she accepted a challenging job abroad which allowed her to explore her Aquarian North Node. The relationship had, however, inspired her to explore her own spirituality and ability to love unconditionally; and had connected her back to the old temple knowledge and skills including 'paranormal' abilities and awareness of the spiritual dimensions and forces inherent in the universe. She was able to harness the positive energies of her Jupiter and Neptune and incorporate them into her way of life.

Tracy Marks[30] feels that a North Node contact to another person's planet is indicative of a soulmate connection, but points out that much will depend on how the energy of the planet is being manifested. The soulmate connection does, however, underlie the contact and it is a definite point of growth, but the relationship may not necessarily be an easy one or one of conventional 'lovers'. In chart after chart I have seen a pattern in which the Sun or

Venus, or one of the other personal planets, conjuncts the North Node in what outwardly seems to be an ideal relationship and yet may suddenly fall apart 'for no reason'. I am conscious, however, of seeing a biased sample of charts, as it is at the point when a relationship has gone wrong that I am usually consulted. I do not often see charts illustrating a relationship which is still 'ideal'. Up to the crisis point there has usually been a great deal of complacency in the relationship, accompanied by lack of mutual growth. The answer to why it has all gone wrong lies in the soul's need to grow.

A woman whose Virgo North Node/Neptune conjunction conjoined her partner's Sun and North Node, described their relationship as 'the sort of fairy-tale romance you read about in romantic novels, as if made in heaven'. It suddenly became catastrophic after she had lent him a considerable amount of money and he had become evasive and unavailable. The negative Neptunian energies of delusion and deceit manifested and she later discovered that he was seeing another woman. She was, however, very reluctant to take legal action to recover her money in case he wanted to come back to her. Her fantasy was that the perfection might be regained. Her Pisces South Node pattern had been to be 'rescuer and victim' and her Virgo North Node was demanding that she move into a more discriminating mode of relating. However, the Virgo energy was obscured by the influence of the Neptune conjunction to the North Node which made her yearn for the unattainable and meant that she was able to overlook the deception and deceit in the search for her lost 'ideal love'.

In another case where the partners had been married for almost forty years, the wife was convinced that one of them had murdered the other in a past life, but she was not sure who did what to whom. There was no astrological indicator for this, but the feeling was symbolic of their interaction which killed individuality. She described their marriage as 'a continual battle for domination': her Venus conjuncted his North Node in Leo. Instead of working on owning and expressing their own individual power, each was trying to have power over the other.

An alcoholic husband's North Node in Libra conjuncted his

wife's Moon. The couple had been separated for years but she still stayed with her husband two or three nights a week on a platonic basis and 'a decree absolute seems to be an emotional trauma'. She felt 'responsible for his security and happiness, feel as a mother'. She was continually moving back into her old Libra Moon pattern, which reflected to him the qualities he was trying to develop. However, she would need to move into her Sun in Taurus and Capricorn North Node which would mean finding security within herself rather than through what she perceived as being her husband's need for her.

Planets which square the nodal axis in synastry can, as with natal squares, pull two ways, resulting in disintegration, or they can assist in the resolution of the nodal conflict. A client had a Grand Cross in her chart (fig. 13). Her Pluto/Mars/Uranus opposition to Saturn squares her South Node/Moon opposition to Venus/Jupiter/North Node. Her ex-boyfriend locked into this Grand Cross, his Pluto/Uranus/Mars conjoined hers, and his Sun was conjunct her Saturn, squaring the nodal axis. He wanted them to get back together again, but she explained:

> There seems to be a lack of communication on some level. I feel like he is not 'seeing me'. There is an uncomfortable feeling, sometimes of sadness or seriousness and I can't put it

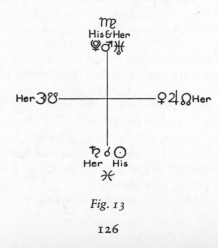

Fig. 13

down to anything that is happening now and here . . . [She also had a] strong feeling of not wanting to interact with the world much [Neptune conjuncted her Midheaven and opposed her Sun and she retreated into meditation]. Everything seems so complicated. At the same time I feel there is something I have to accomplish this time. On a deep level I feel very secure and strong but when it comes to interacting with the world I sometimes feel very lost and lonely.

Those feelings reflected the inherent conflicts of the isolation and discomfort of Saturn in Pisces squaring the Moon/South Node opposition to the Venus/Jupiter/North Node indicative of a potential for a different way of being. Her boyfriend's Sun in Pisces could have shown her a way to integrate her Saturn energies as a channel for Neptunian inspiration. However, he was being typically Piscean and 'not seeing her', his energy was manifesting on the unconscious level and he was not aware of her separateness. The relationship could have offered her the opportunity to move beyond the fear and loneliness of her Saturn energies into her strength and the potential for self-expansion through good relationships which Jupiter/Venus/North Node offered her. She would then have had to deal with the potentially violent and explosive karma between them contained in the Pluto/Mars/Uranus square to her nodal axis and its conjuncting planets. The relationship was a 'fated' one which required a high degree of spiritual evolution and awareness on the part of both partners before it could be resolved.

When there is a North Node to North Node conjunction there can be a very deep soul bond and a unity of purpose. This manifests most strongly in the charts of 'astrological twins' where, of course, not only the Nodes but also the planets are conjunct. A temp worked for a man without meeting him for three months. They communicated through hasty notes and occasional telephone calls. The Personnel Office could not understand how she managed to churn out reams of paper which exactly matched what he wanted to say when no other temp had lasted more than a day or two. They finally met on their joint birthday, a reunion of old friends. They shared many similar life experiences in this life and were connected on a deep soul level. Some of the 'coincidences' in their lives were quite extraordinary. While she was facing death in childbirth, he was in the same hospital (a hundred miles away from where they finally met), on the same day, helplessly watching his young sister die – his Chiron was in the eighth house due to the time difference between them, so the basic experience manifested in a slightly different way. Whilst he considered that her interest in psychic matters was 'non-scientific rubbish' he would nevertheless arrive on the doorstep, begging 'please make my back better'. She commented: 'Somehow the healing for him always seemed so much quicker and more effective than with anyone else.'

Tracy Marks, in discussing the reverse nodal connection (North Node of one chart conjunct the South Node of the other) between charts feels that this is of 'noteworthy karmic and evolutionary significance' as the other person is naturally what we are trying to be. Again, this is a soulmate connection, but as she points out: 'Such a "soul" connection may take the form of friend/friend, teacher/student, parent/child, employer/employee or virtually any other kind of bond. It does not necessarily indicate the potential for marriage or partnership.'[31]

Christine Hartley was my spiritual teacher for over ten years, particularly in the art of 'far seeing', until her transformation to a different level of being – from where she still makes the occasional foray into my conscious awareness. We have a reverse nodal connection between our charts and were spiritual soulmates. We recently had a wonderful reunion in the temple at Philae. On a magical Egyptian evening, as I watched the sunset turn the temple a deep rose pink, I was suddenly aware of Christine beside me. Many years previously we had been given the spiritual message that she should use the power of the red rose to turn the white rose pink, and I can only assume that it was somehow connected to this particular experience. I had followed the time-honoured ritual of paying the backsheesh man for the privilege of being allowed to land 'after hours', and was able to wander without the usual hordes of tourists around. Once again I was able to walk the halls with Christine whilst she instructed me in the inner teachings of the Osiris–Isis Mysteries, as she had done so many years before. It made no difference that the temple had been moved, the energy impregnated in the stones was enough to take us back to that deep spiritual contact.

Many people ask why so many Egyptian incarnations surface in reincarnation memories. When one stops to think that the Egyptian 'temple' age went on for longer than the Christian era has, one realizes the breadth of experience possible in Egypt. Also, the Egyptian 'religion' had so much knowledge about inner power that it no longer seems implausible that so many souls should have taken advantage of the spiritual opportunities and practices of that age.

Christine Hartley was more than twice my age when we met and our charts have, in addition to the reversed nodal connection, Jupiter conjunct Jupiter, and Sun in opposition to the Sun. Her South Node/Mars conjunction conjoined my Pluto/North Node conjunction, and her Chiron conjuncted my Moon. Her Neptune/Pluto conjunction enclosed my Mars. She was the 'spiritual midwife' for my far-memory abilities, and the healer of many of my emotional wounds. We shared many experiences, our lives had a very similar 'pattern'. Despite the age gap we were very close friends as well as teacher and pupil. I first met her, in this life, at the height of summer at Portsmouth Harbour station, just as the London train and the Isle of Wight ferry disgorged their passengers. Among the crowds, we found each other immediately and 'knew' each other. We had been together many times before and would chat about 'the old days' as though it were yesterday. Our contact in this life was preordained: Christine was instrumental in aligning me to my pathway, and for reawakening in me the spiritual knowledge required for my work. She spent many years urging me to take her place in reincarnation work, but it took me a long time to be ready for this step although it would have been easy to fall back into the conjunction of her Leo South Node/Mars to my Pluto, and it would certainly have helped me to own my power as my North Node was urging me to. Our Gemini Mars conjunction to Pluto talked for hours on the subject, but I found it difficult to commit myself to that pathway. When I finally completed my first 'public' reincarnation seminar, some ten years after we first met, she 'died' the following night in her sleep as she had wished, 'just slipping away into the next world'.

Soulmate meetings can be wonderful experiences, but their 'cost' may be high and the lesson hard. A woman who had already had the experience of meeting one soulmate contacted me. Her soulmate had died but she had learnt many lessons from the experience (Pluto was sextile Venus in her chart and she needed to complete the change in her pattern of relating). She had subsequently been told by an astrologer that she would meet her second soulmate (an experience for which her Venus/Neptune conjunction yearned) and that they would have a long and happy life together. She was introduced to a man:

> It was magic, just like the time I met my first soulmate, we felt instantly attracted and each felt we had known one another before. We spoke about reincarnation on our first meeting ... On his third visit he told me he had been diagnosed as having a terminal illness and he feels we need to teach each other some lessons and that we don't have much time. We feel so close to each other he has asked me to be with him when he dies ... How can fate be so cruel.

The nodal axes of the charts (fig. 14) form a very wide Grand Cross out of element, her Aries–Libra to his Aquarius–Leo, so that they may seem to be 'at cross purposes' in their life direction; she is working on herself at the 'personal' level, he at the 'universal'. However, her North Node exactly conjuncts his Aries Ascendant and his Sun trines her North Node; his Venus squares her Nodes, and his Descendant/Neptune/Saturn conjuncts her South Node/Neptune/Venus; her South Node conjuncts his Mars, and his Mars trines her North Node. This does not appear to be the 'long and happy life' and yet it has the potential to be fulfilling in terms of soul growth and companionship. They do have lessons to offer each other through the contacts to the Nodes.

Her initial response to his news was to rush around frantically

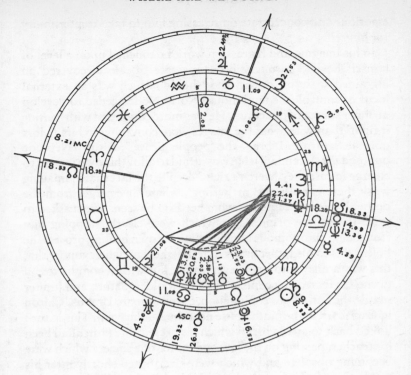

Fig. 14

trying everything for him (his Mars activating her Libra South
Node). He then responded to whatever she initiated (her Mars
activating his Leo South Node). I suggested that one of her lessons
was to learn to 'let go and let God', thereby allowing the quality of
unconditional love to flow. There was a symbiotic, manipulative
Sun/Pluto conjunction and Pluto—Moon trine between the charts
and she needed to release him to be his own unique self. A past-life
contact which surfaced was one in which he was a sickly child and
she was his mother, who literally willed him to live. She was
aware, on first hearing of his cancer, of a strong 'motherly energy'
and of wanting to force him to live. Once she had recognized this
as a past-life pattern, however, she was able to let go of these

emotions and concentrate on releasing him to take responsibility for himself.

In his imaging and regression work he touched upon a level of himself he had formerly been unaware of. He discovered an ingrained sense of 'ought' and 'should' which was an external locus of control (the tenth house North Node needed to develop an inner source of direction). He was more concerned with 'getting it right' than with what the images were conveying to him (Mars quintile Saturn in Libra – the 'people pleaser'; Saturn/Neptune opposed the Ascendant). He was afraid to allow his own images to emerge in case they 'weren't right' despite the fact that in imaging work there is no 'right' or 'wrong', whatever emerges from the deeper levels is accepted as what needs to be seen. When asked to trace the source of messages which were clearly stopping him from being autonomous and directing his own healing process, he linked this to his father and to a feeling he had, when young, that this was a man who knew everything, but with whom he found himself in increasing conflict as he grew older (Saturn and Jupiter sextile the Sun/Pluto conjunction, Saturn square Uranus, Chiron in Capricorn in the ninth house near the Midheaven). This in turn linked back to an old life in which his present-life father had been his teacher, passing on the law and mores of a society which were becoming obsolete and which were overturned shortly after his death. Once he had worked on this block on his Will, he was able to concentrate on contacting his own inner locus of control and self-healing power.

He needed to learn to take hold of his own Will and power (Sun conjunct Pluto), while his soulmate (and his family) needed to perceive that he was quite capable of doing so, and that unless he was motivated enough to make the initial contact no 'treatment' was going to help him. He was way beyond the stage when conventional therapies could 'cure' him. His one chance was to contact the energy within himself responsible for him manifesting the cancer, and then to use his own power of self-healing to reverse the process. However, his soulmate was offered the opportunity of sharing the compassion and acceptance of the Libra South Node conjunction with him through unconditional love, instead of losing herself in the relationship. She has Neptune conjunct Venus and the South Node in Libra, indicating that she was seeking to merge back into her 'ideal relationship', but showing also that the planetary energies might be expressed in a higher relationship in which the soulmate relationship would be that of companion and teacher. Such a relationship would also help with her North Node need to 'develop herself unselfishly' and release her from the manipulative past pattern of the Pluto sextile to Venus and the overly adaptive and accommodating Libra South Node.

Part of his karmic lesson and purpose, indicated in the tenth house Aquarian North Node, is to help in the evolution of his own inner authority and of mankind, and part is to resolve his seventh house Neptune/Saturn dilemma, and the difficulty in relating resulting from the detached, unconventional Venus/Uranus conjunction in the fourth house. In order to do this it may prove necessary for him to 'scapegoat' himself through death to facilitate both a family (tenth house) and wider 'group' (Aquarius North Node) realization that death can be a growth-enhancing process and is not, in any case, The End. His parents have already faced death ineffectually through the loss of a baby and of his elder sister, and he now feels that he has a lesson to teach them through their coming to terms with his life-threatening illness and sharing in his 'death' – he looks upon it as his gift to those with whom he has shared his life. Conversely he may need to take his knowledge out to the world himself, particularly if he succeeds in correcting his 'dis-ease', in order to teach that one must take responsibility for oneself and that death can be a creative activity. His soulmate companion can offer him support in taking this step, providing that the Mars–Node contacts are used courageously and do not invoke the aggressive, ego-conflict level of functioning.

In resolving his Mystic/Pragmatist dilemma (Neptune/Saturn) he may well pull her back into her old Libra pattern for a while as it conjuncts her South Node, but in so doing he will be offering her the opportunity to explore her spiritual roots. His Venus/Uranus conflict may well assist her in exploring the inherent contradiction in the relating style of her Aries North Node and Libra South Node conjunct Neptune/Venus. They can both learn the lesson of unconditional loving and living creatively until the day they 'die', whenever that may be.

RESOLUTION OF THE NODAL DILEMMA

Engaging in a dialogue with the Nodes and planets aspecting and transiting the Nodes can result in an understanding of the underlying purpose, and indicate a way forward into synthesis. In her book *The Astrology of Self-Discovery* Tracy Marks puts forward, in addition to penetrating insights relating to the nodal function, worksheets and questions specifically designed to reach the heart of the nodal dilemma and point the way to unification:

> The nodal axis is like an alchemical factory within our psyches through which we are capable of transforming the raw material of past lives and deeply ingrained behaviours into new sources of energy. When our North and South Nodes operate cooperatively, we experience a continual mobilization which catalyses our growth.[32]

Attunement and alignment to the karmic purpose is a crucial stage of evolution, providing boundless energy for change. It can be achieved through fully understanding, integrating and living the nodal axis.

NOTE   In natal charts where the South Node is in the same sign as the Sun the North Node in the same sign as the Moon, or the Sun and Moon are in the same sign, then the challenge and lesson is to do what has been done before but to do it more constructively, and to develop more of the positive qualities of the sign, capitalizing on the skills that have already been developed in using the energies of the sign in the past.

Chapter 3

SIGNPOSTS ALONG THE WAY

The path to sainthood goes through adulthood ... Our identity must be established before it can be transcended. One must find oneself before one can lose it.

M. SCOTT PECK, *THE ROAD LESS TRAVELLED*

The Sun, Moon and Ascendant can be seen as signposts on the karmic journey, indicating characteristics which have been brought back from the past and attributes to be built into the present. The negative qualities of the sign in which the Moon is located indicates karma to be overcome. The positive qualities of the Moon and Sun sign energies are to be incorporated into the incarnating soul's new way of being. Chiron is also a useful pointer in karmic work as it signifies the location of a deep wound from the past.

The Moon reflects instinctual feelings and reactions carried over from past lives. It is passive and receptive. It relates to the incarnating soul's deepest security needs and to how it will seek to satisfy them; it has a deep-rooted connectedness to the Mother, which is primal and immediate. It is the expectation of, and response to, nurturing. It is unconscious, rhythmic and cyclical. Impregnated by the character of its sign, subtly motivated and incited by past experience, it is a causal factor in emotional life. It is what the soul has been.

It contrasts sharply with the Sun: the conscious Self into which the soul is endeavouring to grow, the qualities it is trying to develop here and now, the autonomy it is seeking to manifest, and the ego strength it must gain before it can be merged into the greater whole. The Sun is active and outgoing, it initiates and forges new experience into a tool for its own growth. It is what the soul must be.

THE ASCENDANT

The Ascendant is both a mask with which to face the world and an inchoate perception based upon past experience which will colour that world: for example the Scorpio Ascendant tends to view the world with inherent suspicion and hides behind a mask of secrecy, the Sagittarius Ascendant, on the other hand, is naturally optimistic and open. The Ascendant is a way of interacting with others, it is what is first perceived and yet may be totally misleading. An Earth-sign Ascendant may appear to be practical, a good organizer who is well grounded, and yet, if there is no other Earth in the chart, this may be a protective outward projection, the mask, to cover an inner feeling of being totally out of touch with the practicalities of daily living. 'The world' demands that these be handled competently, and so a competent façade is erected. The Ascendant can be seen in karmic terms as representing the compensatory, balancing, positive qualities available to be built into the *persona* and projected out on to the world:

The positive Aries Ascendant can develop individuality, leadership, ego strength and a pioneering spirit. It can balance out previous procrastination, egoism and selfishness, or too much giving up of itself.

The positive Taurus Ascendant, being grounded in the body, can utilize practicality and sense perception to interact with the environment. It has the opportunity to develop the quality of endurance. It compensates for previous fixity, indulgence, materialism and possessiveness, or for ignoring the physical level of being.

The positive Gemini Ascendant is concerned with communication, information gathering and processing knowledge. It can develop an adaptable approach to the world in order to compensate for over-rigid beliefs held in the past. Its difficulty is that it can fall back into hypocrisy or lack of concentration, inattentiveness and superficiality.

The positive Cancer Ascendant has the ability to offer nurturing, protection and sensitivity to the world. It can overcome any previous tendency to 'smothering', manipulation and insensitivity. However, it needs to guard against possessiveness and sentimentality.

The positive Leo Ascendant can be powerful, authoritative, and heart-centred. It compensates for previous autocracy, dominance, self-centredness and intolerance.

The positive Virgo Ascendant is rational, learning to give discriminating service, and to become fruitful. It can balance out a previous undiscriminating acceptance of 'life'. Its difficulty can be in being overly fastidious and hypercritical.

The positive Libra Ascendant is concerned with relating, harmonizing, balancing, compromising and adapting. It balances out selfishness and self-centredness, but may fall back into indecision.

The positive Scorpio Ascendant can develop the qualities of penetration, insight and healing. It can either fall into the trap of, or compensate for, suspicion, hostility, vindictiveness and destructive emotions.

The positive Sagittarius Ascendant is philosophical, optimistic and expansive, it is the eternal seeker after truth. It balances out previous narrow-mindedness, bigotry, moralizing and insouciance.

The positive Capricorn Ascendant can develop a personality which is responsible, authoritative, successful and prudent. It needs to avoid old patterns of control and repression in order to overcome emotional isolation. Its difficulty may lie in confusing materialistic success with spiritual fulfilment.

The positive Aquarius Ascendant can be detached, perceptive and humanitarian, initiating social change. It compensates for too much attachment, but may fall back into an old pattern of amorality, anti-social behaviour and eccentricity.

The positive Pisces Ascendant has the potential to develop mystical, intuitive and empathetic qualities. It is offered the opportunity to balance out a previous pattern of untrustworthiness, insincerity, lies, immorality or opportunism.

THE MOON THROUGH THE SIGNS

The Moon has been seen, in some schools of esoteric astrology, as the sign in which the Sun was placed in the last incarnation. However, Mary Devlin[1], who has researched past-life charts (obtained from birth data given under regression), appears to make no connection between the last-life Sun and the present-life Moon, nor did she find evidence to support the related concept of the Ascendant as the past Sun or Moon sign. The concept, however, is a useful one to bear in mind when exploring the role of the Moon in bringing forward powerful influences from the past. The instinctual pattern of the Moon is a deeply ingrained one and must have arisen through considerable experience of the sign in which it is now placed.

A Moon which is out of sympathy with the rest of the chart – for example a Water Moon in an Earthy chart, or a Moon in an inharmonious sign such as Capricorn, which is uncomfortable with feelings – is an incompatible Moon. It will drastically affect how the rest of the chart functions and will continually fall back into the old pattern delineated by its sign, which is detrimental to the expression of the Sun energy. This type of imbalance is a major cause of difficulty in the present life until the positive, life-enhancing qualities of the Moon are allowed to rise into consciousness, overcoming the destructive, life-failing negative tendencies. Tracy Marks explores patterns of parenting and expectations of nurturing relating to the Moon sign and identifies twenty-two positive versus negative expressions of the Moon's energies, including sensitivity/over-sensitivity, nurturing/over-protectiveness or smothering, healthy/unhealthy eating patterns. Her book offers suggestions for improving emotional well-being through moving into the positive expression of Moon energies. She also explores the neglected healing power of lunar darkness and points out: 'One of the lessons of the Moon . . . concerns the healing capacity of consciously chosen unconsciousness . . . we need to relinquish our solar attempts at order and control, to open to darkness not in order to remain in darkness but to awaken our lunar consciousness and its healing energies.'[2]

It is this descent into the darkness of the instinctual Moon-self which enables the incarnating soul to bring forward forgotten wisdom to facilitate the flowering of the Sun-self. Within this darkness the detritus of outgrown consciousness can make fertile compost for the growth of new awareness, provided that the cyclical light of the Moon is allowed to shine when appropriate. Compost without light and air becomes a stinking, crawling morass of decay. Regularly aerated, it becomes a rich and nourishing source of goodness. Tracy Marks also makes the point that 'we must not interrupt the incubation period within us'. It is important to recognize when light is required in the darkness, and when it is inappropriate. Anything new which is growing needs time in the darkness in order to root and sprout, and pulling it up to see how well it is doing kills it. The Moon has natural cycles of darkness and light; attunement to these inner cycles will indicate the time for inward reflection, the moment when the old has to die, the period of dormancy, and the springing into new life.

The unconscious, unaware Moon energies manifest as a compulsive pull back into the past, the consciously expressed lunar energies nurture the growth of oneself and others, rectifying the karmic imbalance.

Moon in Aries

The negative manifestation of the Aries Moon is selfish, self-centred and isolationist; it is emotionally self-sufficient, fearing the 'weakness' of dependency, unable to make contact with others. It demands nurturing for itself, seeks ego-boosting dominant relationships, and lacks commitment to anything outside itself.

The positive expression of the lunar energies centres around the Self, recognizing its deep needs and being able to self-nurture by meeting those needs: it indicates an individual who has strength and validity because the totality of the Self, including its connection to others, has been rediscovered and is known intimately. Aries is the archetypal knight in shining armour on a white charger, defending the weak and helpless, righting wrongs and battling for good. It is caring, concerned, and able to initiate positive change, handing over its creation when it is appropriate for others to carry it on.

Moon in Taurus

The negative side of the Taurus Moon is manifested as tenacity in holding on to emotions. It harbours a grudge for almost as long as Scorpio and exudes the same kind of brooding resentment. It is a past master at repression, particularly of anger. Like the elephant, it never forgets. As with the Taurus South Node, it seeks sensual gratification and security through the body from people and objects – particularly food. It is fixed, immobile, resistant to change even when obviously hurt by its circumstances. Changing itself is never seen as an option: 'they' are at fault, 'they' must make amends/forgive/alter their behaviour. As a mothering energy it is dominant, overpowering, symbiotic; there is no separation, it is the instinctual Earth.

The positive lunar aspects are the ability to nurture through the physical environment, to provide for the needs of others. It finds security within itself. It is loyal, enduring, and perseveres long after everyone else has given up. The Moon in Taurus is often seen in the charts of psychics and healers as it can channel the intuitive levels of awareness down to the earth. It is grounded in the body, a totality of mind/body/spirit/emotions, utilizing all the senses to interact with the world. It is the earth mother who nourishes and sustains her children, but is then able to let them go at a time appropriate to their growth.

Moon in Gemini

The unconscious Gemini Moon is superficial, fickle, restless, uncommitted, and cerebral. It is cut off from the nourishing source of its emotional energy, and inclined to verbalize out of existence any feeling which does surface.

The consciously expressed lunar energy is able to communicate its feelings freely, without being overly emotional. It holds a balance between the body and the emotions, mediating through the intellect in order to recognize and acknowledge its emotional roots.

Moon in Cancer

The destructive side of the Cancer Moon energy is overly sensitive, possessive — those crab claws do not let go easily; clinging and dependent. It has a hard shell of seeming indifference covering an inner feeling of extreme vulnerability. It obliquely demands emotional nourishment for the needy child who is protected by that shell. As a mothering energy it smothers, allowing no autonomy or separation. Its own needs can be totally subjugated to the concept of 'The Family'.

The positive expression of the lunar energy is an unsurpassed capacity for nurturing. It is caring, protective and sympathetic, providing emotional nourishment for all. It mothers, in a growth-inducing way, not only its children but anyone who is needy. It is attuned to the life-giving energies of the feminine, the Goddess.

Moon in Leo

The deeply instinctual Moon in Leo is autocratic and overbearing. It demands the admiration which is essential to its emotional sustenance. Its great sin is 'hubris', too much pride. It cannot cope with feeling neglected or helpless, and will unashamedly exert its considerable authority in order to be rewarded by feeling needed and powerful.

When the Leo Moon becomes conscious it is capable of deep loving and generosity of spirit. It becomes centred in its heart, showering benevolent warmth and affection on all people. It knows that 'genuine love is a self-replenishing activity [which is] volitional rather than emotional'[3].

Moon in Virgo

The unconscious Moon in Virgo is cold, critical and overly analytical. It is not comfortable with emotion and will attempt to rationalize feelings. It seeks order as a means of exerting control. Everything in its conscious mind is pigeon-holed, clean, neat and acceptable. Anything else is firmly excluded, relegated to the hold labelled 'Not Wanted on Voyage'. It is sterile.

When the Moon in Virgo is manifested consciously, it taps a wellspring of fertile, creative energy. This sign above all else indicates truly altruistic service springing from an inner state of love and relatedness. It is virgin within the old meaning: 'intact', integrated and whole. Virgo is the sign of the harvest, fruitful and abundant.

Moon in Libra

The old pattern for the Moon in Libra is one of over-compromising; adjusting too much to the needs of others, the soul with this placement is a 'people-pleaser'. It avoids confrontation and assertion and thereby stifles its own emotional needs. Its very 'niceness' is untrustworthy because it can explode unexpectedly when its deeper needs demand to be heard.

The new lunar pattern opens up to true relationship, interaction with an equal. It is capable of harmonizing and balancing its own emotional needs with those of another effecting a creative compromise. It has reached inner emotional equilibrium and is centred on itself and therefore not afraid to be honest and truthful in expressing feelings.

Moon in Scorpio

The deeply mistrustful Scorpio Moon harbours old jealousies, anger, pain and passion. It is resentful, suffers from inner feelings of inadequacy and guilt, and elicits rejection as a defence against the risk of opening up to another person. Its greatest fear is that someone else will have power over it and it therefore never expresses its feelings directly, not even to itself. It is 'paranoid', seeing persecution around every corner: 'they are out to get me/won't let me be happy/are waiting to punish me' are just a few of its inner messages. Emotions are deeply repressed and erupt from time to time in a monumental outburst that bears no relation to the size of the 'trigger' as it has the full weight of the past behind it. That past is a traumatic, unsafe place in which to venture.

The positive Scorpio Moon has the power to penetrate the depths, the taboo areas where others fear to tread. It is able to go through the pain and trauma and emerge with insights about its own, and others', healing and progress. It is intensely passionate and can harness its creative energy to accompanying others on the journey into their own darkness, acting as a guide and catalyst for their growth. It is deeply intuitive and is attuned to the cycle of birth, death and regeneration.

Moon in Sagittarius

The negatively manifesting Sagittarian Moon is 'out to lunch' whenever any emotional demands are made. Its response to emotional pressure is to travel, preferably physically, but if this is not possible, mentally. Although it will enjoy exploring the rhetorical question: 'Why do we need feelings?', it will not enjoy exploring those feelings other than in a purely philosophical manner. It is a dual Moon, when it does allow itself to feel emotions it can oscillate between two emotions or two people; this is an unfaithful Moon.

The positively expressed Sagittarius Moon is open, honest and trusting in its relationships and sharing of feelings, allowing joy to manifest in its life. It lives by a philosophy which incorporates feelings, intuition, and an old knowing into its philosophy of Being.

Moon in Capricorn

The unconscious Capricorn Moon is cold and judgemental, unresponsive and afraid to express emotion. It gives out a message of isolation and self-sufficiency — 'approach with caution' — and retreats into 'safe' material expressions of its feelings. It cares financially for its family, often at the cost of emotional closeness. It carries a stultifying burden of responsibility and duty, eternally 'shoulding' on itself. As a mothering energy the Capricorn Moon is severe, controlling and often incapable of physically expressing its maternal feelings.

The conscious Capricorn Moon is steadfast, responsible and authoritative, offering dependable support. As a mothering energy it offers consistent discipline leading towards maturity and self-control.

Moon in Aquarius

The negatively expressed Aquarian Moon is self-contained, out of touch with its feelings and its past and yet profoundly motivated by both. The soul with this placement finds one-to-one relationships difficult, preferring to relate 'to the whole' in a very detached way, or to retreat into an unreal fantasy relationship in which it perceives very little about its partner's feelings and responses. The Aquarian Moon has a non-close, distant and formal pattern of relating and takes refuge in a very cold, lonely place whenever it is threatened emotionally.

The positive Aquarian Moon is an expression of universal love. It is connected to the whole, interacting from an objective perspective, unattached to the outcome, and yet capable of expressing its very real feelings of love for the microcosm, Man, and macrocosm, Mankind. It is the true humanitarian. It is detached from the emotions and not swayed by emotive arguments and can therefore evaluate what is most beneficial to the whole. The Aquarian Moon is intuitive and perceptive, attuned through old contacts to the philanthropic ideals behind the new Aquarian Age.

Moon in Pisces

The unconscious Pisces Moon slips into the same old scenarios as the Pisces South Node, falling back into a martyr/victim or saviour pattern. It is self-sacrificing and self-immolating and induces guilt with facile ease. It too is a dual, unfaithful Moon, although it deceives itself into believing it is not capable of hurting anyone and that, 'in any case', if no one knows, no one is hurt by the emotional games it plays with two lovers, for example. It cannot bear pain, wallows in self-pity and sympathy, makes promises it will never keep, and then goes its own sweet way.

The conscious Pisces Moon is the natural mystic and medium of the zodiac, bringing unconditional love and inspiration to the world. It is empathetic but discriminating, connected and yet independent. It recognizes that 'love involves a change in the self, but this is an extension of the self rather than a sacrifice of the self'[4]. When called upon, it can make great personal sacrifice for the good of the greater whole, but this is not an involuntary reaction, it is the final step in self-integration with the cosmos.

THE SUN THROUGH THE SIGNS

The pathway to true integration and release from the karmic round requires that the question 'Who am I?' be addressed. The instinctual Moon offers one answer, but a conscious shift into the Sun sign energies allows for an expansion of the incarnating soul into the Self – the totality embracing the whole being – where an altogether different answer emerges. Although the following is portrayed as a journey around the zodiac, the intention is not to imply that an incarnating soul progresses inexorably from the preceding sign to the next. The signs are areas of experience which will be utilized when required and as appropriate in order to balance out previous incarnations. Several experiences may be needed in one particular sign or element before its lessons are properly assimilated; other lessons come easily and a very short experience may be all that is required. The zodiac is a spectrum through which the soul progresses in accordance with its own innate pattern, evolving towards its Highest.

Sun in Aries

Aries is a sign of birth and isolation. There is an intense awareness of separateness, of being an individual conscious-ness, surrounded by a vast otherness.[5]

Born into Aries, the incarnating soul becomes conscious of moving from the syncretic consciousness of the between-life state of being, as opposed to the separateness of individual identity. It moves from an innate attunement with all those with whom it shares its space in the spiritual realm into a sense of 'otherness' and alienation from that sense of oneness. In Aries the incarnating soul enters into recognition of being an 'other', an individual. A young Norwegian client (eighth house Sun in Aries, five planets in Earth) asked: 'I would like to know from where in the universe I come, and when did I come here. Finally I am interested if there is someone in family or nearby who has been in connection with me during past lives.' He had a third house Neptune and felt separate, not a part of his family of origin. He was viscerally aware of his discreteness, an alien being incarcerated in the body of a stranger with the task of discovering himself.

Aries is concerned with the development of the ego: 'the conscious, thinking subject'[6], the Will: 'desire of sufficient intensity that it is translated into action'[7], and the Self: 'own individuality or essence'[8]. The incarnating soul may evolve through the pathway of identification with itself on the level of individuality; a selfish, self-centred pathway concerned only with 'Me' which generates karma, or through merging with the essence: an unselfish pathway concerned with expression of the eternal 'I' which is beyond karma.

Aries is also concerned with issues of assertion and Will. The Will may be developed in the service of the ego or of the self. When associated with the ego, it is wilful: 'compulsion or ignorance or accident cannot be pleaded as excuse, intentional, deliberate, due to perversity or self-will, obstinate, headstrong, refractory'[9], and concerned only with self-interest. In the service of the self it is concerned with self-growth and self-determination. Aries must master the lesson of transmutation of the base impulses of self-will and aggression which are linked to its ruler, Mars. Assertion is the higher octave of the aggressive, violent urge towards destruction. It is concerned with affirmation of the Self, with growth and construction. Courage is an Aries quality, defined by M. Scott Peck as 'not the absence of fear, it is the making of action in spite of fear, the moving out against the resistance engendered by fear into the unknown and into the future'[10].

It is this experience of travelling out into the unknown which will develop the innate Arian leadership potential and pioneering spirit. However, wisdom is required in order to circumvent disaster brought about by those other Arian qualities, foolhardiness and over-impulsiveness. Aries must learn to think before acting, but not fall into the trap of procrastination. A middle course must be steered between action and dilatoriness, guided by the compass of the Self.

Sun in Taurus

Incarnating into Taurus, the soul becomes aware of being cloaked in a physical body which is equipped with senses through which to interact with the earth environment. Discarnate beings describe inhabiting worlds where the spirit is lightly clothed and where each thought or emotion is clearly visible to all. Bishop Pyke's son described, in his communications through the medium Ena Twigg, a place where all desires could be satisfied. By the act of desiring something, it was there. Sexual intercourse was a fusion of two beings, not just bodies. Small wonder then that Taurus is so involved with the physical, sensual and sexual level of being. The soul needs the experience of utilizing its senses and its physical body as part of the totality of Being: there must be no separation between the Self and its vehicle. If it gets stuck on the purely sensual level however, karma will accumulate which will have to be balanced out later. If it learns to move into that fusion of being on all levels which Jeff Mayo describes as 'organic relatedness'[11], then its karmic task is completed.

Taurus is one of the fixed signs, it is obstinate and unmoving, and learns the lesson of perseverance and endurance. Where Aries moved on, Taurus stays long after others have given up. However, it must learn when it is appropriate to 'hang on in there', and when it is merely digging for itself a deeper and deeper rut which will eventually become its grave. Taurus must evolve, slowly and steadily but relentlessly, or expire from inertia.

One of the main lessons that Taurus must learn is to find

security inside itself, in who it is, rather than identify with what it owns or possesses. Time and time again I have asked a Taurean client what kept her, or him – it makes no difference – in a marriage which was clearly over years before. The answer is always the same: 'Well, there was the house . . .', and of course the marriage, no matter how dead, was something known and familiar. Fear of change and of the unfamiliar conspire to keep many Taureans in their rut. When Taurus feels secure within itself, it has a stable base from which to venture out on its journey into the unknown.

Sun in Gemini

Moving into Gemini the incarnating soul finds itself inhabiting a 'mental' realm of intellect and communication. It is concerned with gathering in information about the world it inhabits and the people it meets, and with processing these facts to make order and sense out of a jumble of perceptions. Human beings are bombarded with sensory input every moment of the waking day, Gemini learns to select only the information relevant to the immediate activity on which it is focussing its awareness. It 'files' the remaining data out of consciousness. Its essential function is communication: what has been processed must be passed on. It is ruled by Mercury, mediator and messenger for the gods. Singer Julie Felix (Gemini with Scorpio rising, first house Scorpio North Node, and ninth house Venus/Pluto in Cancer) experienced jealousy consciously for the first time at the age of fifty. She promptly wrote a song 'Graduation Day' to express her pain and new understanding out to the world.

> I guess that you could say
> That this is graduation day
> Cos I just stand here and hear you say
> Like the lines from a play
> That you slept with her
> That was a promise that you kept with her
> You slept with her.

I know we both agreed
That if we ever felt the need
To explore some karmic debt
With a person that we met
That we could sleep with them
If there were dreams that we could reap with them
Then we could sleep with them.

Its funny how the human heart gets broken
No matter what precautions we might take
Its not until those painful words are spoken
That reality defeats philosophy.

How did it feel inside
Was it guilt or was it pride
What was it that you said
To make her crawl into your bed
And sleep with you
And were your feelings really deep and true
To have her sleep with you.

And now you're by my side
And you held me while I cried
Until somewhere deep inside
I felt the turning of the tide
And you slept with me.

Other songs have communicated her evolving spiritual awareness, and her protests at the exploitation of the earth and its people.

Gemini is flexible and adaptive, able to adjust easily to changing circumstances. The danger is that it can be too mercurial, constantly and restlessly seeking new experiences and not allowing itself time for the ingestion and integration of what it has already learnt. It can be the 'butterfly mind' alighting here and there as the whim takes it but never completing a task and dissipating its energies in a fruitless search for satiation. The lesson for the soul attuned to the Gemini Sun is to discipline its restless mind and focus it on communicating fully all that it has learnt, then it will be free to move on.

Sun in Cancer

In Cancer the soul enters the world of the emotions and encounters the eternally nurturing energy of the Great Mother. It meets and comes to terms with its own inner archetypal feminine and matriarchal energies, and consciously integrates these into its being. Just as Taurus has to learn the lesson of endurance, Cancer has to learn when to nurture, and when to let go. It must recognize when it is appropriate to be sympathetic and supportive, or supported, and the point when growth becomes impeded unless the person is able to stand alone. This is a very specific lesson for Cancer mothers as they can fall into the role of the eternal mother, inhibiting both their own growth and that of their dependant – whether physically related or not – by blotting out separation and difference. They need to differentiate between mothering and smothering, love and possessiveness.

A man (twelfth house Sun in Cancer square the Moon in Libra) was brought up by a mother (Moon in Cancer) who smothered him with 'love'. 'Have you got your hanky, dear?' she would ask as she waved him off to school, age sixteen and six feet tall. He was a sensitive, withdrawn child, absorbing the repressed emotional ambience of a dysfunctional family, his only outlet was music. His father was a womanizer and the family moved continually to escape from the latest affair but the problem was never acknowledged: both parents were Pisces. At the age of eleven, apparently in response to pressure to pass his eleven-plus examination, he developed night-time epilepsy. Twelfth house Venus in Gemini conjunct Uranus/Mercury in Cancer square to Mars indicate an old disruption in the brain-wave pattern, but no brain malfunction or injury could be found to explain it. Many years later it was discovered that, when sleeping, he would literally stop breathing and convulsions would ensue. Breath is one of the ways we nourish ourselves and he was manifesting his symbolic suffocation. This always occurred during a period of emotional distress within the family: failing to breathe was his way of withdrawing from the unacknowledged stress. He has a 'split' chart with Pluto sextiling Neptune but neither planet aspecting any other, so the withdrawal was an unconscious and dissociative, reflex action. The episodes were always preceded by the same terrifying 'dream' (twelfth house Uranus/Mercury communicating an old terror).

Apart from visits to a psychiatric hospital for tests, his problem was never validated within the family by being discussed – a typically Piscean, and twelfth house, response to a difficult situation. His doting mother was terrified of the convulsions and never went to him during an attack. He married a Taurean 'earth mother' type, whose Sun conjuncted his North Node and who tried to give him the nurturing he lacked and to ground him in his body. Although the epilepsy subsided, it recurred whenever the family could no longer be ignored. It was only at the age of forty, on his Uranus opposition, that he was able to reassess the problem and begin to live a life freed from the unconscious parental pressures and his own desperate, little-boy, need for them to nourish and protect him. So far, however, he has not explored the karmic implications of his twelfth house, which could possibly release him from his incarnational difficulties.

When the Cancer Sun energy functions positively, it works through vocations and activities which nurture and nourish others, and which are undertaken by those who know how to ensure that their own needs for nurturance are also met. It encompasses sensitivity and puts it to work in order to understand the emotional needs of those it meets on its journey. It is the universe's social worker in constructive action.

Sun in Leo

In Leo the soul enters the arena of power and develops the urge towards expression of personal authority. Leo is the king of the zodiac and its rule may be despotic, autocratic or benign depending on how that urge is acted out. Leo's lesson is to own the power deep within its Self. As Liz Greene[12] points out Leo's initial challenge is to find out why it is 'uniquely itself', and its life-long task is to discover within itself the self-esteem it so needs. She sees Leo's main purpose as making the journey within.

This journey into the centre of its own being is linked to the Leo need to be heart-centred. Traditionally Leo rules the heart and a stressed, frustrated Leo is prone to cardiac problems. When Leo becomes centred in its heart, the love energy becomes its source of power both for the inward and the outward journey. It is empowered. However: 'When power is clearly moving through us, energy pours through and we become "larger than life". If it is not let go of afterwards then we begin to misuse it and we become puffed up, "on a high horse".'[13]

As Debbie Boater points out, it is through the attachment to power, trying to hold on to it instead of letting it flow, that problems arise. When Leo is conscious of owning its own power, it knows that paradoxically it is not its own: 'owning power is an acknowledgement that there is nothing to own'. A Leo who is grasping at power demands admiration and praise, a Leo who owns power commands it naturally. Watch Leo enter a room: if it is secure its presence lights it up. It has centre stage. A Pisces woman grumbled, about a good friend: 'When Bren walks into a room it's just like a magnet, every man in it gravitates to her.' Bren was middle-aged and overweight, but she was also Leo. Secure in her own power, she radiated love and warmth and everyone responded, including the Piscean who 'couldn't help herself'.

When not comfortable with power, Leo snarls like a bad-tempered old lion protecting his pride from a young challenger. If it is comfortable with power, Leo basks in its warmth like a contented pussycat stretched out in the sun. The aware Leo naturally radiates its Self out to the waiting world. It has become conscious of its creative power. It has authority. The process of becoming aware of itself as an individual is complete.

Sun in Virgo

In Virgo the incarnating soul begins the process of reintegration with the whole, and enters into service as an expression of its interconnectedness. Having been acknowledged for its own power in Leo, the soul now submits to the authority of divine love and offers itself in unselfish, altruistic service as an outpouring of that love.

One of the ways in which Virgo can give service is by entering the world of medicine and healing. Virgo is the intellectual Earth sign and mention has already been made (Chapter 2) of its need to understand the body/mind link and the psychosomatic causes of disease — why and how the soul being ill at ease will manifest within the physical body as pain and discomfort.

Virgo is also the craftsman, the creator on the physical level. Its symbol is the Virgin holding an ear of corn, and it is linked to the old earth goddess and the rituals to ensure an abundant and fruitful harvest. It is part of the fertility cycle and deeply attuned to creative energy. It has an inherent urge towards perfection. Jeff Mayo sees Virgo as having a primal impulse towards the skilful use of energy which avoids wastage or dissipation, and which incorporates self-sufficiency and independence. A purity of Being which is the true meaning of virgin: whole and intact. He sees Virgo's task as to analyse everything until the pure essence is perceived and assimilated. This purity of essence is essential for Virgo as from it springs detached service, service which is concerned only with what is needed, not with regard or recognition. In true humility Virgo honours the creative love force underlying life and carries it out to the world in loving service.

Sun in Libra

In Libra the soul seeks to expand through relationship with others. It is ready to move out on to a pathway that requires its own boundary be temporarily expanded out to include, or be penetrated by, A. N. Other; to enlarge its consciousness beyond individual separation into loving interrelation with the self of another.

> There is no alternative . . . to bringing into being a truly conscious relationship with another person. Inevitably it hurts; any birth does. One must dare to suffer the death of illusions, and the dissolution of projections. One must dare to be mistaken. One must dare to be vulnerable, to be inferior, to be magnanimous enough to allow for the failings of others because one is prone to them oneself; and one must dare to incur (and inflict) pain and wounded pride . . . And one must be willing to accept the element of unconscious

collusion in all situations, however much they may seem to be the fault of the other. Nothing comes into a man's life that is not a reflection of something within himself.[14]

This is the karmic task of Libra; to enter into an aware relationship with another human being with all the failings and foibles, the needs and aspirations on both sides taken into account and allowed expression. To take two separate individuals and to create between them a third entity, the relationship, in which neither partner is diminished into one half of a couple but which has life and energy and nurtures the growth of both partners equally according to their need. Where there is conflict of interest, then the Libran soul must learn the art of creative compromise, ensuring that its own needs do not become submerged under pressure from the other and that a way is found to encompass both.

Libra also attains emotional equilibrium through its relationships, in the widest sense. It learns to accommodate both its own feelings and those of another soul, and to recognize that while both have validity and value, neither are of overwhelming importance. Conscious awareness of motivation and of where those feelings are coming from will allow a choice to be made, whether to go on feeling that way or to decide – decisions being something Libra is notoriously bad at – to incorporate the new point of view which is being represented by the other. In this way Libra is able to grow through its interaction and develops an inner harmony and balance which is reflected in its relationships outside itself.

Sun in Scorpio

In Scorpio the soul makes its descent into darkness. It must retrieve its cognizance of the 'shadow' side of life and integrate this into its awareness.

As with the Scorpio Moon and Node, the Scorpio Sun can venture into the depths where others fear to tread, the taboo areas of life wherein lurk death and annihilation; and will bring back insights to aid those 'others' on their particular journey. It has an atavistic understanding that here, in the darkness, is where the deepest roots of creativity lie, here is the energy for renewal and new growth. It also has an old knowledge of the fertility cycle, the seasons of conception, birth, death and rebirth and it knows that it dies many times, physically and psychically, only to rise again to new life. And from those depths it brings back an awareness of the purpose of its Being.

Scorpio experiences the sexual act as a transforming and regenerative process intimately linked to the energies of creation, an act of mystical union with another soul which incorporates 'death' through temporary self-forgetfulness and immolation. Through that union with an other which is an act of integration, the Scorpio soul fuses with the cosmos and the source of life itself. It is thereby uniquely attuned to the on-going, ever-present process of death and rebirth intrinsic in existence.

The depth of emotional power which Scorpio generates is also unique and must be harnessed to the evolution of the Self as otherwise there is a danger that it will be self destructive. It is in gaining mastery over this power, and losing the fear of death, that Scorpio fulfils its innermost purpose.

Scorpio has many levels of being. There is the instinctual level of the scorpion who lashes out indiscriminately, destroying everything in its path including itself, 'because it is its nature to do so'[15]. There is the level of the eagle who can soar high above the earth, gaining an overview through its penetrating eye and homing in on its target, often with lethal intent. And then there is that of the phoenix, that legendary being who goes through the purifying fire so that all the dross is burnt away and the golden essence is revealed. This is Scorpio at its most evolved: no longer into emotional games, no longer needing revenge for the past, lethal no more. It has entered into relationship with the darkness, mastered it, and brought it into light. Scorpio is then empowered to bring forth the healing and insight necessary for the regeneration of mankind.

Sun in Sagittarius

Sagittarius is the eternal traveller engaged in unceasing exploration of the physical and philosophical worlds. The Sun in

Sagittarius soul is a free spirit who ranges far and wide in its search for meaning. It is the ancient philosopher and the Renaissance man for whom there was no division of knowledge. The arts, sciences and humanities were one. Religion was promulgated in answer to Sagittarius' urgent questions: 'Who am I?', 'Why am I here?'.

These are questions to which Sagittarius must still apply itself today and, having found its answers, must then share that knowledge with the less philosophically inclined soul and lead it forward into its own understanding of eternal truths. Sagittarius's resources are intuition and old knowledge. Its symbol is the centaur, half man, half beast, a synthesis of instinct and rational thought, capable of making a spontaneous, intuitional leap into the unknown which pulls ever onwards. However, like its polarity Gemini, Sagittarius needs time to ponder, space to assimilate and formulate a belief system which offers a way to Be. It must live out its beliefs by Being. A centaur paying lip-service to ethics is a hollow shell, purposeless and untrustworthy. A Sagittarian who is what it believes is a sage who leads mankind onwards into knowledge of itself, its world and other dimensions of being.

Sun in Capricorn

In Capricorn the soul meets the archetypal patriarchal energies of 'God the Father' and must assimilate these into its being. It is offered the opportunity of exploring inner discipline in relationship to leadership and authority. Capricorn can draw on internal strength, resilience and a disciplined Will in order to establish its own inner authority, which is then translated into and expressed externally as leadership. In the unevolved Capricorn, such leadership can often lack spiritual vision and owes too much to a strict adherence to an inflexible set of principles to live by:

> Here the unconscious intuitive search for meaning in life is structured and crystallised by the senses into dogma, which attempts to define God, put spiritual reality into concrete form, and translate the numinous into sacrosanct objects — and adherence to the letter of the law, in other words, an obliviousness to its spirit.[16]

When Capricorn finds within itself sufficient confidence in its own worth and authority, it can be enabled to venture out of the bounds of fixed dogma and into the realms of experiential spirituality and vision. Dr Martin Luther King, Jr, Baptist preacher, winner of the Nobel Peace Prize and Civil Rights leader, was a Capricorn who had not only vision, but also the authority and personal charisma (Sun conjunct Midheaven) required to lead his oppressed people out of the prison constructed from the outmoded concepts of the society (Uranus square Saturn) in which they lived:

> Now is the time to make real the promises of democracy. I have a dream that one day this nation will rise up and live out the true meaning of its creed: 'We hold these truths to be self-evident, that all men are created equal'. I have a dream that one day . . . the sons of former slaves and the sons of former slave-owners will be able to sit down together at the table of brotherhood.[17]

Dr King was a pacifist who believed in non-violent action. He had a wide Sun–Pluto opposition, Sun inconjunct Mars, and Saturn opposing Mars. His karma was concerned with the nature, and proper utilization, of power and assertion. He believed in the transforming power of spiritual love (Venus in Pisces): 'Only through an inner spiritual transformation do we gain the strength to fight vigorously the evils of the world in a humble, loving spirit.'[18] His trine of Ascendant conjunct Jupiter in Taurus to Neptune in Virgo combines idealism with practical action taking him, through his vision, beyond the limits of the environment in which he is operating.

> Violence brings only temporary victories; violence, by creating many more social problems then it solves, never brings permanent peace. I am convinced that if we succumb to the temptation to use violence in our struggle for freedom, unborn generations will be the recipients of a long and desolate night of bitterness, and our chief legacy to them will be a never ending reign of chaos.[19]

That twelfth house Uranus has old knowledge of revolution, but his vision of spiritual community and love freed from oppression, is one which every Capricorn can share.

Sun in Aquarius

The soul incarnating into Aquarius marches to a slightly different drum beat to the rest of humanity. It is one step ahead, the social visionary who is able to conceive of new ways of being in which the needs of all of humanity will be met. However, in spite of this it is acutely aware of its connection to its 'brother man'.

The unevolved Aquarian is, in the words of Martin Luther King: 'A reformer . . . whose rebellion against the evils of society has left him annoyingly rigid and unreasonably impatient.'[20] The evolved Aquarian has become truly centred in his Being, no longer attached to the emotions, the mind the servant of the Self: the intuition has blended with rational intelligence to attain true wisdom. The Aquarian Self is attuned to the vibration of universal love and brotherhood which permeates and underlies the functioning of the cosmos. This universal love is expressed by the Aquarian soul through humanitarian ideals and an originality of thought which ushers in Progress. Mankind is now entering the Age of Aquarius, the time when man can move into conscious, caring brotherhood not only with mankind, but also with the rest of creation. It is no accident that politics have turned 'green' and are aligned to ecological and conservation issues: the Aquarian Age ordains that this be so, together with a shift into husbanding the resources of the planet and its people. According to Genesis, Man was given dominion over the earth and appointed to be steward, a position of responsibility, not despoiler. Brotherhood extends to both creator and creation, including the furthermost stars and planes of being. The Age of Aquarius will ensure a return to the state of harmonious interconnectedness of the organic whole, and the Aquarian energy will be there, leading the way to universal Being.

Sun in Pisces

In Pisces the soul completes its journey back to the Source. It transcends the material world, reaches out to the spiritual realm, and attains union with the divine. It is once more merged into the totality of Being.

The evolved Piscean develops its powers of unconditional love and compassion as it ministers impartially to those around it. It is moving towards a state of grace, the point where karma is balanced out, obligations sufficiently repaid, potential adequately fulfilled. Release from the wheel of rebirth is a distinct possibility. M. Scott Peck describes this state: 'The call to grace is a call to life of effortful caring, to a life of service and whatever sacrifice seems required. It is a call out of spiritual childhood into adulthood, a call to be a parent unto mankind.'[21]

The Pisces Sun is striving to merge into its greater Self and the journey towards integration with the Self appears to be indissolubly connected to the testing process known as 'The Dark Night of the Soul'. When one is seemingly at last reaching a point of enlightenment, one is plunged into periods of spiritual blackness. For Pisces in particular this may well be linked to the need to avoid 'spiritual pride' (especially when the Sun is in the twelfth house) as this can negate any progress made towards achieving the state of grace. It is a humbling experience to suddenly find that, just as one feels one is getting somewhere, one falls into deepest despair, apparently without cause or reason. In her book Christine Hartley points out:

just because in one sense we know so much, so are they [these states of despair] the more bitter for us than for the unaware because we know that we should be able to conquer the despair and the gloom. But we cannot. To each man must come his Gethsemane, the saints and saviours all experience it and the greater the saint, in all probability the greater the despair. Unless a man has cried 'My God, my God, why hast thou forsaken *me*?' he cannot understand the despair of others . . . only by our own suffering can we truly learn how to help suffering humanity, and only by our acceptance of it and our transmutation of it can we show the world our belief that it is only a moment in the eternal passage of time.[22]

It is the karmic task of Pisces to achieve this transmutation of suffering into a state of grace, and in so doing surrender to the divine and merge and become One.

CHIRON: THE WOUND OF THE SOUL

Chiron is a seemingly minor body in the constellation of Sagittarius, located between Saturn, his mythological father, and Uranus, his mythological grandfather. However, its influence is not limited by its size, as it indicates both the presence of a wound from the past – which can be very large indeed – and the means to heal that wound. Although this is not intended to be a comprehensive coverage (readers are referred to Melanie Reinhart's book *Chiron and the Healing Journey*[23]), there are several karmic factors which I have noted time and time again in connection with Chiron. It must, however, be borne in mind that the placement of, and aspects to, Chiron can also link with other issues not covered here.

Chiron was the product of an illicit union between Saturn and Philyra, daughter of Oceanus, the primeval deep. Caught *in flagrante delicto* by his wife, Saturn changed into a stallion and galloped off. When Philyra gave birth it was to what she perceived as a monster: half man, half beast, a centaur who represented the fusion and reconciliation of the bestial nature and the higher nature of man. Philyra prayed to the gods to have her child taken away, and she was answered. Chiron was raised by Apollo and the other gods who taught him many skills but principally those of healing and warfare – another reconciliation of opposites. He became a famous teacher and healer, and was given the gift of immortality. His gift, however, became his curse when he was accidentally wounded with poison from the Hydra. The wound could not heal, and being immortal Chiron could not die. He underwent a long period of agony until he was able to give up his immortality by taking on the burden of Prometheus, he who had stolen fire from the gods and been condemned to forever have his liver pecked out. Chiron descended into the underworld but was then elevated to a place in the heavens by the gods.

As Howard Sasportas points out in an excellent chapter on Chiron[24], Chiron's first wound was rejection by his mother, equating with the expulsion from the womb into separateness and new life. He then became a maker of heroes and it was one of those heroes, Hercules, who wounded him. He was therefore wounded by his own creation.

In karmic work Chiron not only shows where the incarnating soul has its wound but also indicates where it is attached to suffering and must release from the old pain. The reward is to be elevated, but letting go cannot be contingent upon reward. The soul must make a conscious, informed choice as Chiron did, freely relinquishing its hold upon the world it has known and, where necessary, choosing to go through death of the old self in order that something greater may emerge.

CHIRON IN ASPECT AND HOUSES

As previously mentioned, Chiron indicates a wound, and planets which conjunct, or aspect, Chiron, take on karmic pain in varying degrees according to the nature of the planet, the house placement and the aspect.

Chiron–Mercury

Mercury aspecting Chiron can indicate an old wound in the area of communication or related to how the intellect has been used in the past. I have seen this aspect in a child born with a cleft palate ('retributive' karma) and in someone who regressed to a life in which his tongue was cut out as a punishment for informing.

A client consulted me because of her lack of confidence. After the reading she told me that she often had to speak to small groups of people but when she opened her mouth, nothing came out. She had Chiron in Gemini in the eleventh house, opposing Mercury. The first past life which I picked up on was described as follows:

I had a very strong impression of a nun in a silent order, and when I say silent I really mean this as all the prayer times were silent and there wasn't even any chanting to relieve the total silence. I don't feel you used your voice for many many years. You also seem to be totally alone, you slept in single cells and didn't even have the companionship of the other nuns. There is also this feeling coming forward of being so unworthy, a sense of sinfulness and being inadequate in the Lord's eyes. As though you wanted to be perfect spiritually and yet felt that you failed so often, when really it was the standards that were so impossibly high no human being could ever reach them. Also because there was no companionship with the other nuns, and no shared worship in the sense that each joined with the others − prayers were communal but silent, individual − there was no shared spiritual dimensions to give you strength. In fact the spiritual dimension seems to be the most devastating and most lacking of all, as though the real purpose behind the convent's existence had been forgotten . . .

The other life which I'm picking up strongly on was diametrically opposed to this. This is probably Tudor times but I have the sense of you being 'Mistress' to someone quite exalted. You look very pretty but there wasn't much in the way of brains there, in fact there's an almost childlike innocence with this despite the obviously sexual side of the relationship. You seem to have lived for pretty clothes, jewellery. And this very besotted male seems to have supplied them in great abundance and shown you off whenever possible − but as a 'possession' not a partner. There is the impression of 'smile and show everyone how ravishing you are, but don't dare open your mouth'. Although at the time this did not upset you at all, I'm sure that later when you were reviewing the life it left an inhibition and a feeling of being stupid which is no longer appropriate for you but which has lingered beneath the surface.

Her feedback, made as notes at the time of listening to the taped reading, is enlightening as to how experiences are carried over into the present incarnation:

I was pulled into this world (breech) to the sound of swearing and screaming as my mother lashed out at the doctor for hurting her so badly as he hauled me out.

When I was born I was unable to cry at all. Apparently I made all the motions of crying but it wasn't until I was six months old that any sound came out. Then I let the world know of my existence, but my mother couldn't bear the sound of babies crying and as soon as I was fed in the morning she would put me in the pram and push me way down the bottom of the garden behind the woodshed and leave me there until it was time to be fed again (could this be the reason for my occasional resorting to comfort eating in times of stress?).

At one year old I had a head-on collision with my older brother and I remained concussed for two days. When my mother finally managed to wake me up I went into convulsions and in her panic she rolled me up in a blanket and laid me out on the garden path whilst she fetched a neighbour to help her. I had two fits in all and she was told that a third could be fatal and therefore she was not to be left alone with me as she was well into her next pregnancy. So the neighbour took to looking after me until I eventually was out of any further danger (what a start in life). [She has the Moon bi-quintile Pluto on the Ascendant, an aspect of 'fate' related to mothering and being mothered, and a close brush with death in her 'past'] . . . Being the oldest girl it was always my task to look after the latest baby in the family and I loved every minute of it. They were my own real-life dolls . . . When I was eight years old a baby died as it was premature. I can still feel the terrible disappointment and bewilderment that I felt when I saw my little newborn sister, who weighed 2 lb, lying in her coffin ready to be taken away to be buried. Up to that time I had always thought that only our farm animals and birds and cats and dogs died and got buried . . .

When I am with others I can talk reasonably freely one to one until I sense their gaze intent upon me. Then I feel stripped naked, vulnerable and go to pieces.

There seems to be a strong tie in between the nun incarnation and my silent entry into this life. I still have a need to have a 'quiet time' at each end of the day in which to relax, pray and meditate. I feel quite cheated if my husband comes to bed at the same time as me, and equally if he is in a chatty mood first thing in the morning.

Chiron—Mars

The pain of Chiron in aspect to Mars stems from violence, or misused Will or assertion energy, and it can involve a violation of trust in the past. This aspect can, for example, fit in with the priest/healer who commits an act of violence or blasphemy; it can also indicate karma resulting from having taken part in 'Holy Wars' or crusades, or indicate membership of one of the military orders of monks, such as the Knights Templars or Knights of St John. Unfortunately, despite the vows of obedience, poverty and chastity, many of the sieges carried out by the Crusader Knights led to the sacking and pillaging of towns and the slaughter of the populace. This aspect could also delineate a soul who has been the 'victim' of a war or other violent confrontation in a prior life. The 'root cause' can be indicated by the sign in which Chiron is placed and other aspects in the chart.

A client travelled many thousands of miles to attend a workshop in order to explore her compulsion and repulsion around becoming a healer. Her chart had Chiron exactly conjunct the South Node in Gemini, very widely opposing Mars in the ninth, and exactly squaring Neptune in the seventh. In a regression she went back to being a doctor in a prisoner-of-war camp who was forced to carry out surgery which (s)he felt was totally unethical. Eventually (s)he was shot for refusing to cooperate further. At the 'between life' stage she said that she was coming back to atone for all the blood that had been wrongly spilt. During the regression she kept trying to wipe off the blood which covered her arms and when the regression was completed she had to shower in order to symbolically cleanse herself. This particular experience may well have connected to ancestral karma as Chiron was in the fourth house (see Chapter 5).

Pluto–Chiron–Mars

A client (fig. 15) with Pluto opposing a Mars/Chiron conjunction in Aquarius, Venus/Moon in Pisces inconjunct Uranus, and Sun/Mercury/South Node opposing Neptune/Jupiter/North Node had power and assertion issues and was plagued with psychic visions:

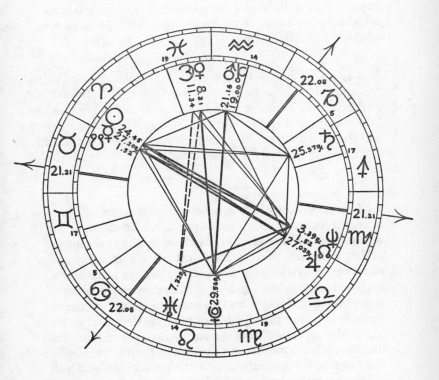

Fig. 15

As a qualified nurse I have become rather more than surprised at the many occasions I have witnessed and actually 'seen' a presence on the ward.

I have the same kind of experience at home and since the age of nine years old several of my friends have been somewhat unnerved by quote 'the strange goings-on' when they are with me.

A close friend of mine bought a very old house and moved with his family. I had never seen the house but I sensed very strongly that the children were in danger when playing in the garden. So much so that I felt quite sick and faint. To cut a long story short, we unearthed a deep cesspit which had been overlooked by the surveyor. My fiancé has witnessed various things, he says I occasionally hold conversations with him when I seem to belong to a past era. He says I have a magnetic hold over him.

This was an instance of uncontrolled psychic abilities being 'contaminated' by emotional and psychiatric difficulties both from this life and from the past. It was suggested to her that she should undergo therapy for these problems and at the same time attend classes which would teach her how to control her psychic abilities. A relevant past life which came up was one in which she had:

used her powers unwisely in order to ensnare a man she was attracted to, and in so doing attracted the attention of the witch-finders. She seemed to have been totally at the mercy of her emotions and to have lost all the training and common sense which she had before this man came along. She had been a 'white witch', using her powers wisely up to that point and doing a lot of good. There was a sense of being involved in the worship of the 'great mother' a very old tradition dating from before Christianity which was handed on from mother to daughter to keep it 'pure'. She went against this tradition in order to 'get her man' and it all rebounded on her and ended in her death. There was a lot of resentment coming forward, with frustration and anger [Pluto opposing Chiron/Mars] that she did not get what she wanted. There was deep emotional trauma because afterwards the depth of her emotion and the lengths she was prepared to go to get this man really surprised and frightened her — there was a picture of her in a cell locked up awaiting 'trial' and suddenly clearly seeing what had been going on as though she had been a different person while in the grip of this emotion.

Although I had been asked to look at the older interaction with her fiancé, this was one occasion when I felt that it was inappropriate as they needed to:

> learn to relate to the here and now, to have a relationship based on love rather than on obsession and compulsion, on freedom and acceptance of each other as individuals rather than one trying to mould the other by and to her Will' [There were a total of eight inconjuncts in the synastry between the charts, her Pluto opposition to Chiron/Mars squared his Mercury and her Neptune/North Node opposed his Sun].

First House Chiron: Chiron Conjunct Sun

The first house Chiron, or Chiron conjunct the Sun, incarnates with a deep wound in its experience of itself. It has been through soul- or ego-shattering experiences in its past lives, or may go through this prior to a transformation in the present life, and it must now heal its sense of Self, reconnecting to its own eternal, indestructible essence. A client with Chiron in Scorpio in the first house 'remembered' having been tortured and brain-washed in a previous life until he lost all sense of identity and 'babbled like an idiot'. He had died under that torture without regaining his shattered sense of who he was. In his present life he had encountered a series of traumatic events and mental breakdowns, following which he was painstakingly rebuilding himself.

Second, Sixth or Eighth House Chiron

Chiron in the second or sixth house brings back an old knowledge of healing and the possibility of release from suffering. Elisabeth Kubler-Ross, who was motivated to begin her work with dying patients by her experience of 'cleaning up' after the Nazi death camps, has Chiron in the second house, an old resource coming forward. Chiron in the sixth may bring over from the past a need to be healed as a catalyst for its own healing power to emerge. I have repeatedly observed the Sun conjunct or opposed Chiron in these houses in the charts of healers, and also in the eighth house – a house which can also be linked with how resources are shared with other people, including sexuality issues. Again there is that same sense of a fundamental loss of identity, a need to heal the very deep split between the ego and the Self which arose in past lives and is reiterated in the present-life childhood. Once this wound is healed, an integration is achieved which is then passed on as healing for others.

Christine Hartley, who was trained in past-life recall and esoteric work (over many incarnations), had Chiron in Scorpio on the cusp of the second and third houses. Her Jupiter in the twelfth house indicated very old links with Egypt and the role of priestess and her Virgo Ascendant that she had incarnated with the intention of being of service to humanity. Although her Chiron pointed to resources carried over from previous lives to help in the present incarnation, and to a need to communicate her knowledge through teaching, the placement of Chiron in Scorpio indicated that she herself had some very deep wounds connected with previous incarnations. During a past-life 'far seeing' she and two colleagues encountered a life in ancient Egypt. Christine described what happened:

> A. was instructed to take the lead and develop the story. She began by picturing the Nile with a dying moon shining on the land but leaving the river in darkness. Downstream was being propelled a boat or barge with about four or possibly six men plying the sweeps. On the barge was a sarcophagus

and seated behind it were herself and F.P.D. wrapped in cloaks . . . During this period I was completely out of the picture and found it almost impossible even to follow the scenes . . .

The boat went on up the Nile to a temple which was described as looming very large and black against the night sky. There was a hidden water entrance to it, through a sort of backwater between banks of undergrowth, terminating in an arched and locked door. It was as they described the boat coming to this point that I woke up, fully conscious. It was horrible. I was in the sarcophagus and the blackness and the sensation of fear were terrible. Dimly I heard F.P.D. give a password at the door and it swung back and I knew that we were in a great hall filled with water and that I was still shut in on the barge. I could hardly control the agony that filled my mind . . . They took the lid off the coffin and then an inner shell and there I lay, with the blessed light on my face, my body bound round with grave clothes and no strength left in me. I was still dizzy from the drug I had been given to make me simulate death.[25]

This particular experience explained the life-long claustrophobia which Christine had suffered (Pluto on MC) and it helped her to live with it. It was never, however, completely cured. When I knew her some thirty to forty years after her regression to the past she still could not bear to be in a confined space or to have the door to a room closed. Even in the depths of winter a window had to be open when she travelled by car and she would always choose a bus or cab in preference to the Underground. She was not afraid of death and gave doctors at the local hospital strict instructions that she was not to be revived if she was brought in 'dead', although she did choose to return after two heart attacks as her work was not finished. She was nevertheless extremely anxious that her coffin should not be nailed down until it was certain that she was definitely deceased. Her memory of that old experience was too vivid – the Chiron wound is deep. Christine also had a horror of horses, but she did overcome that after she had seen herself killed under the hooves of a stampeding horse and, at the age of eighty-three, was very proud of herself when we managed to walk through a field of horses.

Her work in the present life involved writing, lecturing and teaching. She not only delved into past lives in order to heal people but also, on the occult level, battled during the Second World War with what she described as 'the powers of darkness' in order that mankind could survive. She felt called upon (Virgo Ascendant offering service) to confront personal, collective and archetypal wounds and release humanity from its suffering and pain through the resources of Chiron.

Third House Chiron

Chiron in the third house can experience a wound in its ability to communicate. Christine Hartley's book was in a sense before its time. During her life it did not sell well and the publisher consistently refused to republish, although Christine felt that it contained knowledge which was part of her karmic task to pass on to others. After her death there was a resurgence of interest in karmic matters and the book was reissued in paperback.

As the third house is also the house of siblings, the karmic wound may involve a confrontation with or through a sibling, or with a wounded sibling. The Cancerian epileptic mentioned earlier has Chiron conjuncting his sister's fourth house Moon. The latter was instinctually deeply aware of his and their parents' pain despite the conspiracy of silence. Her Chiron is in the third house (Virgo), indicating both being wounded by, and having, a wounded sibling. Her mother had always wanted a son and shortly after her brother's birth, at which she experienced a sense of abandonment and considerable rejection, she developed a psychosomatic, life-threatening illness (Virgo Chiron) which was virtually ignored by her mother. Her brother later took over the function of 'identified patient' and released the family stress through his 'dis-ease'. However, she had to live with the deep, dark secret of his illness which was never mentioned by the rest of the family and friends.

Fourth House Chiron: Chiron–Moon

In the fourth house Chiron indicates a karmic wound located deep within the home environment, and Chiron–Moon aspects can signify deep pain around being parented. A sister and brother who both had Chiron in the fourth grew up from a very young age 'knowing', in the way that children do, that their father had cancer. It was always denied, however, and they were never helped to come to terms with the prospect of his death. He died, leaving behind a deep fear of pain and feelings just as they were entering adolescence. The son became a doctor who felt that he had 'failed' whenever someone died. His attitude to death was very different from that of Elisabeth Kubler-Ross, who has Chiron in Taurus in the second house, indicating an old resource brought back to help in the present life. She understands from a very deep level that death is 'the final stage of growth' in this incarnation, and as such a creative and life-enhancing activity.

Fifth House Chiron

A fifth house Chiron has a wound in the area of creativity, which may or may not include children, and there may be a lack of confidence in the power to create. It may also indicate pain carried over from an old love affair. An aspiring and very talented young artist, who appeared strangely reluctant to paint, regressed back to a time when all her paintings were destroyed by a jealous, sadistic, teacher – who was also her lover in that, and the present, life.

Seventh House Chiron: Chiron–Venus

The wound for the seventh house Chiron, and for Venus conjunct Chiron, is in the area of relationships. A client with Chiron conjunct the North Node in the seventh asked: 'Why do I keep attracting such unsuitable men into my life since my husband's death?' The solution to her problem lay in giving up the suffering attached to unsuitable relationships, a karmic pattern, and focusing instead on dealing with the pain of her husband's death.

I have noted a close correlation between Chiron–Venus aspects and women whose husbands die or disappear at an early age.

An elderly client had Venus conjunct Chiron in Aquarius in the twelfth house, trine Pluto and sextile Saturn. She had, in the past, been working on changing the obsessive, manipulative quality of the Venus–Pluto relationship pattern, and her painful difficulties around being loved and loving: the Venus/Chiron sextile Saturn brought back a feeling of inherent unlovableness as well as a deep pain around relationships. Hers was, historically, a prominent, tragic family. Her relationships had a peculiarly fated quality to them. She married late, at the beginning of the Second World War, and after only a year or so her husband was reported missing. It was almost two years before his death was confirmed – after many stories from escaped prisoners saying that they had seen him alive. Some years later her son and heir went missing from a sailboat in the Caribbean; he has not been seen or heard of since, and is presumed dead. She has a fourth house Neptune square twelfth house Sun/Mercury, representing confusion and misinformation, and with a Sun/Mercury quintile to Pluto and the Moon quintile Saturn she had to confront death and loss head-on, the quintile being an aspect of destiny.

Eighth House Chiron

The eighth house Chiron experiences a significant life change after a death. This is usually connected to having suffered a particularly difficult or formative transition to the spiritual realms in a past life. It can also indicate an old ability to communicate with the 'abode of spirits', which is carried over into the present life. In two instances mothers with this placement became mediums following the death of their daughters. In each case the daughter 'knew' that she was going to die and she is now helping communication from the other side. And in each case the mother felt that she herself had undertaken this role before. In another 'disappearing husband' case a woman, having previously led a very sheltered and protected life, was liberated by the declaration of her husband's death seven years after his disappearance.

Ninth House Chiron

With the ninth house Chiron one would expect the wound to be in the area of religious beliefs and values. One client regressed to a life during the English Reformation in which he had been a monk and, at the time of the dissolution of the monasteries, he had been turned out. He was involved in a similar experience in his present life – the turning out of elderly inmates from psychiatric hospitals into an inhospitable and unwelcoming 'community' – as he was an administrator involved in the reorganization of psychiatric services. In that past life he was totally disorientated and incapable of fending for himself. His pain arose from the fact that his God, in whom he had placed all his trust and obedience, had seemingly abandoned him.

Tenth or Eleventh House Chiron

The tenth and eleventh houses indicate interaction with the outside world, and Chiron in these houses incarnates with a wound linked to its experience with the outer planes. In the tenth house the suffering may have been in the realm of 'business affairs'. In the eleventh house it may, for example, have experienced betrayal by a 'friend' and carry deep scars from this experience. A man with tenth house Chiron regressed to being the 'scapegoat' on whom a major financial disaster had been blamed, and an eleventh house Chiron experienced considerable pain in a previous incarnation in which he had, initially, been 'blackballed' by his club during the days of British India, and then had been drummed out of his regiment as a result of his taking up the case of one of the local people. His disgrace had been engineered by those who, opposing his stand, had taken action 'for the honour of the regiment'. He, not unnaturally, reincarnated with severe difficulties in trusting a group.

Twelfth House Chiron

The roots of the Chiron twelfth house pain are very deep and very old indeed, and they can be difficult to trace. They may include a close identification with the collective, ancestral and individual suffering of humanity and a need to work towards healing the splits that recur throughout time, as is shown in the following example which has a symbolic twelfth house Chiron in the sunrise chart:

Omm Sety

One of the most interesting and detailed manifestations of karma is contained in the life of the extraordinary English lady Dorothy Eady (fig. 16), known for most of her life as Omm Sety, who had the Sun conjunct Chiron and Mercury. When she was three she fell downstairs and was to all appearances dead. Sometime later, however, she recovered, but from that time on she wanted to go

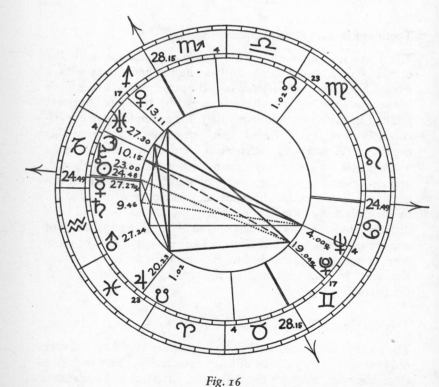

Fig. 16

'home'. 'Home' turned out to be Egypt three thousand years earlier. In her teens she began to receive visitations from the Pharaoh Sety I, with whom she had had a love affair in that previous life. Then she had been a young priestess of the temple of Isis, and as such sacred, virgin and untouchable. When her pregnancy had been discovered by the priests, they had questioned her at length. She had not revealed the name of her seducer, whom she loved more than anything and who was not immune, even as Pharaoh, to punishment for his offence against the goddess. In the end the young priestess had committed suicide in order to protect her lover. For his part in the affair Sety had been condemned by the gods to wander in darkness until he found her again. He had searched unceasingly for three thousand years — this synchronistically being the time span allotted by the Egyptian *Book of the Dead* for a soul to transmigrate from species to species until it is able once again to take human form. Sety could well then have expected the soul who became Dorothy Eady not to take human form again until the twentieth century. In the course of his search Sety explored most of the solar system and other planes of being until this was forbidden by the gods.

Omm Sety was a very determined soul (Uranus sextile Mars has a strong Will) who knew that she just had to return to Egypt. She married, and was divorced from, an Egyptian, and lived and worked in Egypt for the rest of her life. She revealed an uncanny knowledge of how things had been in ancient Egypt and an amazing ability to read previously indecipherable hieroglyphic inscriptions. She began an incredible, secret, sexual (Mars trine Neptune) affair with the 'dead' Pharaoh who manifested to her physically in the present life, but the sexual side of the relationship came to an end when she moved back to her temple at Abydos and became once more consecrated to Isis (the Mars–Neptune aspect works on attuning to the spiritual purpose and Will). She displayed a remarkable knowledge of the temple, pinpointing among many other things the site of the old, previously unknown, temple garden in which she used to meet the Pharaoh in her other life. She adhered to the old religion, kept the festivals and made votive offerings to the gods. She also became an expert in Egyptian magic and healing, curing many ailments with water from the Osirion (a sacred well) and local herbs, and could inflict an effective curse on anyone who upset her. Although His Majesty, as she called him in her diaries, continued to visit her frequently, and she him in the 'astral' realms, in order to reverse the karmic sentence laid on him they had to remain celibate for the rest of her earthly life while she fulfilled the reneged vow of temple service. In time she passed on to Amenti (the Otherworld), where it is to be hoped she was reunited with her Pharaoh.

Omm Sety had Chiron conjunct Sun/Mercury in Capricorn, that most down-to-earth of signs. Many people have wondered whether the early fall had in fact damaged her brain in some way which either gave her delusions or enabled the past life to break through. Her biographer, Jonathan Cott, discussed this question with psychologist Dr Michael Gruber:

> I think it would have been an extreme loss to have seen her simply as someone who was hallucinating or who was out of touch or split off – it would have been a diminution of her being . . .
>
> The adventure she acts out is not only her own. She is not selfish. We have to remember that Omm Sety had an uncanny sense of Abydos, so she wasn't acting out just a *personal* myth . . . that's the interesting thing to me. The way she seems to have processed the light that entered her after her fall afforded her an intuitive or imaginative glimpse of knowledge that, after all, was only available to initiates during an entirely different period of history. This seems to me to somehow 'speak' beyond a personal mania or just an acting out of a personal myth . . .
>
> To accuse Omm Sety of 'mythomania' or 'schizophrenia' is to analyse away her experience. Her experience, as we know it, yielded a meaningful life. If our criterion of health or sanity has to do with whether one can live in a creative, compassionate, and disciplined way, then Omm Sety surely did that . . .
>
> It is important to remember that Sety first appears to Dorothy Eady as a mummy. Both of them have to go through a kind of purification and rebirth process so that

Sety can appear as a man, and so that Dorothy Eady will not be simply victimised or ravished, as she was at fourteen. For Omm Sety and Sety are involved in a process of remembrance that's also atonement for what they had transgressed together during a 'previous' lifetime and, on her part, an atonement for her own sense of not being *at one* with the 'masculine', energetic form that is called 'Sety' [The Chiron conjunction in Capricorn indicates a fundamental split in her sense of self]. It is this sense of at-one-ment that is connected to the notion of the 'heavenly marriage' of Isis and Osiris . . .

Whatever the inspiration or even 'otherworldly' origin of Omm Sety's vision, it's important to reassert that she found a way to make that vision meaningful, creative, and of this world. She was able to be faithful to her love at the same time that she loved the world that she was living in. Her life had meaning to it, it embodied values . . . that is what I think important – rather than whether she was sane or insane, or whether her vision was real or unreal. For those questions may reveal more of the questioners' insecurity about their own sense of reality.[26]

Omm Sety was extremely psychic and had many OOBEs – her Capricorn Moon opposes Neptune with the orb widening as the day progresses (there is no time of birth available). As she had been a priestess this would have been an old skill and the orb does not need to be a close one. She has Venus opposing Pluto, an aspect which frequently means that the soul experiences the death of a lover as a way of changing old, obsessive, ways of relating. Omm Sety appears to have turned this around so that her relationship was with someone who was 'dead' but with whom she was nevertheless working out an old karmic pattern. Her North Node is in Libra and her karmic purpose worked itself out through this most unlikely relationship with a 'dead' Pharaoh, which is also indicated in the Grand Cross of the Nodes squaring the Moon opposition to Neptune. Neptune has an ability to see beyond the physical plane and can carry on a relationship with a discarnate spirit (as happens in channelling for example).

Neptune–Moon can idealize, or idolize, a relationship or a person. Omm Sety appears to have done this in both lives as, in her eyes, her Pharaoh could do no wrong. It also has the potential to sacrifice itself for the beloved as she did when she committed suicide rather than reveal his name to the priests. She also has Jupiter in Pisces forming a T-square with the Venus opposition to Pluto, a link to the Egyptian priestess who, although chosen to represent Isis at the Mysteries, sacrificed all for love.

The chart also has a wide Moon inconjunct Pluto, indicating that she had an old karma around mothering. In her incarnation as the priestess Bentreshyt, Omm Sety had been abandoned at the temple following the death of her mother. Her father, a soldier, had been unable to look after her and she was brought up by the priests – her Capricorn Moon had experienced a 'religious' figure as a surrogate parent and when she herself was about to become a mother she was judged by that 'parent' for breaking her religious vow. She has Saturn sextile Venus, indicating an old feeling of unlovableness and certainly in her English incarnation she was distant from her parents as she believed they were not her real family: they in turn found it extremely difficult to understand this stranger who was suddenly in their midst. The difficulty around mothering re-emerged in the present life, her son was taken to another country by her husband, who considered her a most unsuitable mother. She never saw her son again – in this life. As Dr Gruber points out, Omm Sety worked on the issues of healing and mothering (both connected with the Moon–Pluto inconjunct) in the present life, specifically through the area of childbirth:

> She ministered to the people in the village where she lived – even if her healing techniques were unorthodox and came from some personal interpretation of certain ancient magical texts (though she also used natural medicines and herbs). In addition, she helped women reinstitute faith around the crucial cultural issue for women in Egypt – childbearing. She was able to help in a compassionate way that allowed them to fulfil what they considered to be their proper role.[27]

Omm Sety used 'spells', incantations and offerings to Isis to cure childlessness and impotence and was usually present at village births as a kind of talisman – although she recorded in her diary that she doubted that she was of any real use during the physical process of birth.

The life of this unique woman depicts the creative balancing out of an ancient pattern and, as Dr Gruber pointed out, it does not matter whether the *facts* of that previous life were *true*. What matters is that Omm Sety was enabled by her belief in that life to fulfil her destiny in this life by making a substantial contribution on many levels, including knowledge about ancient Egypt which could not have been obtained from any other source.

Chapter 4

BURDENS AND BAGGAGE

I am ill because of wounds to the soul, to the deep emotional self.

D. H. LAWRENCE, 'HEALING'

The incarnating soul carries over burdens and baggage from past lives which are mapped out in the natal chart and may manifest physically as illness or handicap, or as emotional difficulties and problems in handling the daily business of living.

THE KARMA OF HEALTH

Chronic health problems or handicaps frequently reflect an underlying karmic basis. The incarnating soul may choose to undergo the particular experience to reverse previous patterns of bodily abuse, misuse or neglect, or to offset emotional imbalance. When this is the case disease should more properly be written 'dis-ease', as it signifies a basic disharmony creating lack of ease between the different levels of being. Conversely, the soul may need to go through the experience to change an ingrained attitude or to develop qualities such as courage, fortitude and acceptance. The experience may also be an unselfish act to facilitate the growth of another soul as well as its own, as in the case of the handicapped child whose parents grow through caring for him or her. Karmic astrology can identify the old pattern underpinning illness or handicap and indicate how best to respond to it.

'Retributive' karma is carried in the sixth house and describes how the energy of a planet in this house has been used, or abused, in the past, and how it will manifest in the present incarnation. In Fixed signs the karma has developed over many lifetimes, whereas in Cardinal signs it is the result of a dominant 'recent' past life, and in Mutable signs it is in the making.

In his past-life work psychiatrist Arthur Guirdham found that specific parts of the body were often subjected to repeated patterns of injury, and there have been other reports of this phenomenon.

In a spontaneous regression to a Roman incarnation, a woman uncovered a life in which her chest had been opened up by a sword wound. This experience was confirmed, as far as these things ever can be, by a friend who, when massaging her feet, 'saw' leather armour torn open over a gaping chest wound. The friend 'remembered' being a servant at that time and using massage and herbs to heal the wounds of war. Another friend, who also had past-life recall, suddenly said: 'We were Roman soldiers together and you were wounded in the chest. You were also stabbed in the chest way back before that in Egypt.' Another life involved her being burnt at the stake and choking to death on the smoke. In her current life her karmic chest weakness had manifested when she was a child as bronchial-pneumonia, which had scarred the trachea and caused an on-going 'dis-ease'. This 'weakness' is linked in the chart to an over-emphasis on the Air and Fire elements and a lack of Earth planets (Chiron in Virgo being the only Earth) and to Capricorn on the cusp of the sixth house. Saturn, the ruler of Capricorn, is in Gemini, and conjuncts Mars, indicating an old wound and constriction on breathing. The comment has been made that this person only breathes into her head and is unconnected to the earth – something she had been endeavouring to overcome for fifteen years. Some karmic lessons can take a long time to absorb, and the step between the head cognitively understanding and the heart then putting the understanding into practice can be a long one.

The 'fixed' nature of past-life patterns is shown in the chart of a client (fig. 17) who has had ME for the past fifteen years, following glandular fever as a student, and yet who has the potential to be fully healthy – his Sun/Mars conjunction in Taurus in the sixth house has tremendous drive, endurance and energy available. Although he appears to want to become well, he

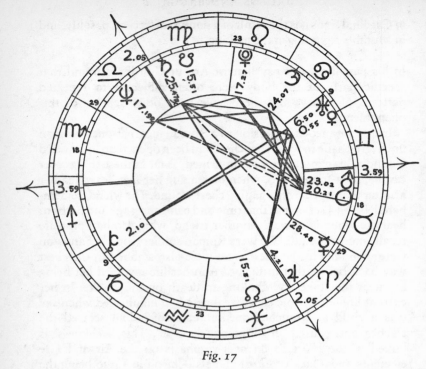

Fig. 17

is constantly sabotaged in his attempts by an unconscious need to stay weak and helpless (Neptune inconjunct Sun/Mars, and Sun/Mars square Pluto and trine Saturn). Both Saturn and Neptune can take the role of saboteur: Saturn out of ingrained fear and Neptune because of old illusions and lack of clarity. His karmic pattern is one of abuse of the body as, for example, when he was a monk and fasted and scourged himself constantly to escape from the 'evils of the flesh', and in another life when he over-indulged his appetites. In the present life he cannot digest his food and his weight is down to seven stone. His Saturn in Virgo indicates chronic fear and worry affecting the digestive system. He speaks of a 'permanent problem of disorientation [Neptune], hearing a voice, seeing a body and yet not being part of it'. With his Sun in Taurus in the sixth house and his Saturn in Virgo, one of

182

his karmic lessons is to become aware of the psychosomatic component of disease: he must recognize how the mind, the emotions, and underlying beliefs, affect the physical body and how inner disharmony will manifest as illness. He also has to learn how to be at one with a physical body and how to integrate the four levels of being – physical-emotional-mental-spiritual – into himself.

There are old power and anger issues in the Pluto squares, and he also needs to deal with the Will (Saturn trine Mars); it is only when he truly recognizes on the inner level that it lies within his power to become well and accepts his own responsibility (Saturn) in this process, that a change can take place. He is strongly defended against his feelings, having been subjected, in addition to past-life problems, to the emotional chaos of a very unstable mother (tenth house Neptune square Moon in Cancer). His chart is weak in the Air element with only Neptune in Libra, but his intellectual function is overdeveloped. Talking and rationalizing (Virgo South Node) are his defences against feeling, and he used to take refuge from the body in meditation (Neptune) until he recognized and closed that escape route.

He is a chronic over-breather, hyperventilating through anxiety, and yet is not utilizing his breath to ground and nourish himself. His present condition is linked to the lack of control over the Air-element function, and to the old grief and disharmony embodied in Neptune inconjunct Sun/Mars.

Working with the body through bio-energetics was one of the most successful therapies of the many he has tried. And yet he 'lacks the energy to carry through the exercises' as the ME makes him physically weak. With the Sun/Mars in Earth conjunction and three planets and the Ascendant in Fire, he could, if he persevered, actually build up his stamina and reserves of energy through exercise, and release the physical blockages which have built up within his body as a manifestation of his old dis-ease.

He has had, karmically, a lack of relationships, and relating is a source of great difficulty for him (Chiron opposing Venus/Uranus in the seventh house). The wound of Chiron in this case is opposing the uncommitted, unpredictable Venus/Uranus style of relating in the house of relationships. The T-square of Venus to the Saturn opposition to Jupiter indicates an old inability to perceive himself as lovable, and the tendency to go to extremes within a relationship. The sexual area in particular gives him problems. Although he does feel mentally aroused, he has too little physical energy or drive to carry it through. Saturn–Mars aspects frequently indicate sexual problems such as a lack of sex drive and fear of one's potency. My first astrology teacher, Robert Tully always drew Mars afflicted by Saturn with a drooping arrow: he described it as 'brewer's droop without the need for alcohol'. Under the Neptune, Saturn and Uranus transits of his Chiron this client experienced the birth, life and death of his first ever 'proper' relationship. The break-up of the relationship is now affording him an opportunity to finally face his feelings and deal with his pain and grief. A breakthrough seems likely in his disease and distress as the planets – those representatives of his own inner energy – by the very nature of the heavyweight combination which has been hitting him 'force' a resolution and a new way of being upon him.

An example of bodily karma-in-the-making which was reversed is illustrated by the brother of a client who was interested in alternative therapies. The brother had Pluto in Virgo in the sixth and all the symptoms of multiple sclerosis, but the tests proved negative – Pluto can indicate an illness which is extremely difficult to diagnose or attach to a cause. He was due for more tests and my client persuaded him to work with his strong Jupiter through the power of creative imaging. His symptoms cleared and he became well again.

PLANETS IN THE SIXTH HOUSE

The energies manifested by planets in the sixth house are particularly relevant to bodily 'health' karma. They also indicate what type of energies are available for working on the body and how they may be utilized. These energies may manifest negatively as 'disease', ultimately leading to physical or mental illness; or positively as old wisdom and skills, or a sanguine attitude which can in turn be used to overcome disease. Aspects from other planets, and the sign on the cusp of the sixth house will affect how the karma manifests. The placement of, and aspects to, the ruler of the sixth house should also be taken into account.

The Sun

The Sun in the sixth house, or difficult aspects to the Sun when it is the ruler of the sixth, indicates that particular attention should be paid to the body in the present life as it may have been misused, or abused in a past life and that the gross physical material needs to be to a 'higher' level of functioning. Planets aspecting the Sun will illustrate the old pattern. For example, Jupiter aspects show that the body is now reaping the effects of over-indulgence or impracticality in the past; Saturn aspects indicate the results of previous over-disciplining or rigid repression of the body; and Pluto may indicate the results of past compulsiveness or cruelty. The Sun is also linked to the heart and to old emotional patterns such as impatience, arrogance and pride. In the present life the soul is then offered the opportunity to transmute these energies into love, kindness and compassion.

The use of energy is particularly important for the Sun in the sixth house as this placement can be a power-house resource to call upon in times of need, or may produce an unconscious 'leakage' of energy. In a Fire sign energy can easily burn itself out if the incarnating soul fails to pay attention to the body's need for sufficient rest and recharging. However, with this placement it may also have learnt to handle stress well in the past and thus have a seemingly inexhaustible fund of energy to draw upon. The Earth Sun in the sixth may well have a pattern of putting all its energy into work, particularly of the physical type, and ignoring the need for relaxation and play, or of having over-indulged in the so-called 'finer things of life' in the past. Ultimately the imbalance will result in physical or mental dis-ease. The Water sixth house Sun imbalance is often expressed through an excess of emotional energy, which literally drains the body. Women are particularly familar with the 'washed out' feeling which follows a crying jag, but men can experience this through inner tears; similarly intense

THE KARMIC JOURNEY

fatigue accompanies an angry outburst which has been 'buried'. A similar reaction can occur from the Air sixth house Sun, who can be into mental benders – bouts of excessive mental activity – and suddenly finds that it is totally exhausted even though it 'hasn't done anything'. Nevertheless, once these are seen as old patterns repeating themselves, a more constructive use of energy can be made.

The Moon

The Moon, or Cancer, in the sixth house, or difficult aspects to the Moon, may relate to 'disease' passed on through the mother. They are particularly significant for women and can indicate the possibility of a reproductive system malfunction stemming from old problems with sexuality, menstruation, pregnancy, etc. They may point to a hereditary disease which is genetically passed via the mother, or there can be an ancestral attitudinal pattern carried over from the past. If the great-grandmother, grandmother and mother have all seen menstruation and childbirth as a painful curse, then it is likely that the daughter will inherit this belief and manifest it physically. If Mars and Pluto are in aspect to the Moon, then pent-up rage or frustration from the past can have a physical manifestation as painful cramps, fibroids, etc. Where old resentment or guilt has come forward, it may present itself as a cancer 'eating away inside'.

It should be borne in mind that the guilt and repressed emotion behind disease are not necessarily from a past incarnation. They can just be from 'the past' – although the *potential* for the disease may well have been laid down in past lives through failure to learn the lesson of a continuing pattern. A woman with the sixth house Moon in Mutable Gemini, square Neptune, lost her husband and son within a very short time of each other (Moon sextile seventh house Chiron, a wound around relationships). She then became involved with a man she described as 'almost psychotic', but whom she could not leave because she believed that she could 'cure' him by loving him (Neptune square Moon is prone to this type of delusion). She became pregnant and 'was diagnosed as having Idiopathic Thrombocytopenic Purpura, my immune system had gone haywire'.

Idiopathic means of unknown cause or origin (Neptune squares the Moon, obscuring the emotional cause of the disease) and the blood and immune systems are involved in the illness (Mars inconjunct Moon, Mars opposition Saturn/Uranus). A doctor has pointed out that this is an auto-immune disease, the proclivity to which can run in families so that she could have 'inherited' it (Moon aspects). It is also more usually a disease of childhood, which may indicate that the stress she was under reduced her to being a child again:

> I was producing antibodies against the platelets in my blood. I began to miscarry the baby and had to go on to massive doses of steroids to stay alive. I feel very strongly that the disease was the result of the terrible strain of living with this man, but also the fact that when my husband died the pain of grief was so terrible I kept running away from it. The same pattern occurred with my son's death.

However, she continued to live with this violent man until eventually her deceased husband told her, through a medium, that she must not stay with him as he was destroying her. She subsequently refused to go on with orthodox medical treatment, which consisted of steroids and the removal of her spleen – in Taoist medicine the spleen is linked to the negative emotion of worry, as is Virgo, the sign also indicating psychosomatic illness and the body/mind link. There was considerable danger of a spontaneous haemorrhage and she was particularly frightened of having a stroke and being helpless. She specifically requested information in her reading on what she should be learning from the present life as she felt that was what she should be concentrating on – although she had virtually answered her own question already. It was suggested to her that she should work with a therapist through her grief and pain and tackle the guilt which her sexual relationship had engendered. In that way she could perhaps connect to why she had 'punished' herself by attracting this violent, psychopathic man into her life, and gain insight into the resulting illness.

Another side of the Moon energy presented problems to a young girl who consulted me. She had Pluto/Uranus/Moon in Virgo in the sixth opposing Saturn/Chiron in Pisces and had never known her biological father. Her mother had married another man before she was born and the latter had a strong sense of owing the child a debt from a previous lifetime. She was extremely psychic (Pluto/Uranus/Moon indicates an old ability carried forward) and was having difficulty handling the strong energies which were emerging as minor poltergeist activity and spontaneous past-life recall. The hormonal changes linked to menstruation, pregnancy and menopause can, in susceptible women, bring about the onset of psychic experiences. Her problems were focused physically as dysmenorrhea following a very late onset of the menses – the effect of the Saturn/Chiron opposition to the sixth house planets and a carry-over from her mother's emotional trauma at the time of her pregnancy and childbirth. She 'saw' herself in many lives as the priestess of the ancient Mysteries, sometimes involved in sexual rites, at other times in sacrifice, and using her psychic powers as an oracle. She said that she had grown to hate the men who 'used' her and had been glad to see them sacrificed – her sixth house planets were sextile Neptune in Scorpio in the seventh. She was aware of having been killed as a witch, and was frightened of her psychic powers as these had been the direct cause of that earlier death. Her breakthrough came when she began to use her creative energy in the present life in a different way. She wrote and illustrated a children's book which was snapped up by a publisher, and her physical and psychic problems disappeared.

Mars

Mars in the sixth house, or difficult aspects to Mars, particularly when it is the ruler of the sixth or twelfth house, indicates inner feelings of long-term anger and frustration which will eventually manifest physically. The body's defence mechanism may then attack itself, producing problems such as Aids, ME, arthritis,

Parkinson's disease, cancer, ulcers, etc. The liver, although ruled by Jupiter, is the organ related to anger in the Taoist system, and is susceptible to diseases resulting from internalized anger, blocked rage (particularly when there are aspects from Saturn), and over-indulgence (particularly when Mars is in Sagittarius or Taurus, or has aspects to Jupiter). Liver 'disease' in the present life may be linked to a past-life alcohol or other over-indulgence problem (particularly when Mars is in a Fire sign). Too much rich fatty food may then trigger liver dysfunction or heart trouble, depending on the sign in which Mars is located. Alcoholism usually produces cirrhosis of the liver, and alcoholics tend to be very angry people although this is frequently repressed unless 'under the influence'. Aspects of Mars to the Sun, Jupiter, Uranus and Neptune are common in the charts of alcoholics. Guilt from 'the past', linked to Neptune/Mars, is also an underlying feature of both alcoholism and repressed rage, and can produce the symptom of throat or digestive-tract cancers (particularly when Mercury is in the twelfth house or adversely aspected). It is as though on an inner level the alcoholic, or cancer sufferer, bitterly regrets the angry things that may have been said in the past, whenever that was. On the other hand the 'victim' may have suffered in silence while 'it made my gorge rise' or 'the bile of bitterness was hard to swallow', or gulped down emotions whenever they threatened to surface. It may take several lifetimes before the physical symptom of this inner 'swallowing' of the emotions manifests.

Old injuries also come forward with the sixth house Mars or Mars as the ruler of the sixth, and 'retributive' karma may result from injuries inflicted on another person. I have very rarely seen a chart in which an illness, injury, or handicap appeared to be a direct consequence of 'an eye for an eye' in the sense of a man who had put out the eyes of another in the past being born blind in the present life – probably because people requesting readings tend to have evolved some way along the spiritual pathway. However, Edgar Cayce did once warn one man who was deaf in this life never again to close his ears to cries for aid and I have seen examples of this type of 'attitudinal' karma returning as a physical handicap. I have also seen a man with Mutable sixth house Mars become deaf, literally shutting himself off, because he did not want to communicate with others following the death of his wife – an example of karma-in-the-making.

There can be a link between old injuries and attitudinal karma. A Taurean woman with Mars in Capricorn in the sixth burnt with a very slow fuse as she had been taught as a child that it was 'wrong' to show anger. However, when she finally 'blew' she took her anger out on her daughter by beating her across the upper back. She had a long-standing back problem centred on this area herself and felt constant fatigue linked to blocked anger. When regressed, she went back to a life on board ship as a sailor in which she had been pinned down by a spar falling across her upper back. Paralysed as a result, she had spent many years nursing her resentment and anger, taking them out on her daughter through angry words. Her daughter, however, would simply walk away and refuse to listen. In the present life the mother was connecting to that old resentment whenever she felt angry with her daughter. Following the regression her back problem was 'cured' and she became more able to express her anger as and when appropriate. This allowed the fatigue problem to clear.

A blind musician who attended one of my workshops was asked by a participant, in a rather arch way, what he thought of karma. He gently replied that he thought the question told him rather a lot about the questioner's beliefs. He did not feel that his blindness was a 'punishment' but rather something which he had chosen to experience for his own growth. He had learnt to see with inner vision and had developed his other senses and his music to compensate. He did not feel deprived in any way and his blindness was certainly not a 'handicap' – he had travelled from Ireland to London, entirely unaided, in order to attend the workshop. As a traditional Indian saying goes:

> *Who is blind?*
> *The man that cannot see another world.*
> *Who is dumb?*
> *The man that cannot say a kind word at the right time.*

Who is poor?
The man plagued with too strong desires.
Who is rich?
The man whose heart is contented.

Jupiter

Jupiter in the sixth or twelfth house, or difficult aspects to Jupiter, can reflect a past misuse of the appetites, particularly sensuality (aspects to Venus–Mars), or over-indulgence (frequently linked to Taurus and, surprisingly perhaps, to Capricorn). They can be linked to food allergies or compulsive-eating disorders, especially when attached to the Water element or Saturn aspects in which case there may be an old compensatory pattern of starvation/overeating. They can also be linked to liver dysfunction/'disease' as a result of old, inappropriate, eating patterns. If Jupiter is in an Earth sign, then there may be an old blockage around the body image which needs to be adjusted as otherwise it can manifest as anorexia, etc., (particularly if aspects to Saturn or Neptune are involved). Also, if Jupiter is in an Air sign then the body image may be perceived totally differently from what it really is. Neptune aspects add to such confusion, which may also be a consequence of previous 'religious' lifetimes during which the body was kept clothed all the time and never seen. Jupiter, particularly when in the Water element, may indulge in 'comfort eating' in order to quell emotional unease, or to stave off old remembrances of deprivation. Jupiter transits may trigger off these old patterns so that the weight fluctuates in accordance with the season and sign in which Jupiter is located. Jupiter transiting Taurus, for example, will tend to manifest as weight going on to the body, adding substance; transiting Gemini it will roll off again, only to return as Cancer seeks comfort in food.

A woman who had Jupiter in Gemini in the sixth, squaring Neptune in Virgo in the ninth, had a long-standing weight problem which fluctuated between too fat and too thin. During an imaging session it became clear that her body image was totally distorted. She was regressed back to a very harsh life in a convent during which she had always been on the verge of starvation. She was never allowed to be naked; even the cold bath which all in the convent were subjected to was taken in a coarse linen shift. Her hair had been cut off and her feet were all deformed with chilblains and arthritis. Her present-life mother appeared in the regression as the Mistress of Novices who was responsible for cutting off her hair. In the present life her mother had hacked off her waist-length blonde hair in a rage when she had started seeing a boy at the age of fifteen. Her 'beautiful feet' were now this woman's pride and joy, the only part of her body which she considered acceptable, and she always pampered them with expensive shoes, even though the rest of her clothes came from Oxfam. In order to change her body image she had to visualize stripping off her nun's clothing, burning it, and discovering the body underneath. She then imaged putting on luxurious, silky underwear and attractive outer garments. This was followed by several massage treatments in which she learnt to take pleasure in her body again. And her weight stabilized.

On the positive side Jupiter is a powerful tool to use in healing: through creative visualization old disharmonies can be balanced out, the body image adjusted to a realistic one, and the body encouraged to fight off the invasion of 'aliens' such as viruses, against which conventional medicine has, so far, not found an effective defence.

Saturn

Saturn or Capricorn in the sixth house, or difficult aspects to Saturn, can indicate a rigidity carried over from the past which leads to immobility. Its root cause may be found in inflexible attitudes or behaviour, or deep suppression of anger. It may be linked to fear or paralysis of the Will which, having prevented the soul from making progress in the past, is now manifesting physically. On the other hand, the disability may have been taken on in order to learn patience, self-control and acceptance. It may also be linked to the incarnating soul's refusal in the past to take responsibility for its own health, or a shirking of its duty to care for another. This placement indicates a need to explore the body/

mind link and to understand psychosomatic and chronic illness. The lesson may be learnt through caring for, or nursing, the chronically sick, or may be encountered in one's own body. Past-life attitudes such as having 'a chip on the shoulder', or 'refusing to bow down to anyone', or looking down on those weaker than oneself, may manifest physically as scoliosis, etc. Saturn in this house may also point to the potential for a career in osteopathy, chiropractic, physiotherapy, etc., which deal with the underlying structure of the body.

Uranus

Uranus in, or as the ruler of, the sixth can be linked to an old disruption of the vibrational pattern of the body, an inner 'dis-ease' and misalignment carried over from life to life which may go all the way back to Atlantis and the 'high-tech' medicine practised there. A client with Huntington's chorea – a hereditary disease passed on through the mother – had Venus conjunct Uranus in Taurus in the sixth house, inconjunct Mars and trine the Moon. It is typically Uranian in that Huntington's chorea cannot be detected before the symptoms strike, usually in middle age. From that stage on the progress of the disintegration into senility and of the physical loss of control can be rapid and irreversible.

On the positive side, sixth house Uranus signifies a deep understanding of the subtle effect of vibration in realigning 'dis-ease' and restoring harmony, and it can lead into many related fields of healing.

Neptune

Neptune or Pisces in the sixth house is wide open to outside influence. It acts like a 'psychic sponge' soaking up everything around it, including other people's diseases and environmental stresses. It points to a high susceptibility to reaction to ingested substances such as food or drugs, which can cause allergies and illness, or to emotions and vibrations given off by other people. It also indicates a need to learn to use the aura as a barrier to external influences, and to control substances which are taken into the body. An organic detoxifying diet and homoeopathic, rather than allopathic, medicine are essential as otherwise minute traces of 'alien' chemicals can lead to biochemical imbalances and disturbances. A lack of trace elements and essential nutrients can lead to similar problems. The glands of the body, the endocrine system, are liable to inefficient functioning due to the non-synchronization of the physical and 'etheric' bodies. Such disharmony may stem from past-life abuse of alcohol or drugs (aspects to Mars), mental states (aspects to Mercury), occult practices (aspects to Pluto), or spiritual initiations which 'failed' (aspects to Uranus). The process is always from the etheric body into the physical, the imbalance exists on the higher level before it reaches the lower. It may manifest in a subtle way as neurological disorders such as multiple sclerosis, motor neurone disease, etc., or through diseases with a biochemical basis such as adrenal failure or over-activity, parathyroid malfunction, early kidney or liver failure, etc., depending on the planetary aspects.

Cellist Jacqueline du Pré (fig. 18), who died at a young age from the effects of multiple sclerosis, had sixth house Jupiter in Virgo and Neptune conjunct Chiron in Libra. Her illness, which appears to have been rooted in an old disregard for, or over-indulgence of, the body, was subtle and resulted from an old wound to the soul.

There is an indication in her chart of a previous contact with both parents. The Moon's placement in the third house shows that her mother may well have been in a sibling relationship with her in a prior life, and the Sun in the tenth that her father may well have been her father in a former life. Jacqueline's mother was a very powerful influence on her present life (fourth house Pluto and Cancer Moon/North Node) and she nurtured the development of her early talent. However, from the chart it would appear that Jacqueline was a child valued for what she achieved rather than for herself (Moon very widely conjunct Saturn, and Saturn inconjunct the Sun), and her consequent sense of unworthiness may have driven her on in her need to succeed (tenth house Sun/Midheaven in Capricorn). On the other hand, these aspects also indicate that she was capable of great self-discipline and of dedication to her music. When no longer able to perform, she utilized her previous-life ability to teach and communicate her

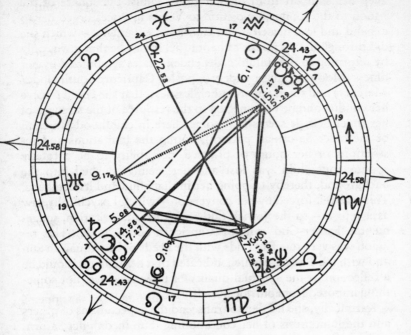

Fig. 18: Jacqueline du Pré

skills through her Masterclasses (Saturn, the teacher nurturing the
talent of others, widely opposing Mercury, the sixth house ruler,
and Capricorn South Node). An over-developed Saturnian self-
discipline may have compensated for a lack of confidence and a
feeling of unlovableness, as well as for a previous lack of discipline
(Jupiter). Her present-life need was to love, nurture and accept
herself (Moon/North Node in Cancer), and to be valued by others
for who she truly was (the aspects to Saturn), and part of her
karmic task (Pluto opposing the Sun) was to reclaim the power she
had projected on to her father, or other powerful males, and own
it for herself. She could have achieved this through her work and
in spite of having become physically powerless as a result of her
illness.

Cancer is a very emotional, instinctual sign, but Saturn acted to keep her shut off from the emotions, whilst the square of the Moon to the Jupiter opposition to Venus in Pisces urged her to expand and lose herself in her emotional experience – which she did through the discipline of her music. It may be that it was only by returning to the childlike, dependent states symbolized by her illness (Moon in Cancer widely opposing Capricorn South Node/ Mercury) and to an apparent helplessness, that she could resolve her conflict and be reconnected to the resource of the strength of her inner Self. It seems that somewhere in childhood (an echo of the older Saturnian pattern), within the limitations and restrictions of her hours of practice, her ability to be a totally spontaneous child was lost and her feelings pushed into the background, thereby trapping her in that child and its demands. This was reinforced by her conversion – which I psychically saw as a return – to the Jewish faith, with its authoritarian, judgemental 'Father-God' symbol (Capricorn South Node). This religion was very much at odds with the needs of her Aquarian Sun and with the T-square which indicated that her religion should be a reflection of the spiritual quality of universal love, not something imposed from outside herself.

Karmically, she needed to transcend the expectations of others and the limitations of her conditioning (Sun inconjunct Saturn, and Moon conjunct the Cancer North Node) to find her own inner freedom, which is the freedom to be her Self. Thus her illness can be looked upon as her Self engineering time for meeting herself face to face. A great deal in her chart points to the expression of the collective vision (Aquarius and the Kite) and to her needing time to look inwards in order to find all the pieces of herself that were left unexpressed in her great creative outpouring, thereby nurturing and integrating herself through the reconciliation of the Cancer–Capricorn and Aquarius–Leo axes. The sixth house Jupiter/Neptune/Chiron conjunction forms part of a Kite configuration (with tenth house Sun in Aquarius and first house Uranus in Gemini and the Sun opposing Pluto in the fourth) indicating a susceptibility to vibration and dis-ease as well as a very subtle disruption of the biochemical and neurone functioning.

Conflict is repeated throughout her chart and her past lives, together with a lack of balance and harmony between the different facets of her life and her Self which was reflected in her 'disease'. Having on the one hand to express the immense creativity of her Kite and the all-encompassing vision related to it, she also needed to come to terms with the everyday needs of her body and their emotional expression on the physical level (Taurus Ascendant, the T-square, and Virgo on the sixth house cusp). But, more particularly, she had to learn the effect the emotions and environment have on the body and health (Virgo). It would appear from the chart that, always racing to express her creative side, she was so caught up in the impetus of her first house Uranian energies that she was too impatient with the slow plodding of the Taurus Ascendant — except where it gave her the discipline to practise — and its need to learn about the physical senses and the material world. This frenetic effect is exaggerated by her lack of Fire; the little Fire there is would have a tendency to burn itself out very quickly and be unable to regenerate energy.

It could be said that her illness developed to anchor and focus her on the body (Taurus is connected to roots and can be so fixed and slow-acting that it results in immobility despite enduring for so long). She needed to surrender to Neptune and Chiron, to go with the flow, secure in the knowledge that everything was exactly as it should be for the stage she had reached, and for the life lessons she had come to learn. This need to surrender was, however, different from a passive acceptance of fate because it contained within itself the dynamic seeds of action — a readiness, through Uranus, to do whatever was necessary to bring about changes, so that rather than trying to force and mould her life to a rigid pattern, as an Aquarian she needed to attune herself to her own life-plan and the music of her own soul.

The pain of her situation had value in that it was genuinely and uniquely hers to experience and share in a very direct and courageous way. Nevertheless, with that sixth house Jupiter/Chiron/Neptune and the Sun opposition to Pluto, she had to let go of past ambitions and compulsions in order to explore the present. She also had to receive acceptance from everyone she was intimately connected with, including herself, of her karmic need to be the way she was and to perceive her opportunity to explore new ways of being, of getting in touch with those energies she had ignored or overlooked in the past – not to sigh for what might have been, but to see the value in what *is*. In that way, she could be supported and share her new perceptions, the thoughts and feelings which she had such a deep need of expressing. But at the same time, she needed to take responsibility for that expression, so that she would be able to control and direct what she allowed to *be* not cushioned from its harshness nor shut off from its pain, but following the impetus towards self-knowledge and growth with a willing heart.

Pluto

Pluto indicates a very deep-seated illness, with roots way back in the distant past, usually defying diagnosis in the initial stages, and this type of illness brings the soul face to face with the possibility of death. As with Neptune, it may be related to food or drug allergies – particularly the side-effects of drugs taken, perhaps, many years previously – or to repressed emotions. The reproductive system can be affected, in men or women, and an over-bearing, possessive mother or a past life in which this was a feature may be a contributory factor.

This placement is also linked to past-life compulsions and obsessions. It featured in the chart of a woman who believed that a breast tumour she had was 'the manifestation of her dead lover within her breast'. She had for many years been obsessed by an eighteenth-century poet with whom she believed she had a very unhappy, compulsive love affair in a past life. She would not allow surgery on her tumour as this would have meant separation from her love again – he had committed suicide in the past life. Strangely enough, the tumour did not seem to be life-threatening, presumably being benign, as she lived for at least ten years like that and may well still be alive today.

Pluto or Scorpio in the sixth house also has the potential to heal, particularly through therapies which involve exploring depths of the psyche and dealing with the subtle energies which govern 'health'. For example, the Bach Flower Remedies may be utilized to gently ease out old emotional disorder, or homoeopathy to bring the soul back into balance and reach the subtle imbalances which lie at the root of Plutonian 'dis-ease'.

SEXUAL MALFUNCTIONING

Other karmic factors related to bodily malfunction, particularly in the sexual areas, are aspects of the outer planets to Venus and Mars, or a strong placement of Pluto. Pluto has difficulty in letting go, in opening itself up to another person, and the soul with a strong Pluto placement may experience sexual difficulties linked into old power, manipulation or abuse issues whereby it fears that the sexual partner will, in its most vulnerable moment, 'have something over it'. In women this can result in difficulty in relaxing enough to achieve orgasm. Strong Pluto aspects – particularly to Mars – can also indicate the masochist who is pre-programmed to find pleasure in pain. In men these difficulties may be expressed as a preference for masturbation – which may include the use of a female in order to achieve orgasm but not to share feelings, the sadist who receives his pleasure by inflicting pain, or the man who uses his sexual power in order to achieve mastery and who cannot fully allow himself to join with his partner on the inner level and therefore always remains vaguely dissatisfied, but blames his partner. In both sexes Plutonian difficulties in attuning and opening to another can lead to promiscuity as the person 'chases' fulfilment through a series of partners instead of looking within for the release which would heal the difficulty.

Saturn in aspect to Mars expressing itself as impotence in men has already been touched upon. Women with Saturn–Mars aspects may be anorgasmic, as their inability to reach orgasm may be due to repressed anger. Saturn–Venus contacts can also be frigid or non-orgasmic because in its heart of hearts the soul with this aspect believes itself to be unlovable, or sinful, and is therefore incapable of responding. In her book on Saturn, Liz Greene explores the links of Saturn–Venus aspects to prostitution, prostitution not only meaning the selling of one's body to a stranger. As she points out, many wives 'prostitute' themselves to their husbands in return for the housekeeping money. However, a past life may well include prostitution or repressed sexuality as a contributory factor to the present-life sexual difficulty.

Premature ejaculation can be linked to Uranus aspects to Mars or the Sun, or to Aries energy, particularly in the eighth house, and it may be linked to a past-life persona who was always in a hurry, rushing here there and everywhere and never taking time to finish anything. It may also connect to guilty or 'sinful' encounters during which it was felt, usually for religious or moral reasons, that what was happening was 'wrong', and therefore something to be got over with as quickly as possible. It may also relate to 'stolen' sexual experiences where discovery may have been imminent, often a feature of teenage sex in the present life. One man regressed to 'screwing the maid in the linen cupboard at every opportunity but we had to watch out for the old girl [wife/housekeeper?] coming so it had to be quick; on one occasion she caught me with my trousers down and gave me hell and sacked the poor girl'. In the present life his sexual experiences had started with furtive fumbles in his bedroom, on which his mother may have walked in at any point. It immediately triggered off the past-life reaction.

I have only ever met one person who admitted to being a nymphomaniac; she happened to also be a dipsomaniac. She had Neptune conjunct Mars and Venus and always swore that her condition was the direct result of having been 'unwillingly locked up in a convent with a load of bloody women' in a past life!

Sexual difficulties connected with violence or cruelty may arise from past-life causes when linked to Pluto–Mars aspects, and/or to abuse as a child in the present or a past life. In the 1987 Cleveland child sex-abuse case, 197 children were taken into care in a six-week period following allegations of parental abuse. Dr Marietta Higgs, one of the doctors involved, has Mars trine Pluto, Scorpio Sun conjunct the South Node, and Pluto sextile Neptune/Mercury. Although the initial investigation into her allegations of abuse exonerated the parents, she did perform a valuable service to the community at large by bringing to public attention the whole question of child abuse and the way it is handled by society (her Saturn is sextile Uranus). It could be that her Pluto—Mars and Scorpio energy was tuned into abuse as it would appear to be an issue which she had been working on in former lives. However, her Neptune conjunction to Mercury appears to have 'obscured' the issue and she arrived at a conclusion which may not have been warranted by the physical 'evidence' – and may well have been influenced by her own far-past experience of abuse. The continuing demands for re-investigation into the whole affair nicely illustrate the effect of Neptune in creating confusion in this Plutonian can of worms.

A man with a Pluto—Mars contact remembered dozens of incarnations, all of them as a man. He said that he 'just loved incarnating back into a physical body'. When regressed back to being a woman in ancient Greece, he relived a mass rape, after which he had sworn that he would never return again as a woman. In the present life he had been 'interfered with' by a man within the family as a young child, and had difficulty in achieving a 'normal' sexual relationship with a woman as he inwardly craved and fantasized violence.

A surprising number of people with Pluto—Mars aspects have come to expect violence and need the adrenalin rush which fear and violence present to them. A friend took in a girl who had a violent husband. In the middle of the night she was shaking and begging to be hit as only violence could end her withdrawal symptoms. She went back to her husband the next day.

GENDER DIFFICULTIES

Difficulties with sexual identity or gender problems often relate directly back to past-life experiences. A soul who has had many incarnations as a man, for example, may decide that it needs to learn about the feminine perspective and therefore incarnate into a woman's body. However, if masculine traits carried over from the past are strong, then adapting to being a woman will not be easy: there may be a powerful animus energy linked to the past 'male experience' which requires to be integrated into the 'new personality'. Furthermore, the incarnating soul may well retreat back for several incarnations into taking the masculine role, either as a dominating woman within a heterosexual relationship or within a lesbian relationship, until it becomes comfortable with the receptive, passive feminine energies. Similarly, a woman who incarnates into a male body might then become the highly sensitive 'bitchy', anima-possessed, feminine male who so often appears in stereotyped portrayals of homosexual men, but who is based nonetheless on a very real person, and can also be linked with over-identification with the mother and the Moon energies.

Some charts have a strong imbalance of positive and negative energies, or the Sun, Moon, Venus or Mars in the 'opposite' quality to that it is attuned to (Mars in Pisces or Venus in Aries, for example), which indicates that the soul is trying to change sexual role and overcome a past pattern, but which can manifest as a blockage in present-life functioning as 'male' or 'female'. Although feminists would probably argue that such stereotyped roles have to change, we are not looking here at the roles within society, we are examining how the energy functions within the person. Both male and female need to learn how to manifest their negative 'feminine' energy in a sensitive, nurturing, caring way; conversely both sexes need to express their positive, outgoing 'masculine' energy, particularly when the opposite energy has been expressed throughout many incarnations. This is a stage on the road to integration of both types of energy within one soul, leading to wholeness. However, integration can be a very difficult lesson to learn as the soul continually falls back into the old pattern, aided and abetted by cultural expectations and role models.

One woman had nine planets in negative signs and yet looked like a, not very good, female impersonator. She was dominating, aggressive, and totally 'unfeminine': nails bitten down to the quick, hard skin, short hair and stocky body. She had married late in life and never adapted to the role of housewife – many women with her kind of personality prefer not to marry, finding their fulfilment in the 'masculine' business world, as she had until her marriage. Inwardly, however, she felt that she needed to work on her softer, more receptive qualities. She became a reflexologist, but used her positive energy (Sun/Mars conjunction in Pisces) to 'force' a physical healing, flooding the patient's system with toxins which resulted in an overwhelming 'healing crisis'. Her work was at its best when she teamed up with a spiritual healer who worked on the non-physical levels, adjusting the imbalances on the etheric body. However, she was unable to take an equal position in this partnership, she simply had to dominate. One patient complained of being the yo-yo in the middle, bounced back and forth by the underlying conflict. Needless to say the partnership ceased and she returned to her solitary 'masculine' pathway.

This is the type of ferociously mannish woman to whom Emma Jung is referring when, in a discussion on the animus[1], she points out that there are those women in whom not only has the integration of the masculine principle failed to occur, but the animus has actively become predominant, resulting in an overly aggressive, non-feminine approach to life and loving which is set apart from the feelings. This is the virago or shrewish termagant we are warned against by the old morality plays. At her best, she may successfully fulfil a male role in society under the guise of escaping from the stereotyped female role. At her worst, she is destructive and inwardly sterile, because she has sought to replace men rather than to allow her feminine qualities to complement and be fertilized by the male energy within herself which is represented by the animus.

As Emma Jung points out, women need to resist the unconscious invasion by the animus in order to maintain their creative, feminine power. When the animus is successfully integrated, however, the soul who has incarnated into a female body can function on the highest level and in the fullest sense as 'woman', thereby fulfilling her destiny for the present incarnation.

The eternal Self appears to be non-sexual in its function and composition, integrating both masculine and feminine within its Being, but the portion which incarnates as the soul takes on, to a greater or lesser extent, the gender characteristics of the physical body into which it incarnates. It can be argued that the anima or animus is composed of all the qualities which the soul learnt whilst inhabiting the physical bodies of the opposite sex. The same argument can apply to the particular archetype to which the soul is attuned. If it has had considerable experience as, for example, the Puer who refuses to grow up (Mercury) then it will manifest those qualities when incarnating within the male physical body, or will be attracted to those qualities in a male if it has incarnated as a female. The man who has incarnated many times in the physical body of a woman and carries within himself the archetype of the 'devouring mother' (Moon aspects to Pluto) will attract such a mother to himself and carry this over into his marriage, choosing a partner who carries similar archetypal characteristics. He may think he needs, and is choosing, someone very different, but his burden from the past will manifest time and time again as confrontation with a dominating woman until he resolves the conflict within himself and attunes to a different archetypal energy.

AIDS

With perfect synchronicity, as I was writing this section the charts of two men who had contracted Aids arrived on my desk, both having Sun in Leo with Chiron conjunct the Midheaven, and both having most of the planets 'squashed' into a very small section of the chart, one 'extrovert' (top half of the chart) and one 'introvert' (bottom part of the chart). The chart (fig. 19) shown is an 'angry' chart. Aries is on the cusp of the 'empty' sixth house. Mars, its ruler, being in Taurus in the seventh widely squaring the nodal axis. It is through the Will, or assertive energy, that the karmic purpose will be resolved. It has the feel of a 'fated' chart. He has chosen to take this path because he has to take this path for his own evolution: Mars is exactly quintile Pluto (an aspect of fate or destiny) and there is a Finger of Fate (Uranus inconjunct Moon, Moon inconjunct Pluto/Jupiter in Leo), indicating old emotional karma to be resolved. The Sun, North Node and Chiron are also in Leo, so that there is an emphasis on the heart energy and on

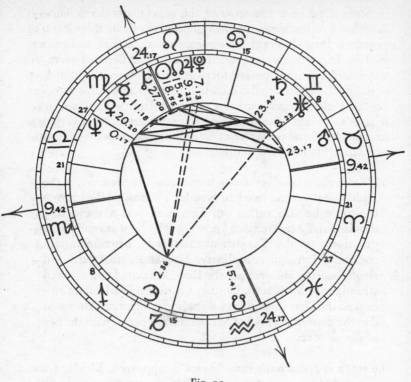

Fig. 19

empowering. With Mars trining Neptune in the eleventh, this man may not have faced his destiny in the past but he has been working on this issue. His Ascendant is Scorpio, indicating that he must penetrate to the depths of the taboo areas of life and bring back insights to help in the evolution and survival of mankind.

Various theories have been put forward to account for the arrival of Aids, many of them judgemental and concerned with 'the visitation of a plague as retribution from On High for unnatural practices'. The 'practices' in question, however, appear to have existed since the beginning of time and to have been glorified by cultures such as the ancient Greeks and, in a non-physical way, by the Sufis. One only has to read the official (modern) Turkish *Guidebook to the Shrine of the Sufi Mevlana Celaleddin Rumi* to appreciate how different the approach was, and is, to brotherhood and love between men. Love and the Beloved were an inseparable spiritual reality for Rumi and the concept of love should not be limited to the English interpretation of this complex activity. Unfortunately, sources differ on Rumi's birthdate so no chart is available. The following excerpts are quoted verbatim from the delightful prose. The first describes Rumi's meeting with his teacher, Shemseddin Tebrizi:

> He [Mevlana] was returning home from the Medrese, in the middle of the street two hands suddenly grasped the reins of the mule he was riding on. This man was a wandering dervish, and Mevlana not knowing who he was replied the questions of the Dervish without any ornamentation, sophistication and complexity. This straightforward and single-hearted answers got the Dervish excited and spurred stimulation in his soul. Getting off his mule Mevlana embraced the Dervish and they went home together. After that day the door of the soul of Mevlana was opened with the key of divine-love.

The story is a dramatic one: Shems disappeared, Mevlana was devastated; Shems reappeared, Mevlana was ecstatic, and the followers of Mevlana became jealous of the influence Shems had on him and had Shems murdered:

> Mevlana's lonesome bruised heart and confused mind never calmed then . . . The absence of Shems influenced Mevlana deeply and was burnt by a flame of melancholy and trance, so that he was dragged into love's spell in an everlasting mystery. [However,] while he was living in a gloomy forlorn darkness without Shems, one day another Shems arose in his horizon . . . Mevlana praised him so . . . 'The Radiant Light of God among the human beings'. He also said that the set sun in the existence of Shems rose again in the being of Selahaddin . . . Reverend Mevlana passed many happy days

full of joy and love. [But then tragedy struck again and Selahaddin died.] Sometime after the death of Selehaddin, Mevlana found another sun . . . because he couldn't live any longer in his loneliness . . . supposedly the spirit of Shems had resurrected in the Being of Husameddin.

Mevlana was married and had a family, and yet it was accepted that he needed the spiritual companionship and love of another man in order to achieve union with God. As Talat Sait, a Turkish commentator on the Dervishes, points out:

> This sequence of events was, in fact, a perfect mystic phenomenon. For Mevlana, Sems constituted the embodiment of God as well as the symbol of humanity. He in effect found God and became part of the Godhead. The disappearance of Sems had its correlative in God's abandoning mankind, in Sems absence Mevlana was to undertake an arduous mystical search . . . (when Sems returned) symbolically Mevlana had found God again, this time to merge his soul utterly and inseparably.[2]

As the spiritual teacher 'Jesus' pointed out in a channelling:

> Aids is a healing opportunity for all who have it and even for all in fear of having it. Aids is a blessing and spiritual opportunity for one to advance in his or her soul growth. It is not evil, bad or sinful to have Aids. This disease is a natural result of sexual guilt, fear and judgment. It is a form of self-punishment . . . Aids is a way for individuals to learn self-love and love for family, friends and life. Aids is a planetary disease to open up compassion . . . It is time that sex be seen as an expression of love and not just lust, power or pleasure . . . Aids is a sexually transmitted opportunity to know one's self as a divine expression of God or love![3]

Other theories to account for Aids include one which says that, having incarnated into a minority group, the soul is not happy within the physical body and the body therefore 'turns against the soul' (which could well be linked to Mars). Yet another theory, says that many souls, before their present incarnation, elected to 'sacrifice' themselves (Neptune), through Aids, to raise or to awaken the world's consciousness to a more moral standard, and to encourage the development of compassion instead of superiority. At the time of the changeover to the Aquarian Age casual sex may need to be abandoned in favour of the more committed, and spiritually based relationships required by the New Age – relationships which would equate to those of Mevlana and his companions of the soul, and yet would incorporate the body, so that it would be a true merging on the physical, emotional, mental and spiritual levels.

To return to the Aids chart, Chiron is in the tenth house and it may indicate that the family of origin (Russian Jewish) did not fit into society, or that this client will not fit into the society to which his family 'belongs'; either way there is a family wound which manifests through the soul's interaction with the outer world and which may include the family disowning the fact that their son has Aids. This wound may, however, open the way to the family displaying love and compassion, and facing in unity the prospect of death – another Aids client described his death as a 'gift' which he offered to his family in order that they may learn from it to be together and to love each other fully and openly.

Mars in the seventh house indicates old karma and pain coming from an aggressive relationship, particularly as Mars squares Chiron on the Midheaven. Mars trining the eleventh house Neptune indicates that the soul has been working on spiritualizing the Will and forgiving itself, and possibly working towards some kind of reparation for past 'misdeeds'. Neptune in the eleventh does indicate the potential for sacrificing himself for the good of the greater whole.

Uranus is on the cusp of the eighth house, square Venus; it is an ambiguous, ambivalent, unconventional energy which often indicates confusion around gender identity or sexual orientation – I have often found it to be bi-sexual rather than homosexual, taking refuge in celibacy as a way of escaping from long-standing difficulties. For the subject of this chart, contracting Aids in the present life effectively cuts off indiscriminate, 'unsafe' sexual contacts if he exercises the responsibility towards others called for by his eighth house Saturn. Taking into account the Finger of Fate, this is an old emotional pattern which needs to be resolved. Mars quintile Pluto would seem again to indicate some kind of 'fate' or 'destiny' at work in the confrontation with death and the challenge of making this 'final stage of growth' in the present incarnation, a creative one. Aids involves meeting this challenge, as does the eighth house Saturn, which also squares Neptune bringing in the need to resolve the mystic/pragmatist dilemma.

The need to make death a 'creative choice' is outlined in the channelled teaching of 'Bartholomew' regarding Aids:

> Death can be a moment of absolute heroic wonder, beauty and clarity *when experienced from an empowered position* ... It is empowering to say: 'I've got five months to live – and I am going to live like a warrior. I am going to get my life in order ... to be powerfully alive to the end.' That is a dynamic and aware way to die.[4]

This chart therefore indicates that the incarnating soul has the potential, whilst working on its own karma, to aid the evolution of mankind. The level of unselfish, unconditional loving and caring which can exist in a relationship between partners with Aids, and their families, certainly fits into the Leo North Node need to work with the heart energy, and satisfy the ninth house Node need for a new way of Being. The Leo heart energy may well be involved in a resolution of the 'dis-ease'. The Sun rules the Thymus-gland, situated close to the heart (Leo Sun) and a deficiency of Thymus dependent T-cells is responsible for the body's vulnerability to invasion (Mars square Chiron) by foreign bodies such as bacteria, viruses, mutation of cells, etc. If the heart energy could be merged with the Mars energy and channelled into regenerating the Thymus activity, the cells could be given new life and the aggressive energy required to fight off infection. Jupiter, and the power of the creative imagination, could be the tool used to fuse these energies and bring into being a balance and ease within the body.

PATTERNS OF 'DIS-EASE'

Some charts carry within them a pattern of fundamental dis-harmony and 'dis-ease'. The chart shown here (fig. 20) is that of an alcoholic manic-depressive woman who ended up in an institution suffering from total disintegration of the personality. There is an emphasis on inconjunct aspects, including three Fingers of Fate. This is the picture of a disunited soul. A line spoken by a psychiatric in-patient in a Radio 4 short story *Survivors* seems to sum up the difficulty this woman had in relating and explain why she withdrew from the world: 'We come here to escape from love. They make love safe here. They make it manageable.'

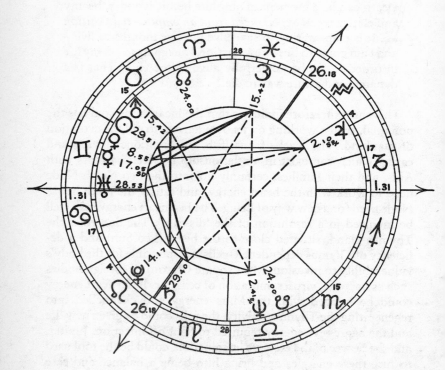

Fig. 20

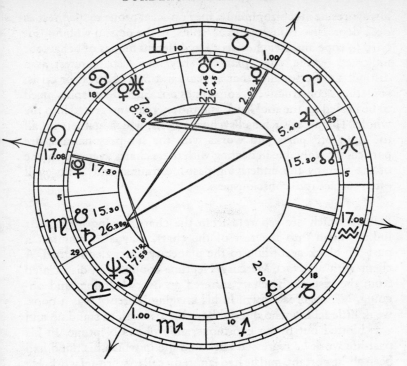

Fig. 21

Another fundamental pattern of 'dis-ease' is that of the 'split' chart where there are two, or more, distinct and separate parts to the chart. The pattern shown here (fig. 21) manifested as schizophrenia. As the person concerned, pointed out: 'I was hospitalised and given electric-shock treatment for what you get paid for.' He heard voices from the past 'persecuting' him. Pluto sextile Neptune/Moon represents old psychic abilities and delusory emotional states, and the 'split off' from the Uranus sextile Mercury energy represents the electric-shock treatment misused to 'treat' it. In this case it also linked back to torture inflicted on him in a past life. Such charts are indicative of old conflicts which manifest as separate personality styles or traits. Although they do not always result in schizophrenia, they do seem prone to manifest as deep depressive troughs and as 'splits' in the person who finds it hard to cope and switches between different modes of behaviour indicated by the 'split' planets. They may also manifest as a distinct sub-personality that appears in times of stress or crisis, sometimes constructively, sometimes not. Such deep 'splits' need to be healed on the soul level, and the energies integrated into the whole. Therapies such as Psychosynthesis, which 'gathers in' all the 'split off' parts and works with the sub-personalities, are particularly valuable in dealing with these charts as in the course of the therapy the underlying past-life trauma and 'splits' will often surface into consciousness.

Planets which are separate from the chart, having no aspects linking them into the rest of the chart, may also manifest a past-life block according to the planetary energy concerned. A client with an exact Mercury/Neptune conjunction dissociated from the rest of the chart suffered an overwhelming, and on-going, mental breakdown. In his imaging Mercury was a poor, weak little fellow who did not have the strength to stand up and was blotted out by an enormous, amorphous Neptune. In his past-life work he regressed back to a life in which his mind had been all-important, and he had ignored a call to spiritual work. He then went into a life in which the mind was totally subjugated to a 'spiritual' concept. Unfortunately his rational mind had kept rebelling against what it was being asked to believe in, and finally he had broken under the strain. He then came into the present life with the energies in very tight aspect, and was in the process of continuing the conflict. Gradually, through the use of imaging it was possible for him to negotiate a 'time-share' in order that Mercury could regain his strength, and he learnt to blend the two energies so that they could work in harmony.

As past-life hypnotherapist Glen Williston points out:

Illness is not always a simple past-life repression of some emotional pain that refuses to be subjugated any longer.

Other reasons for disease that are related to past-life conditions [astrological indicators have been added for clarification] as well as to the needs of the Greater Self include:

1. General lack of empathy for others in past lives, bigotry. [Difficult Saturn aspects, Saturn in aspect to Neptune. Saturn in the ninth, strong Earth or Water imbalance.]

2. Unwillingness to help others who are debilitated by disease in a past life. [Twelfth or sixth house Neptune or Saturn, Air imbalance.]

3. Unwillingness to develop creative potentialities that are struggling to be expressed. [Fifth house Saturn, Jupiter square Saturn, Saturn in a Cardinal sign.]

4. Conflicting energies of many past selves that interfere with present-self focus. [Sun and Moon and/or Venus and Mars in conflicting signs, planets in hard aspect, strong twelfth house, 'split' or dissociate charts.]

5. A strongly negative past self trying to live again emotionally in this time frame (negativity is a breeding ground for illness). [Planet, particularly Saturn or Pluto, conjunct the South Node.]

6. A specific affliction or impairment from the past that is influencing the present self, a direct carryover. [This will be obvious from the karmic houses and aspects, aspects to the South Node, or from the first house.][5]

THE 'SINS' OF OMISSION AND COMMISSION

Not all karmic burdens and blocks are physical or psychological in manifestation. Many involve the so-called 'cardinal sins' and also the 'sins of omission' where the soul has refused to face up to issues over many lifetimes; such 'sins' are ubiquitous and universal and, as Richard Coates of the Findhorn Foundation pointed out in a lecture: 'If everyone openly admitted their sins and fears, the biggest complaint would be lack of originality.' These 'sins' can be indicated by both planetary aspects and placement.

The Ninth House

The ninth house is the house of moral, ethical, philosophical or religious attitudes or beliefs carried over from the past which may be a burden or handicap when dealing with the present life. Saturn can indicate a past attitude such as bigotry or a rigid adherence to a conventional, restrictive religion which tends to equate pleasure with sin. The soul has carried over a sense of being sinful and feels a need for 'punishment' or reparation. It may appear to have a vocation towards the Church in its present life, but may find it too constricting to its spiritual growth. A French client with this placement began his career as a minister of the French Protestant religion. He made a shift of awareness and ended it as an 'astrological counsellor offering structure and meaning to the perplexed'.

Pluto in this house may indicate coercion or experience of the fanatic, someone who forcibly inculcated his belief system into another person – either as victim or perpetrator. In the present life the incarnating soul may try to continue this pathway, or to become concerned with, for example, environmental issues and trying to transform the public conscience and heal the planet. Neptune in the ninth, on the other hand, is the mystic, or the escapist, who now has to find a way of expressing his innate sense of the oneness of life.

The dual signs of Gemini, Sagittarius and Pisces, or Libra, in the ninth may indicate past 'sins' of hypocrisy, insincerity or two-facedness about beliefs coming forward from the past, particularly when there are, for example, difficult aspects of Mercury to Neptune or Saturn.

The First House

The first house planets (see Chapter 5) can also indicate burdens of unfulfilled obligation, or responsibility or fear (Saturn), which have been carried over from past lives. The incarnating soul may not have taken up this burden in a past life, or the burden may be one that weighs very heavily because it is a continuation of a past experience. In either case a child with this placement is one who is old before its time: it often becomes younger as it gets older and the burden eases. Such a placement usually indicates a burden picked up at a very young age in the present life within the family into which the soul incarnates. It can involve deep loneliness as in the case of the child of elderly parents, when the 'generation gap' is virtually uncrossable, or there may be no other young children within the family or social circle, so that the child is cut off from its own generation. Caring for a sick or aged parent, or younger children, or living in poverty are just three examples of how the Saturn burden can manifest. This burden often appears to be punitive and relentless, but it has its positive effects, as Stephen Arroyo points out: 'A remarkable inner strength can develop from Saturn's pressure, a strength that comes in part from knowing that we have done the required work, earned the results, and taken full responsibility for our own development.'[6]

Neptune

Neptune on one of the angles of the chart can bring back with it the burden of addiction or of being too open to 'possession' – undue influence from another soul whether living or dead, and not necessarily in physical proximity. This type of possession is often the result of having been trained in past lives to open up psychically and merge with another soul, or of having undergone a total mental breakdown: having become unsure of its own boundaries the soul will not be able to put up any barrier to the 'take-over'. After a drug trip, one client experienced what she termed a 'walk-in' from an alien being who needed a physical body to manifest through. Although she did retain partial consciousness, she acquiesced, if somewhat unwillingly, to this 'other being' utilizing her faculties, as she felt he was very wise.

A case of 'possession' by a person living contemporaneously on earth was experienced by a girl who had Neptune right on the Midheaven. She had had old occult contact with the man, and was now in unwelcome telepathic contact with him across an ocean. He manipulated her to the extent of affecting physiological processes in her body. The lesson she had to learn was that no one has the right to take over the body of another person in this way, and she also had to strengthen her defences and bring her Will energy into being to ensure that the 'possession' ceased. Her position was 'weakened' by an element imbalance within the chart involving an over-emphasis on Water and a lack of Air, which left her vulnerable on the unconscious feeling level and lacking in objective perception.

THE ELEMENTS

The four elements of the chart each equate to a particular function of consciousness and describe the incarnating soul's previous pattern of experience with these functions, as well as the present-life attunement to these creative energies:

> Air signs are correlated with the mind's sensation, perception and expression, especially related to geometrical thought forms. Fire signs express the warming, radiating, energising life principle which can manifest as enthusiasm or love or as ego. Water signs symbolise the cooling, healing, soothing principle of sensitivity and feeling response. Earth signs reveal an attunement with the world of physical forms and a practical ability to utilise the material world.[7]

The element balance within the chart indicates areas for the incarnating soul to work on, or to overcome. Lack of an element may mean that it has been successfully developed in the past, or it may indicate that this is a very important area to begin working on. When assessing this from the chart, it can be helpful to look at the balance of planets within the element houses. If, for example, there is a lack of Water and the fourth, eighth and twelfth houses are 'full', then there may be a need to become conscious of, and develop, the Water function further. If there is a lack of planets in Water signs and these houses are 'empty' then it may be that the feeling function has been balanced out in the past.

Fire

An over-emphasis on the Fire element represents the need to control impulsiveness and to cultivate the balancing qualities of receptivity and stillness. It can also be helpful to develop sensitivity and thinking with one's mind instead of one's mouth, in order to counteract a tendency to be hasty and tactless. A very disciplined utilization of energy is called for as otherwise 'burn-out' can occur, although the Fire element usually has reserves of stamina available in a crisis. The habits of circulating energy around the body or 'cat-napping' can be useful ones to cultivate to counteract the tendency to scatter too much energy outwards.

Too much Fire can also indicate a fierce independence carried forward from the past and an inability to ask for help when required – the 'sin' of pride may have featured in a previous incarnation. It is important to balance this out by learning to gracefully accept assistance when it is appropriate. It may be 'more blessed to give than to receive', but someone has to be on the receiving end in order for the blessing to flow, and becoming receptive is an important spiritual lesson. An old lady, with a preponderance of Fire, developed cataracts in both eyes and, although she had always refused any aid before, found that she simply could not manage alone. Once she had recognized and learnt the lesson that could be learnt from her situation, her cataracts were operated on and her sight returned. She commented that she had also learnt the invaluable quality of patience at long last – courtesy of the NHS who had kept her waiting so long.

Too little Fire can frequently manifest as a lack of energy and initiative. This is reflected in very passive past-life experiences in which the soul was always under the control of another person, as in the elderly companion who was 'totally lost' without her bossy employer to tell her what to do. Far from resenting the bossiness and control, she had welcomed it and had found the same type of relationship again with her husband in the present life. When the latter died, she was again lost, not even able to organize herself to shop for food without someone else suggesting it. Conversely, the incarnating soul may have a history of wasting energy and come back depleted.

The lack of energy experienced by the low Fire chart can be counterbalanced by physical exercise, even if only a brisk walk. When the person feels least like exercising is when it will do the most good: that brisk walk will result in an uprush of energy which can then be utilized to carry on with the task in hand. A daily exercise programme can be particularly beneficial in balancing out past lives in which either too much or too little energy was expended. Stephen Arroyo points out that the Fire-deficient body cannot digest heavy concentrated foods and that therefore diet is also an important factor in combating the lack of Fire.

Air

The element of Air needs to combine disciplined thought processes with action. Too much Air can indicate an over-attachment to ideas and the intellect, and too little connection with the feelings. The over-active mind of the Air element can be linked to past lives in which the emphasis was on being academic, or rational and analytical, at the expense of the emotions and senses. There can be a lack of understanding of anything beyond 'the facts', and an old difficulty in trusting to sense perception. A client with a strong Air–Fire chart, and a Mercury/Saturn opposition to Uranus (the intellect versus the intuition), spent years training as a homoeopath. He had an insatiable urge for more and more knowledge. His intuition and attunement to the 'Higher Mind' symbolized by Uranus would tell him within ten minutes which particular remedy a patient required. His intellect, aided by the mistrustful Mercury/Saturn conjunction, would then spend the next fifty minutes of the consultation justifying that choice. Once he learnt to trust his intuition, utilizing his long experience and knowledge to make fast, seemingly non-rational decisions, he became a much better homoeopath, and was able to see many more patients.

Part of the imbalance of the past-life pattern can stem from having been too detached, or too objective, lacking a connection to how both itself and others felt, and therefore cut off from those around it. Spicy foods can help to ground the Air element into awareness of the physical level of being, and sensitivity to the feelings of others can redress the balance.

Too little Air acts on feelings and emotions rather than on rational and logical thought, and is incapable of an objective perspective. It lacks stamina and can experience great difficulty in understanding or cooperating with others as it is incapable of projecting itself into their shoes and of seeing a different point of view. Such an incarnating soul has never lost the omnipotent feeling of babyhood, it still sees everyone else as an extension of its own being. Its past-life pattern may well have been one of puissance, of not having to worry about what other people thought or felt as it had total control over their lives anyway. With an Air-deficient chart the soul must learn detachment without losing its connection to the feelings, and utilize the mind and spiritual awareness to connect to, and understand, the world in which it finds itself.

Water

An imbalance of Water points to an undue influence from the emotions and feelings. A chart with an over-emphasis on Water is literally water-(emotion)-logged, reacting to any and every emotional stimuli in a completely instinctual way, and it is therefore untrustworthy. With such an imbalance, the soul needs to learn to plan ahead and move forward purposefully, to be in touch with, and then to detach itself from, the emotions, so that it can formulate a response to situations instead of endlessly falling back into the old pattern of reaction. Stephen Arroyo, in a very comprehensive treatment of the elements, describes this imbalance as 'cast adrift on the open sea in a small boat with no rudder, no sail, no air, and no compass . . . easily influenced by any wind that blows.'[8]

The past-life pattern is usually full of insecurity and excessive, uncontrolled emotionality. A client with an extremely unbalanced chart, six planets in a large sixth house (Virgo cusp), six planets in Water, one in Fire and Earth, and two in Air, presented a charming façade of intelligent, unemotional competence – Leo Ascendant and Taurus MC which is seen by the world as efficient and practical – although he was not in fact in the least organized. He was very involved with the New Age movement as the organizer for, and facilitator of, 'growth' groups of many different kinds (Mercury/Saturn/Neptune conjunction), and yet he presented the following problem:

> Periodic outbursts of alarming and intimidating physical violence [North Node/Mars square Neptune] towards my wife when mentally [Mercury/Saturn square Uranus] and emotionally frustrated and blocked [Venus trine Uranus]. Difficulties in channelling sexual energy [Mars in Capricorn square her Mars in Aries] within our relationship – sexual frustration. Challenge of creating and channelling prosperity and abundance in our lives despite history of negative attitudes and lack of material means.

Although his chart had many conjunctions, squares and sextiles, it lacked oppositions to act as a focus for the blocked energy contained within it. One of the squares was from the Scorpio Moon to Pluto – a seething mass of traumatic and very fixed emotions from the past forcibly clamped down. He found it difficult to understand, other than in a superficial intellectual way, that it was his own negative attitudes that were manifesting as a lack of material means. He found it even harder to understand that it was his own emotions, of which he was unaware except when they surfaced uncontrollably (Pisces on the cusp of the twelfth), that were the cause of the periodic outbursts. He could relate to the past-life patterns of himself as an emotional person, but not to the present-life picture. To make matters worse he was a 'crisis counsellor' and, with Neptune in the sixth, was soaking up his client's negative and violent emotional energies; he then unconsciously channelled them into the difficult Mars square between him and his wife. Mars was in the ninth house in each chart signifying a fundamental clash of beliefs and values between the two of them, as well as a clash of egos (his Mars conjuncting her Sun square to Mars). When his inner perception of conflict became too much to bear and demanded expression, instead of verbalizing the disharmony he exploded into violence.

Too little Water in the chart does not mean a lack of emotion or feelings, but it does indicate a person who has, particularly in a past life, been too successful at detaching from the emotions and is now out of touch with any motivation springing from that source. This was expressed to the extreme in the chart (fig. 22) of a brain-damaged child with no Water, two Earth, three Fire and five Air planets, and an Air Ascendant. She appeared to lack hearing, although at times it was possible to attract her attention by sound, and her problem seemed primarily to be one of non-attention to

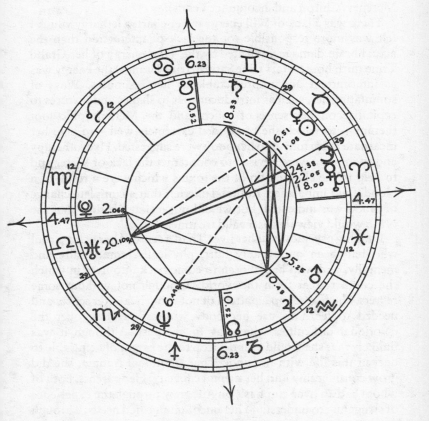

Fig. 22

the messages her senses were sending her. She lived in her head 'in her own little world' of too much Air; she did not speak and her sight was limited. She responded a little to touch and could at times be aware enough of another person to reach out to them. And yet she was totally disconnected from her emotions and very cut off from the world or interaction with the environment (Cancer South Node conjunct MC). She never cried, never laughed, never appeared to vary in her blank, non-emotional response. Had it not been for the handicap, she would have been highly, and moodily, emotional (Uranus opposing Moon/Mercury/Chiron and inconjunct Venus).

There was a lack of Will energy in her chart, a lethargy which I felt was more responsible for the lack of interaction than the actual brain damage, indicated by the 'lazy' energy of her Grand Trine (fifth house Mars trine Saturn, trine Uranus) the energy was as intermittent and unpredictable as her responses. Ways of stimulating her, such as introducing her to shapes and textures to capitalize on her sense of touch, and the Metamorphic foot therapy – to which she responded extremely well – to help her incarnate more fully into her body were suggested. Hydrotherapy and swimming were advised to counteract the lack of Water and to help in the elimination of the toxins which were a result of a blood/fluid imbalance. Robert Tully felt that a complete change of blood was indicated, but we did not feel at the time that the NHS would view this as a valid treatment!

Looking psychically at her lives, I had a sense of her being a soul who had been quite badly hurt, physically, emotionally and mentally, and who had chosen to come back into lives in which she could retreat from the world, although not without some regrets. She had set up a pattern of not using her outer senses and needed to learn to use her body without carrying over the emotional difficulties which lay in her past. Although it was unlikely that she would ever develop to the extent of being able to deal in this life with the underlying emotional trauma, she did grow considerably into her mental capacity. Her parents, both of whom had an over-emphasis on Air, grew through the experience of struggling to understand her uncommunicated needs. Through caring for her with very little response or reward, they also learnt how to extend unconditional love, perception, empathy and compassion to another soul. As a friend who nursed handicapped children pointed out: 'You may look after such a child for ten years, your only reward being one smile at the end of that time. But it is worth it.'

Earth

Too much attachment to the physical senses and survival needs are indicated by an emphasis on the Earth element. An over-emphasis points to prior lives in which material 'things' were all that mattered, or in which the soul may have lost everything, or may have lived in extreme poverty. The lesson behind such experiences is that the security of material possessions is illusory; the only lasting security is the inner one of spiritual attunement and growth. Therefore the Earthy chart needs, whilst retaining its rootedness, to explore the spiritual dimension of life through meditation which will take it beyond the confines of the body.

Any imbalance of Earth, too much or too little, can lead to difficulties stemming from the retention of toxins – physical, mental or emotional – and there is a need for a periodic cleansing of all the levels as otherwise it will ultimately manifest as disease.

Too little Earth is related to the need to become grounded, to cope with the demands of the practical, physical environment, and to learn how to be at one with the body. Many non-Earthed people feel incarcerated within an alien lump of flesh, and this can lead to long-term illness and disease as the incarnating soul struggles to learn the lesson of at-oneness with the physical level. Yoga, tai chi, postural integration and similar physically based techniques or meditations can be extremely helpful in grounding the non-Earthed soul into the body.

A client (fig. 23) with no Earth planets and five Water planets had experienced a very difficult and traumatic life. Her husband had died just before the birth of her baby. As she had Chiron square Venus, Moon in Scorpio and Pluto conjunct Mercury/Venus, she had incarnated expecting to undergo this type of emotional trauma in order to change her pattern. She was the

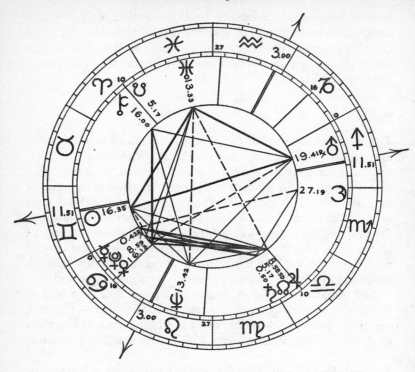

Fig. 23

seventh known generation to carry a very rare, genetically trans-
mitted disease (sixth house Moon). She had a Fire Grand Trine
(Chiron–Neptune–Mars), indicating the potential to align the
Will with the spiritual purpose in order to overcome her wound,
and a Finger of Fate (Uranus at the point inconjunct Neptune and
inconjunct Saturn/Jupiter/North Node – this was a transpersonal, collective karma she was dealing with). With a T-square
from Uranus to Sun opposing Mars, she incarnated intending to
take control and transform her previous-life pattern.

When she first contacted me she was totally paralysed from: 'a
rare, intractable, complex and defeating familial condition; with
no known cause, cure or name'. She had a 'burning desire to end

this misery'. The matriarchal family interaction was a very tight one and it appeared that the same group had incarnated time after time, repeating the difficulty. Her Venus/Pluto contact and Scorpio Moon indicated an old pattern of emotional trauma and mothering karma, and the lack of Earth that she was not attuned to being comfortable within the physical body. She had been taught to view herself as a victim of the family curse from a very early age and was programmed to continue it unless she took control of her life.

She was introduced to the 'carrot meditation' as a way of becoming comfortable within the physical body. The visualization consists of imagining oneself to be a big, juicy, orange carrot, nurtured and cocooned by the warm earth with just the feathery tops waving above the ground. Although it can initially be an extremely uncomfortable meditation for the no-Earth chart, it does stimulate perception of the earth, and of the physical body, as a source of nourishment and support. Incarnation into the body then becomes more harmonious.

Within two years this client had defeated her paralysis – mainly by the use of Bach remedies to heal the emotional trauma of that Scorpio Moon and all her other Water planets. She had travelled to Australia, found a specialist who understood, and, most importantly, named, the condition, which was validated and could therefore be overcome: cognitively it is extremely difficult to fight against something which is not supposed to exist. She founded an association for fellow sufferers, and although there were very few they were at least able to share information and hope of a cure. As she could not resolve the problem of heredity, she hoped that by tackling the cause of the disease within herself, she could prevent future generations from having to cope with such an intractable condition. As she said, although it was valuable for her own development it was 'oh so very wearying, so much, too much'.

The same feeling pertains to all karmic burdens and baggage, and it is the pressure of everything becoming 'too much' which pushes the soul into discarding or dealing with the underlying cause and present-life manifestation. As comedienne Ruby Wax so eloquently expressed it: 'It's not the grossness of the experience that drives people crazy, it's how long you let it ferment inside.'

STILLBIRTH AND SUICIDE

Questions which always seem to arise in reincarnation workshops are 'What happens to suicides?' and 'Can you explain stillbirth or cot death?'. There appear to be a number of answers to both these questions and very little in the way of astrological indications, although certain specific aspects such as Mars–Neptune, Saturn –personal planets, Saturn–Jupiter and some difficult Pluto aspects do seem to share a propensity to suicide.

It appears that for suicides the motive behind the act can be an important factor in determining the next-life conditions. If the incarnated soul feels on the deeper levels that it has worked on its difficulties as far as it can, and then decides to opt out – as, for example, when a cancer patient makes the choice to 'die with dignity' to save other people the agony of watching a slow death – then a different kind of karma is generated from that of a soul who has 'escaped' from a situation it feels it cannot handle, avoiding a lesson which may well be repeated in the next life.

Similarly, a variety of factors operate for both stillbirth and cot death. It has been suggested that some suicides, or accident victims for whom death was sudden and unexpected, need to incarnate again for a very short time in order to have time to adjust to the transition. In the case of some very traumatic deaths a gentle intra-uterine experience may help the soul to prepare for another physical life at a later date. Infant mortality may also be linked to the incarnating soul changing its mind, particularly when conditions have altered within the family environment. Another explanation may be that the soul, having incarnated solely to bring its present-life parents a karmic lesson, or to fulfil their in-built expectation, may not have intended to incarnate for a long period.

Fig. 24 is the chart of a baby who was stillborn by Caesarean section, following a very painful and difficult labour, at the appropriate time of 13.13. The chart has seven planets in Earth, including Mars in Capricorn in the sixth house, which indicate karmic difficulties around being in a physical body, with Mars quintile Pluto which points to the possibility of the 'fate' of a

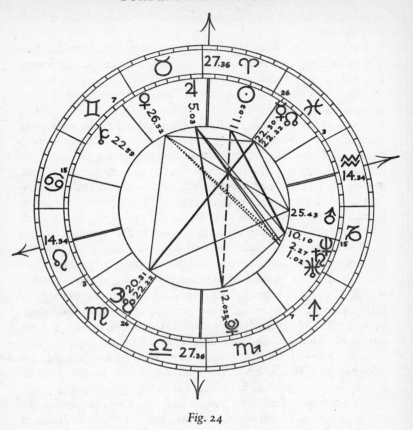

Fig. 24

traumatic and violent death, both in the past and the present life
(Pluto–Mars contacts often signify an old, aggressive conflict,
particularly on the psychological level). The chart for the commencement of labour has the Capricorn Saturn/Uranus/Neptune
conjunction right on the Ascendant, indicating a deep ambivalence about incarnating into the physical body and, perhaps that
self-sacrifice was chosen in order that karmic lessons may be
learnt by others. It would appear from the chart that, had the
baby survived, she could very well have been brain-damaged

227

or autistic: indeed the hospital abandoned resuscitation for this very reason.

The child, who would have been very much loved (tenth house Venus and Jupiter), was clearly bringing a lesson to her young parents as they faced the pain and loss of her death together (fourth house Pluto). Her mother's Saturn, opposing her Moon, conjuncted the child's Sun, and her Pluto conjuncted the child's Moon and South Node, indicating an old debt and mothering karma. The mother's Saturn opposition to the Moon, which shows she lacks confidence and undervalues herself, indicated old emotional pain and isolation as well as her sense of worthlessness, and on an occasion prior to the baby's death she had said that she 'killed what she loved' when referring to her pets, although it would perhaps have been truer to say that what she loved, died. The child's North Node/Mercury conjuncted her parents' Chiron in Pisces, activating their spiritual pain and alienation and the deep wound in their contact with the cosmos: after the baby's death both were convinced that there was no god – a suspicion which both had voiced earlier. Her Chiron also conjuncted her father's Saturn conjunction to the Sun, opposing the Moon, which brought out his underlying emotional pain but also his inner strength. The child's Saturn/Uranus/Neptune squared the father's Sun–Moon opposition, his Uranus conjuncted her Moon/South Node, his Pluto conjuncted her Moon, and his South Node conjuncted her Pluto: his lesson was to let go.

The pregnancy had been punctuated by trauma (reflecting the Mars quintile to Pluto). Very early on a beloved uncle had died; at four months the mother fell downstairs; at five months the car in which the mother was travelling was hit on the motorway by another car; at eight months the husband's car went up in flames while the mother watched helplessly and hysterically. Fortunately, it was stationary at the time and he was unhurt. They spent all their savings on another car which turned out to be worthless, and the shock induced labour. The baby's heart stopped when the hospital intervened in the birth and broke the membranes to speed up labour. The mother had intuitively felt that a Caesarean was needed, but did not have the confidence to say so. After the baby's death, she believed that this baby had just not been meant to be,

and that it had happened for some unknown purpose, but she also
knew that the baby would come back to them when ready to
incarnate.

Fig. 25 is the chart of a child born to the same parents fourteen
months later, again by Caesarean section in life-threatening
circumstances indicated by the Scorpionic Pluto close to the
Ascendant. Labour had been induced (often a feature of Plutonian
births), but the cervix was not dilating and the hospital were again
threatening to rupture the membranes in order to speed up the
process. This time the mother had enough confidence in her own

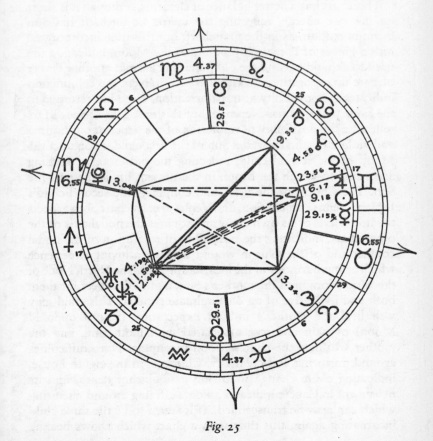

Fig. 25

intuition to refuse: she demanded a Caesarean. Her fear was that the pattern would repeat itself and that she, through her body, would let the baby down at birth (Pluto in Virgo). Her Saturn–Moon opposition meant that she felt inadequate as a mother and she needed to find her own inner strength and resilience. This time the baby lived, but she was initially separated from her mother (Moon square Saturn) by the effects of the anaesthetic (Neptune). However, she was fed by her father (whose Sun in Aries is close to her Moon) immediately after birth (nurturing Mars in Cancer completing the T-square).

This chart has a better balance of elements, although it is short on the Fire energy, reflecting the inertia of birth. It has Sun inconjunct Pluto as in the first chart, but this time incorporated into a Finger of Fate with Jupiter and the Moon, indicating the need to expand beyond the old parenting karma; another Finger of Fate incorporating the Uranus/Saturn/Neptune conjunction indicates the possibility of transformation. Pluto has returned to the same place, as has Neptune, but this time Pluto trines Mars reflecting the possibility of resolution of the issues of old trauma and violent death. The Aries Sun of the first child is conjunct the Moon of the second child, reflecting the old esoteric teaching according to which the Moon in the present life is the past-life Sun. The Chiron of the first child conjuncts the second child's Jupiter/Venus conjunction, and Venus in each chart both aspects the nodal axis of its own chart and squares the nodal axis of the other chart, indicating the possibility of resolution of the nodal conflict and of the Chiron wound through a loving experience which brings harmony to the incarnating soul. The North Node of the Moon conjuncts the mother's Sun, a growth aspect for them both and indicative of an old soulmate contact. This child may well heal the mother's in-built expectation (Saturn opposed Moon) of pain and loss associated with mothering, and the mother will heal the child's Moon inconjunct Pluto difficulties around nurturing and creativity. Chiron is in the eighth house, indicating a life change following a significant death, and its placement in Cancer indicates an old suffering around nurturing which can now be transcended. This seems to be the same child incarnating again, this time with a chart which shows healing

potential to overcome an old sense of helplessness and powerlessness (Saturn/Neptune opposed Mars, T-square Moon, eighth
house Chiron, and the Moon–Pluto–Sun/Jupiter Finger of Fate).
The chart also appears to be typical of one of the Age of Aquarius
old-soul children who are incarnating to help the birth into the
New Age (third house Aquarian North Node). Her chart has
tremendous psychic and healing power from the Scorpionic Pluto
on the Ascendant inconjunct the Moon, Mars opposition to
Neptune, the eighth house Chiron, and a reservoir of old skills and

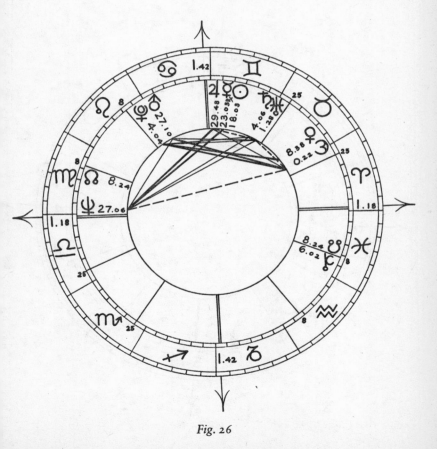

Fig. 26

transpersonal abilities in the second house Uranus, Saturn and Neptune.

Fig. 26 is the chart of an alcoholic who committed suicide in an emotional blackmail attempt which went wrong (Neptune inconjunct the Moon). Although not aware of the fact, he only had a few months to live as he had an undiagnosed kidney failure (Chiron conjunct the South Node in Pisces on the cusp of the sixth house and inconjunct Pluto). Fig. 27 is the chart for his 'death' and transition to another life. The Ascendants are almost conjunct

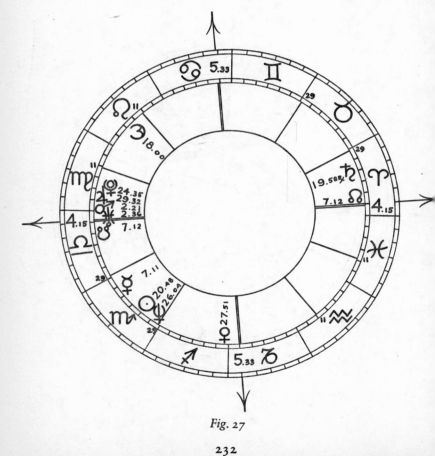

Fig. 27

(there is some confusion about the exact time of death) and the natal Ascendant is being transited by Pluto/South Node/Mars/ Jupiter/Uranus inconjunct Saturn, forming a Finger of Fate with his wife's Moon in Scorpio. Following his death his estranged wife was told by a medium that he would try to return to her. Some years later as Neptune transited her Sun/Mercury, and opposed his natal Saturn/Uranus, she became aware that he was an earth-bound spirit and worked at releasing him. Three months later she miscarried a child on an anniversary of his death and, despite the fact that she was much relieved, she was aware of a

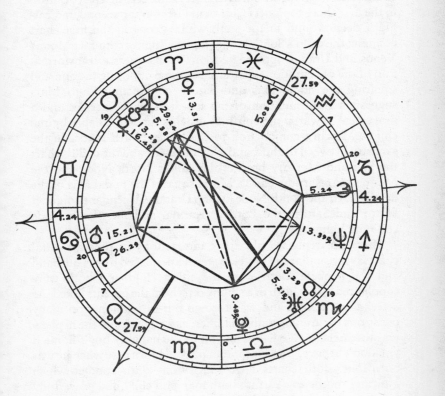

Fig. 28

very deep sadness and of her body grieving for the 'child'. Again, a medium told her that her husband was trying to return to her and would incarnate into her family if she was not willing to mother him.

Nine months later her nephew (fig. 28) was born and she saw him when he was only a few minutes old: her husband looked at her out of his eyes. The child's chart has karmic inconjunct aspects requiring resolution, including a Mercury–Neptune–Mars Finger of Fate. Although not in the same sign, less than a minute separates the Moon in the first natal chart from the Sun in the chart of her nephew, who was a reluctant forceps delivery; Chiron in the first chart conjuncts Chiron in Pisces in the second, indicating a deep wound in the soul, while Venus in the first chart conjunct the child's South Node/Jupiter, Jupiter conjunct Moon/Venus and Uranus opposing Moon/Venus offers a transformation of the old emotional pattern. Neptune opposing the Sun and squaring the nodal axis and Saturn conjuncting Pluto/Mars suggests a transmutation of the self-destructive energies and a movement towards the spiritual insights made available by the child's Mercury conjunction to the Pisces North Node. In the synastry between the husband's 'death' chart and the child's chart the Sun and Mercury bracket the child's North Node and the Moon squares it; the child's Moon squares the nodal axis of the death chart; the South Node/Mars/Uranus/Ascendant conjunct Pluto; and Saturn, the Lord of Karma, and the North Node conjunct Venus.

There are replicate planetary interactions in the two natal charts: very similar life patterns were experienced by the husband and the nephew. Both were the eldest child and both were supplanted by the birth of a sibling on whom the parents doted. As a teenager the husband was thrown out of his home on many occasions for arguing with his father; as a young child the nephew was threatened: 'We will send you to the naughty boy's home if you don't behave,' and his mother packed him a case when he was only four. Both charts have the Moon–Pluto contact which indicates mothering karma; both man and child had powerfully instinctual mothers who held the power within the family. Both charts have Mars–Saturn aspects; both their lives were dominated by another person and both felt helpless and powerless. The man longed to go to sea from early childhood (twelfth house Neptune, Jupiter on the Midheaven and five ninth house planets) and he became a sailor, only returning home to die. The child was fascinated with the stars, and wanted to become an astronaut. Both had the escapist Neptune–Mars contacts. In the man's case these became self-destructive when he died from a mixture of drink and drugs (a transit activated his Neptune sextile to Mars, square to the Sun/Mercury conjunction, trine to the Saturn/Uranus conjunction, and inconjunct to the Moon). The child incarnated with a Finger of Fate (Saturn/Mars inconjunct Neptune, inconjunct Mercury), indicating that he had to integrate and resolve the energies which had proved his 'downfall' in the last incarnation.

Chapter 5

FELLOW TRAVELLERS

*The child lives and breathes in the atmosphere that the
parents create through their relationship to each other.*

STEPHEN ARROYO, *ASTROLOGY, KARMA
AND TRANSFORMATION*

The incarnating soul's earliest relationship is with its biological
family of origin, and it includes interaction whilst still in the
uterus. The natal chart indicates the patterns of behaviour and
expectation carried forward from the past, and the environment
into which these will be projected. It describes how the mother,
father and siblings will be perceived, and how the family will
interact. Parents are selected on the basis of the experiences
required by the incarnating soul, the genetic and attitudinal
inheritance of the family being taken into account. There may be a
direct karmic link between the souls incarnated within the family
unit, or karma related to the type of family interaction. Some groups
of souls appear to incarnate as families time and time again.
Others are much more loosely connected, varying the experiences
explored through karmic contacts and including friendship or
enmity as well as 'love' relationships. Here, relationship is always
used in the widest sense of the word: interaction with another.

Old patterns such as lack of self-worth or conflict with authority figures will be carried over by the incarnating soul from the
past, and the appropriate family interaction will intensify the
inherent difficulties. It is these unconscious patterns which form
the basis of learnt behaviour: they include many defence and
avoidance strategies conceived in order to prevent feelings and
emotions from surfacing, and form part of the 'shadow' side of the
personality and are, therefore, rarely consciously acknowledged
or recognized. The pressure of behaviour based on childhood
circumstances and of experience carried over into adulthood,

however, ultimately forces attention on to the issues involved, and offers the possibility of resolution of long-standing personal and parental karma.

Karma related to individual relationships manifests in the natal chart through the placement of planets in houses and the position of house rulers, and through the planetary aspects – in particular outer-to-personal planet contacts. In this respect even 'easy' aspects such as sextiles and trines can delineate a residue of unresolved karma and, therefore, unless an aspect is specifically designated, the karma can apply to any contact between the planets. The nature of the planets will dictate the type of karma involved. Saturn – particularly in difficult aspect – can indicate deep, long-standing fears and feelings of lack of self-worth and value, an inward sense of unlovableness and anxiety with a consequent inner helplessness which may manifest as extremely tight outward control. Unmet dependency needs may leave an unacknowledged 'aching inner emptiness' which the child, and later on the adult, fixedly seeks to satisfy through a comfort-object or dependent, symbiotic relationships. Power issues and manipulation are a feature of Pluto contacts and it may be a lifetime task to regain power handed over to a dominant parental figure.

The network of karmic ties and obligations pervading the family can be identified through the synastry between the natal charts. Patterns and dilemmas such as dependency/self-determination, possessiveness/separation and freedom/commitment show up clearly in the contacts across the charts between the inner and outer planets. 'Unfinished business', debts to be paid or pledges to be fulfilled can be identified. Relationships may have repeated destructive patterns for many lifetimes, but the karmic interaction can be investigated through the charts, and a way of resolution found.

NATURE VERSUS NURTURE

Scientists and educationalists have long debated the question of nature versus nurture: how much of the personality is attributable to heredity and genetic factors, and how much to family and environmental influences. The concept of reincarnation throws new light on this dilemma. Without reincarnation the baby is a 'blank slate' at the mercy of its genes and environment. With reincarnation it is seen as having an innate disposition carried forward from the past which will affect how it interacts with both nature and nurturing. This concept can also explain why twins who incarnate with virtually the same chart may nevertheless express the energies very differently. The incarnating soul's past experience will colour its perceptions, subtly influencing its expectations and will be reflected in its inherent response to new experiences. The innate disposition is reinforced from the moment of birth. A happy, contented baby is automatically responded to with love and kindness. A crying, discontented one will almost always engender exasperation and, if it continues crying for long periods, may well provoke anger. The mother, particularly when the baby is her first child, may feel inadequate and unable to cope. Thus, the level of nurturing available to that child will be 'poor' when compared to that of the contented child. However, an incarnating soul who is pre-programmed to expect poor nurturing will 'home in' on the occasions when that poor expectation is met, and may totally ignore the nine out of ten times when it received perfectly adequate mothering. On the other hand, the child whose expectation is that its needs will be fulfilled will more easily tolerate the occasional frustration of unmet desires.

FACING UP TO INCARNATION: ASCENDANT AND FIRST HOUSE

The first house is the house of the Self and the Ascendant is the persona or mask the soul dons to face the world (see Chapter 3). The Ascendant and planets in the first house indicate how the incarnating soul will view the prospect of incarnation, birth and nurturing, and how it will interact with those other souls it encounters.

There is a theory which postulates that the womb is *the* most wonderful place in the world. The incarnating soul floats in mystical unity with the mother, cushioned and nourished by its own integral life-support system. However, there is another line of thought which considers the uterus threatening, hostile, non-supportive and a most unsafe place to be. To which school of thought one belongs will depend on one's experiences prior to birth and on the sign and planet(s) on the Ascendant.

Neptune, Venus, Taurus, Pisces and Cancer will usually be identified with the five-star womb, and Pluto, Saturn, Scorpio, Aquarius and Capricorn will probably recognize the no-star variety. The attitude of the Libra or Virgo Ascendant towards incarnation will tend to depend on whether or not Pluto, Saturn and/or Neptune also feature in the equation. With first house Neptune in Virgo on the Ascendant, the soul is likely to incarnate with the dualist view that incarceration into matter is separation from the divine and birth into an 'abode of the damned'. In other words, hell. Saturn in Virgo may well agree that it is 'a place of misery'. The first house Neptune in Libra, however, all other things being equal of course, is likely to enjoy the uterine experience and may continue the symbiosis and non-separation from the mother, and the rest of creation, a long way into incarnation: the umbilical cord of the psyche being much harder to sever than the physical structure. On the other hand, this being Neptune and Libra, it may be ambivalent, but ultimately it must decide whether incarnation was or was not such a good idea after all, and either fully incarnate or withdraw.

Neptune

With first house Neptune, or Pisces on the Ascendant, the soul can experience the difficulty of being born to a mother who either has an undefined boundary of her own or who is knocked out by drugs or anaesthetic and unaware of having given birth. Such an experience may mean that neither the child nor its mother are able to separate psychically. The child may itself be suffering the effects of the drug — a difficulty which may later be recreated through drug or meditation experiences in which the 'child' seeks to regain its lost unity with the mother and the cosmos.

Whenever Neptune falls in the first house, or Pisces is the

Ascendant, the incarnating soul is unsure of its own boundary and needs to learn where itself ends and another begins. As with the twelfth house Neptune, the lesson is to distinguish: 'Who am I? Who are you?' whilst retaining a fundamental sense of interconnectedness to the whole of the cosmos. Neptune can be the planet of the highest spirituality or of the deepest escapism. The incarnating soul can be naïve, too trusting and open to deception. It is the cosmic sponge, soaking up emanations and taking on pain indiscriminately, without separation into 'mine' and 'yours'. The soul with first house Neptune is capable of great sacrifice and yet must learn how to protect itself and how to say 'No' when appropriate, learning that at-onement is more apposite to its spiritual functioning than atonement. Neptune is the planet with integral oneness, but the lesson is one of discriminating unity. The incarnating soul must cleanse and strengthen its 'aura' to provide a protective barrier as in past lives it has been too open.

Saturn

Saturn, or Capricorn on the Ascendant, on the other hand, indicates that the soul has been too closed during previous incarnations. It is repressed and constrained and needs to open up its boundary to interaction with an other. The first house Saturn incarnates with the expectation that life will be difficult as the soul is already carrying a heavy burden. Saturn or Capricorn on the Ascendant, can indicate fear and resistance to birth. The soul often experiences a difficult struggle to be born which necessitates forceps or Caesarean section delivery – a process which confirms all the soul's worst fears. Or, it may undergo a premature birth which necessitates separation from the mother and time in an incubator. The soul feels isolated and alone, and the baby is often met with the hostility or indifference of a mother worn out by the pain of a protracted delivery. This may well have been an unplanned, unwanted pregnancy or the mother may have been experiencing her own fear and isolation during the gestation period. Either way, soaking up these emanations from within another, the incarnating soul is acutely aware of its discreteness; it feels unwelcome and uncared for. Incarnating with the expectation of coldness, rejection and poor nurturing, it inevitably meets physical or emotional deprivation – one can, of course, be physically well cared for and yet emotionally deprived, and vice versa. This may be the child of an elderly, inadequate, chronically sick, or 'absentee' parent.

The soul with a first house Saturn tends to face responsibility early, meeting hardship with fortitude or resignation because it expects nothing else. A woman with Saturn on the Scorpio Ascendant was born shortly after her sister died. Her mother grieved for the lost child continually and paid no attention to the new baby, who received no nurturing from her mother throughout her childhood – which was exactly what she had expected when she incarnated.

The first house Saturn may also need to explore its 'shadow', all those facets of itself which it does not wish to own or acknowledge and which are pushed down into the darkness of the unconscious, from where inevitably, sooner or later, they will demand attention. Such a demand may be expressed as a projection of the undesired quality or emotion 'out there' to another person, which is the dynamic operating in most relationships. On the other hand, it may continually surface as emotional tension until it has to be acknowledged and integrated. A Saturnine soul is therefore prone to incarnating into a family which has carried forward an ancestral 'shadow' pattern and an unspoken edict forbidding certain feelings. This is referred to by family psychologist Robin Skynner[1] as 'screening off' unacceptable thoughts and emotions. The child very quickly re-discovers that a specific response or emotion, for example anger, is simply not allowed to exist. It consequently re-learns to repress what it has found difficult to deal with in its past lives, and ultimately does not even notice it. Nevertheless, not to acknowledge one's unacceptable facets does not make them vanish into thin air. Anger which has been ignored, for example, will remain located deep within the psyche or stored in the physical body as 'dis-ease'. And, from time to time, given sufficient stimulation, it will surface, countered by such thoughts as: 'This is not me, I am not like this.' Part of the lesson to be learnt from Saturn is to acknowledge that: 'Yes, this is me, I can tolerate and accept the darker side of myself.' These are Saturn's great gifts: the possibility of integration and the inner strength which follows acceptance of the totality of the Self.

Pluto

Pluto in the first house indicates that the soul has incarnated with the expectation of trauma, intensity and issues relating to death, as does the Scorpio Ascendant. A woman with Pluto exactly conjunct her Leo Ascendant was hypnotized and taken through the conception-to-birth experience. Contrary to her expectation of being a soul lightly attached to the foetus from conception onwards, she found that she had been instantly compressed to the size of a pinhead and held in the womb. She experienced gestation as a traumatic imprisonment, acutely aware of her mother undergoing the emotional frustration of an unfulfilling, wartime marriage. Towards the end of the pregnancy she endured an intense feeling of constriction and suffocation, and a long process of fighting to begin the birth. Her mother was deeply Plutonian and held on to her until the birth became a very real power struggle and a survival issue.

Many incarnating souls with Pluto or Scorpio on the Ascendant face the issue of death through the loss of a parent, sibling or grandparent, either whilst *in utero* or during childhood. It is part of the Plutonian lesson of the need to let go. Death may also be faced more directly, either at birth or during the early years of incarnation through a life-threatening illness. The soul may also have to deal with rejection, abandonment, guilt and resentment at a very early age. Usually unspoken, but nevertheless clearly heard, the parental message often is: 'If you did not exist, I would be free to be something different,' or 'I am trapped within this situation,' a message which induces guilt, and resentment in the child, triggering an old pattern. Pluto on the Ascendant indicates that the soul is also peculiarly open to abuse by one or both parents. Abuse can be defined as: 'Any behaviour that is designed to control and subjugate another human being through the use of fear, humiliation and verbal or physical assaults.'[2]

Pluto – in any house – has the lesson of finding, and owning, its own power and authority. In the first or twelfth house the incarnating soul may in the past have misused, abused or given away that power. Now it is time to reclaim it and use it wisely.

Pluto on the Ascendant of the mother and an exact Pluto/Uranus/ Virgo Ascendant conjunction of the child to the mother's Chiron featured in a birth by vacuum extraction after the mother's contractions had almost ceased and the baby's heart was slowing. Both were near to death (Pluto). The baby had been conceived during a civil war (Uranus) and the mother had been coping with the breakdown of her marriage. The child had incarnated with the expectation that birth would be life-threatening and that the world was, in any case, an unsafe, unpredictable place to be (Pluto/Uranus). This was reinforced both by the toxic state (Pluto) of her mother's body (Virgo) and the way in which she herself was suddenly sucked out into the world (Uranus). She also had an eighth house Saturn opposing the Moon, showing an in-built expectation of rejection and isolation. Owing to the trauma of her birth, she had to be cot-nursed for forty-eight hours and was denied the comfort of physical contact with her mother. The family moved house constantly during her childhood and she experienced continual disruption in her environment. Her father died early and she was briefly abused by her stepfather. However, she overcame her difficulties around power and abuse, learning to own her power whilst still young. She was then able to move on to dealing with her other karmic lessons, and to face the prospect of change and growth with equanimity.

Uranus

The incarnating soul who is attuned to the vibration of Uranus, or the Aquarian Ascendant, expects to meet chaos and disruption and needs constant stimulation and acceptance of itself as an individual, rather than conventional mothering, which is usually experienced as smothering. It is naturally independent and anticipates nurturing that will support its urge towards self-determination and individualization. Its karmic lesson is to evolve steadily, rather than undergo periodic revolution and total change as its means of growth.

Jupiter

With Jupiter, or the Sagittarian Ascendant, the soul incarnates trusting the process of growth and expecting good nurturing from the cosmos. It has an inherent faith and optimism in this process, which can overcome poor nurturing from its biological parents. The incarnating soul may well have within the family one person, a grandparent or aunt, for example, who will ensure that it receives the nurturing it needs.

The lesson for Jupiter is that of disciplined expansion into fullest consciousness and integration of all the parts of its being into a totality of Self and God. It must recognize that ultimately there is no separation, but for Jupiter, unlike for Neptune, this is a process of expanding awareness, a function of Self-awareness not self-immolation. Neptune is one with the cosmos and unconscious of separation. Jupiter is one with the cosmos, encompassing both separation and integration, whilst maintaining its own integral state of Being.

Personal Planets in the First House

The Ascendant (see Chapter 3) and the personal planets also indicate how the soul will meet incarnation, and describe the dominant energy in its interaction with the environment. For the Sun development of the ego or the Self is paramount; Mercury works through the mind and understanding; Mars meets its challenges with courage, impatience or anger, Venus with an urge towards unity and harmony.

The Moon

The Moon carries with it the opportunity to learn the twin lessons of mothering and emotional equilibrium. A young man incarnated with Capricorn on the Ascendant (conjoined by twelfth house Chiron). The Moon in Aquarius in the first house opposed Venus in Leo in the seventh, forming a T-square to Saturn in Scorpio in the ninth. He was an unwanted, unplanned pregnancy and he was the third child in four years born to a middle-aged mother. His father had left home some days before his birth, but was forcibly brought back by his mother. Shortly after his birth his mother experienced severe post-natal depression (Saturn square the Moon) and entered hospital, returning there periodically over the next four years so that his early nurturing was intermittent and on the whole poor (the expectation of the Capricorn Ascendant). His Aquarian Moon indicated detached, unpredictable and unstable mothering and yet, paradoxically, he was deeply attached to his mother, living with her until his thirties. He was unable to break away from what had become a suffocating bond formed through fear, isolation and idealization (Mercury/Venus square Neptune/Saturn opposing the Moon). He was, initially, very much disliked by his elder brother and sister, who blamed him (a Capricorn scapegoat) for the 'loss' of their mother, teasing and tormenting him throughout his childhood. The children were brought together by the early death of the father, but, even as adults, they remained fixed in a pattern of childish interaction. He had incarnated with an inner sense of worthlessness and lack of confidence (Saturn–Moon) which was reinforced by his uterine and childhood experiences, and the development of a repressed personality. The emotional impact of these experiences was internalized – at one point in his childhood he was hospitalized for chronic constipation, a psychosomatic manifestation of his inner constriction. At the age of eleven he became a Buddhist, finding his nourishment and sustenance in his contact with the cosmos (Sun conjunct Jupiter trine Neptune), and rejecting worldly matters (wide Saturn/Neptune conjunction, ninth and eighth houses). In his mid-thirties he underwent the progressive transits of Saturn–Uranus–Neptune to his Sun, Jupiter and Mars, which enabled him to overcome the past conditioning and to leave 'home'.

EMOTIONAL EXPECTATIONS

The incarnating soul's emotional experience in previous lives will colour its interactions in the present and is mapped out in the aspects between the inner and outer planets. On the whole the 'easy' aspects tend to manifest as slightly less intense or difficult experiences, but much will depend on the stage of consciousness reached by the incarnating soul, on how much it sees itself as at the mercy of 'fate' and on how much awareness it has of its inner dynamics. When it recognizes that it is creating its own reality, the aspects are likely to manifest as more internally centred experiences leading to psychological and spiritual changes. It may be necessary for the soul to reconnect to a particular feeling or emotion, to reiterate its past experience and to accept it as its own before it can let go of it. In such a case the experience may be intense, but it may also be short-lived as acceptance will bring release, integration and change.

It must, of course, be borne in mind that the planets and the aspects represent the part of the psyche which derives from the past-life experience, and although the word 'soul' has been used to describe the principle which carries these patterns, it should perhaps more properly read 'the part of the soul'. It is necessary to examine all the aspects in the chart in order to ascertain the underlying emotional 'themes' which may be in conflict with one another. For example, the Moon square Saturn in Capricorn and Mercury/Venus in Virgo both carry constriction on expressing the emotions. On the other hand, the North Node/Sun in Cancer in the same chart would have a deep need to explore and express the emotions. The different energies represented by the planets and their aspects are experienced as warring factions within the psyche which battle for domination. The incarnating soul's behaviour at any one time will depend upon which faction is in ascendency over the others, but the overall behaviour patterns will present all the underlying themes.

Saturn Aspects

Aspects of Saturn indicate old patterns of constriction and repression, of long-standing inadequacy and fear.

Saturn–Sun

An aspect of Saturn to the Sun is indicative of an inner lack of self-esteem arising out of a fundamental block on the sense of Self and its worth and value. This frequently manifests through an early experience of emotional coldness from, or loss of, a parent, usually the father, and a lack of validity of itself connected to the old pattern which gives the message: 'I have no value, I might as well not exist.' The soul lacks confidence and is unable to express emotional warmth as it has not had the vital experience of receiving unconditional love and affection. Its energies are channelled into its inner defences against deep feelings of vulnerability and into its outward need to succeed to prove to the world that: 'I am here, I do exist, I have worth and substance.' At some point in its journey this soul will have to meet its 'shadow' and integrate all that it has denied for so long into itself.

Saturn–Moon

For Saturn in aspect to the Moon the difficulty tends to lie in obtaining nurturing and affection from the mother. The incarnating soul lacks self-esteem and a sense of self-worth. It makes the assumption that it is unlovable, and experiences a deep constraint in relation to feelings or emotions. The past-life pattern is one of emotional isolation and difficulty. The soul is cut off from the emotional nourishment of the family because it does not know how to receive it, and the family into which it incarnates may well also not know how to give it. It yearns for love like a small child, but is unable to make the contact or feel the warmth needed for mutual interaction. It will often settle for a 'safe' relationship rather than risk exposing its vulnerability.

The soul may also not 'fit' into the family as a result of having had a very poor, or no, previous contact with family members. Liz Greene[3] points out that this aspect has to learn that the security of family ties is an illusory one, the only security being within oneself. It also has to recognize, as a way of moving into interaction with the wider family of man that: 'The bond that links your true family is not one of blood, but of respect and joy in each others life. Rarely do members of one family grow up under the same roof.'[4]

A client with a Saturn/Moon/South Node conjunction in Cancer in the fourth house conceived a child during the Second World War, following the death of her first husband, at a time when she was destitute and homeless. The child, a girl, had to be adopted although the mother later married her father and brought up his teenage children. The mother incarnated with the expectation that mothering would be a source of sorrow and difficulty to her, anticipating rejection (Saturn/Moon/South Node), and she needed to learn to let go of her child, overcoming past possessiveness and a tendency to 'smother' (fourth house Cancer Moon). She had also incarnated with six planets in the twelfth house, including Chiron, and was working on her karmic issues in a very intense way.

When the client's daughter was thirty her adoptive parents died and she traced her mother. The daughter had Moon in Virgo semi-sextile eighth house Saturn, tenth house Neptune square Venus, and Chiron inconjunct the Sun. She also had four planets in the seventh house, indicating that she had considerable relationship karma. Her tenth house Neptune expected elusive mothering and her eighth house Saturn had karma regarding how she shared herself with others. The daughter already had a young child and shortly after meeting her mother again she gave birth to a son. She went into severe post-natal depression and rejected him, and he was subsequently fostered, made a ward of court and eventually adopted. The daughter 'remained in torment, unable to love or make meaningful relationships'. The mother 'tried to help, but was filled with guilt and could find no solution'. At a later stage the daughter refused to see her mother.

Her mother asked whether this was karmic restitution. The interaction between the charts was not heavily karmic, and showed very few contacts. There were personal planets to Uranus interaspects, indicating a freedom/commitment dilemma, and reflecting the daughter's own Sun/Uranus conjunction opposing Jupiter – an aspect which indicated that she may well have grown and expanded rather more through her adoptive parents than her biological ones. A Neptune square to the mother's Moon indicated illusions, guilt, and perhaps idealization of mothering. Saturn opposes Uranus, a change/maintenance dilemma. It appeared as though the daughter had needed to learn a karmic lesson about relationships and had chosen a mother who expected to 'lose' her child, but not a mother with whom she had intense personal karma to work out. With the Sun inconjunct to Chiron it also appeared that she may have had direct karma with the father, although this was not explored as he was dead and the mother was more concerned with the immediate effect of the interaction and the prospects for the future. She found it very difficult to accept that, having once given up her child, the child should return to her and then reject her. This, however, was the expectation and lesson expressed in her Saturn/Moon/South Node which needed to move beyond the confines of the biological family and into a wider understanding of the meaning of relationship. It was also possible that, through the unconditional love offered by the Neptune–Moon interaspect and the empathy from her own experience, she could in time help to heal her daughter's wounds.

Saturn–Mercury

Saturn in aspect to Mercury incarnates with a fundamental difficulty in communicating itself to others. The soul may feel that it lacks intellect or a quick intelligence, or it may reflect very fixed patterns of thought from the past in which it may have experienced perceptual, speech or hearing blocks. It therefore can find communication within a relationship difficult and may incarnate into the kind of family in which children are 'seen and not heard', in which great emphasis and value is laid on 'intelligence' and 'ability', rather than on who the child *is*; or in which individual expression is discouraged or forced into a channel unnatural for that soul. The soul must learn to communicate itself out to the world and to express its own unique self in its interaction with others, as a way of valuing both who it is and what it has to say.

Saturn–Venus

With Saturn in aspect to Venus the soul can have an inherent sense of unlovableness. Because of its past experience, it does not believe it can be loved and it may also feel deeply vulnerable and open to pain through the emotions. It tends to incarnate into a family which will support that perception of itself and experience emotional deprivation and very conditional 'loving'. As a result, it may well retreat into being 'good' in order to obtain what passes for love. Again it is an aspect with which the soul may well settle for 'safe' relationships. Its links with 'prostitution', whether actual or metaphorical, have already been discussed in Chapter 4.

Saturn–Mars

Saturn in aspect to Mars experiences a very fundamental block on its Will (see Chapter 1), often incarnating into a strongly repressive, controlling family with no room for individuality or personal choice. The soul's underlying feelings are helplessness, powerlessness and frustration, with an inability to follow its own pathway. A child with such a placement may well experience violence, physical or verbal, from one or other parent. This experience will then intensify its inability to assert itself in any way, and ultimately will push the soul into lessons centred around aggression, assertion and the use of the Will.

Pluto Aspects

The karmic lessons for Pluto centre around power, symbiosis and separation and long-held feelings of guilt, resentment and rage, as well as underlying issues of rejection and abandonment. As Susan Forward points out: 'Parental love is the only kind of love in which the ultimate goal *must* be separation.'[5] However, for many incarnating souls who are attuned to Pluto the insidious strangulation of the psychic umbilical cord pervades relationships far into 'adulthood'. Mother, or Father, takes on the archetypal role of dominance and authority, acquiring the willing or unwilling projection of power from the child who must later struggle to regain it for itself.

Pluto–Sun

Aspects of Pluto to the Sun involve overt power struggles with the image, if not the actuality, of Father in order that the incarnating soul may regain its lost power. A client, a twin, (Sun in Gemini inconjunct Neptune and square Pluto) was most concerned about her fear and dislike of her father. She described a 'creepy feeling' about him and was sure that he had abused her as a very young child. Now in her twenties she was still experiencing 'interference' from him in the form of a strong mental power over her and deliberate participation in her dreams. Her twin did not experience difficulties to the same extent and she had married and become the powerful partner. It was suggested that both girls should work on cutting the ties with the father, particularly the one who first consulted me, as there were strong past-life links to him. Shortly afterwards she moved out of the family home, something she had found impossible to do prior to this despite her problems with her father.

This aspect is particularly difficult for women, who have traditionally handed over all their authority to a man: first father, later husband. They may well find themselves incarnating into families where powerful, authoritarian fathers still demand absolute obedience, with the consequent enfeebling of the soul's ability to exert itself, and risk of abuse of the child. Repressed rage and anger will then fester into resentment, an energy carried over into so-called adult relationships which may well in turn be abusive or parasitic.

The Pluto–Sun aspect can also indicate difficulties for a male in handling his power. The chart shown here (fig. 29) is that of a man who sued, in the English Courts, for restitution of conjugal rights. His 'split off' first house Pluto in Cancer opposing seventh house Sun in Capricorn indicates power issues manifesting through a relationship. In spite of winning his case, he did not win his power struggle as he discovered that although she had been ordered by a judge to do so, his wife was not going to resume marital relations willingly.

He incarnated with various karmic patterns which led him to believe, unconsciously, that he would find relationships difficult and to anticipate a power struggle. Outwardly he was very confident, but his confidence failed to result in fulfilling relationships. The message contained in the out of element Grand Trine of Chiron/Jupiter–Neptune–Saturn/Moon and the Neptune opposition to Venus is a very mixed one. His Moon conjuncts Saturn, indicating a poor self-image, constriction on emotions, and expectation of inadequate nurturing. His Moon is in Sagittarius and, as his wife pointed out, he may have won control over her body, but her mind and her Self did not have to be involved in the sexual transaction. His Moon/Saturn opposes

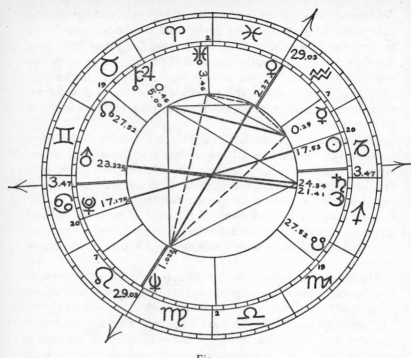

Fig. 29

twelfth house Mars, indicating a Will conflict which leaves him feeling inwardly powerless, as well as an anxiety about his own potency and adequacy in sexual relationships – which he took to a judge (Saturn) for confirmation of his 'authority' (Capricorn Sun opposing Pluto). He also has a Neptune–Venus fourth–tenth house opposition which led him to both idealize and deceive women, particularly his mother. The 'split' pattern of the chart showed up clearly in his behaviour both as a child and an adult. He incarnated into the typical English upper-middle-class home where he reigned as tyrant in the nursery. Cared for by a nanny, he was shown briefly, suitably sanitized, to his adored and adoring mother before supper. She was totally deceived by his little-boy charm, never believing the stories his sisters, and later his wife,

252

told about his temper and autocratic behaviour. He was sent off to a boarding preparatory school at the age of seven, in conformity with his in-built expectation; there he encountered the usual bullying problems but quickly became the bully himself – the Sun–Pluto part of himself preying on the weak.

After his marriage finally ended he used his charm to enter into a pattern of living off women, virtually hypnotizing them into complying (Neptune–Venus) and he 'conned' several extremely intelligent women using flattery and promises he had no intention of keeping. One of these women later commented that, looking back, she had no idea why she had been so infatuated as 'he was a once-a-week man and useless in bed!'.

Pluto–Moon

The power struggles involved in Pluto aspects to the Moon are more subtle and covert, but no less damaging, and are linked to very old traumatic experiences which programme the incarnating soul to expect to meet emotional issues such as rage and resentment, abandonment, rejection, and guilt which are carried over into both childhood and adult relationships. It is as though the incarnating soul carries a tinge of paranoia with regard to a certain powerful, but frequently unspecified, 'they' who are 'out to get me', 'won't let me be happy', etc., which causes the soul to metaphorically look over its shoulder in fearful apprehension whenever it is aware of things going well or of being happy. Pluto has great difficulty in letting go and also stores up resentments and hurts which can well up from the depths of the unconscious with a force which has nothing to do with the present-life trigger event. In particular these negative emotional expectations are linked to karma around mothering and being mothered which the Pluto–Moon soul anticipates will be life-threatening and devouring. The most appropriate symbol for the Moon–Pluto mother is that of the Indian goddess Kali who holds the power of life and death and many souls attuned to the Moon–Pluto energies face death in childbirth at some stage in their journey.

A woman was born into a family in which for at least five generations the Moon–Pluto women's husbands had died or disappeared, leaving them to bring up the children and to look after their own elderly mothers. By the time she incarnated the pattern was beginning to change in that her father was physically, although not emotionally, present during her childhood. Whilst giving birth to her daughter, she was deeply unconscious and in danger of dying (Pluto conjunct Ascendant square to Moon in Scorpio). She experienced a spontaneous regression to a past life in which she was giving birth on a straw pallet in a hut. She had deliberately chosen to die in that incarnation as she could not face yet another mouth to feed in an already over-large family, worn down by grinding poverty. In the present incarnation she was told by the wise being who was with her at the birth that she had to decide whether to opt out or to deal with her karma. She chose life, and both she and her daughter survived although her husband died shortly afterwards and she brought up her daughter alone. Her daughter did not have the Moon–Pluto aspect in her chart, thus breaking the family pattern, although Pluto/Uranus was on her Ascendant, with a Saturn–Moon opposition also present in the chart. Later on in this life the mother met a man who told her he had been her son, but that she had abandoned him by dying young. She was regressed to several lifetimes where there were mothering difficulties. As Pluto began by transit to approach the Scorpio Moon she was told by psychics, palmists and astrologers that should she have a child, it would probably be handicapped or die. Determined to circumvent this, she was sterilized. On the first pass of Pluto over the Moon her daughter informed her she was pregnant. Her baby was stillborn; that Saturn opposition to the Moon had its own lessons to learn. Although she was not taking on her mother's karma, the latter did work through some of her own lessons by seeing her daughter suffer in this way. As a result of the baby's death, she had to face up to many issues she had, hitherto, been unaware of concerning separation: the symbiotic nature of Moon–Pluto contacts was illustrated by the fact that she started menstruating, in the middle of a cycle, as soon as the baby was born. On the final pass of Pluto over the Moon her own mother suffered a life-threatening, although not fatal, disease – issues of abandonment also lie buried deep within the Moon–Pluto contact – and at the same time her daughter conceived again.

*

The challenge with a Pluto–Moon aspect is to be creative, although not necessarily on a biological level. Many women with this pattern are expected to conform to what their mothers have always done and, although they may inwardly feel deeply rebellious, some comply. A considerable number of them are now, aged around thirty-five to forty, asking for readings as they have to face making a decision on whether to have children or not 'before it is too late'.

> Too often women get caught in a restrictive, single vision. Instead of realizing, a woman will concretize. Instead of admitting everything into her totality – waiting, accepting, ripening, transforming and being transformed – a woman will literally conceive and bear a child.[6]

These women have to break free from the past and from their mothers, or from archetypal expectations of women. When women perceive that there are different ways of becoming creative and that their karma may necessitate moving away from the biological level, new choices will open up together with the possibility of overcoming the old, destructive cycle. As the very act of birth can often be traumatic, it can bring up a great deal of the emotions and pain from the past which the Moon–Pluto carries. Pluto signifies that it will be hard to let go on many levels, but especially of the past. It has issues such as guilt to confront – particularly if Neptune aspects are also involved. This guilt is usually all-embracing, non-specific, and cannot be pinned to anything in particular. When analysed, this guilt is found to be partly related to the mother in the present life and partly to the soul's interaction with the mothering energies and emotions in past lives. Psychotherapy may be necessary to deal with this old pain, but the positive side of the Pluto–Moon contact is a healing of those old wounds in the psyche and a release of the inner creative energy.

The possibility of creating anew, without fertilization by external male energy, is one of the issues explored in the literature of the feminist movement:

Rites of Passage have turned inward where they can be lived out as stages of psychic transformation.

A woman need not literally have a daughter to bear witness to the mystery of continuity . . . a child is as much the offspring of the body of your imagination, the treasure hard to attain, as it is the blood fruit of your womb.

It is essential also to let these daughters of imagination go from you – there are mothers in myth who would kill their own children if they proved a threat to their own individuality and passion. It takes great strength to let go of a thing you have created: a child, a work of art . . . but the estrangement, the giving up, the separation are often necessary in order for something fundamentally new to emerge . . .

Perhaps that flowering of women, that gathering of women in our time who choose not to conceive literally, those who choose at a young age to be (paradoxically) *past* the age of childbearing, are those to whom the burden of a cultural labour has fallen. Like the vestal virgins who tended and carried the public fire, these women might be the bearers of a kind of illumination that we have not known before . . . [but] if the mothers who conceive of new forms of language and culture forget their connection to the body, to the real female depth of tissue, to the earth (their Mother), the life they create will be sterile.[7]

However, the impact of Moon–Pluto aspects is not restricted to girl-children. This combination represents the 'devouring mother' in all her awesome power, who will swallow her boy-child whole rather than allow him to separate from her. Roger Waters (Mercury and Moon quincunx Pluto, and Moon square Saturn) articulates the underlying fear of the Moon–Pluto aspect in the Pink Floyd song '*Mother*', in which he perceptively points out that mothers have a habit of making their children's worst nightmares come true. Susan Forward links the misogynist, the man who hates and abuses women, to this 'devouring mother' figure:

The mother who validates her son's striving for independence and encourages him to separate from her when he needs to, gives him some very important tools with which to deal with life. When the mother is willing to let her son establish his own identity, by permitting him to take risks on his own and by allowing him to make mistakes, yet being there for him should he need her, she helps to build a man who is confident about himself and his abilities.

The suffocating mother, on the other hand, restrains and constricts her son's development by over-controlling him and by making him feel inadequate and helpless.[8]

It is this symbiotic dependence in infancy, and beyond, which ultimately forces the incarnating soul to face up to the separation issues and the prospect of abandonment which so terrify it. If these issues are not confronted in childhood, they will arise on the death or loss of a parent, partner or child, propelling the soul back to explore roots either in helpless infancy, or beyond into the previous incarnations which have contributed to this desperate fear of letting go. The challenge for the Moon–Pluto soul is to own its creative power and find a new outlet for its emotional energies. It will then have great healing potential and be able to become a powerful force for transformation and regeneration.

Pluto–Venus

Incarnating with Pluto in aspect to Venus, the soul brings back an expectation of trauma in connection with relationships, and a deep need for intense emotional closeness. This is the emotional black hole which sucks in all the love and affection it can get and yet still demands more. It is 'insatiably greedy for emotional nourishment'[9] and will manipulate and vampirize in order to meet that need. Its old patterns of relationships have been predatory, symbiotic and demanding. It is not only in the sexual relationship that its manipulatory pattern is apparent. For example, clients who respond to my telling them how far down on my waiting list they are by pressurizing, however gently, for me to give them priority, or who ring, 'Just to see how you're getting on with my reading,' will inevitably have Pluto in aspect to Venus. As Stephen Arroyo points out this placement is 'prone to use one's attractiveness or friendliness to gain power, money, or simply to inflate one's ego.'[10]

The Pluto–Venus attuned soul must learn to totally change its way of relating, to fill itself up from the source of 'divine' love which emanates through the cosmos. This divine love will provide an endless source of the nourishment it craves and which no mere 'human' can provide in such abundance. The soul will then be able to give of itself, knowing that its own store of love will always be replenished. And in giving, it will also learn to receive.

Stephen Arroyo also mentions the repeating pattern of Pluto–Venus conjunctions or oppositions in which a fiancé or lover dies or disappears. I see this 'loss' as a characteristic of all Pluto–Venus aspects. At times the cause of the 'loss' is physical death, and at other times it is the death of a relationship which produces the grief and pain: it is as though the relationship cannot continue in its present form and, in order for the soul to learn a new, non-absorbing way of loving, it must learn to let go entirely of its old patterns of relating.

A woman with fifth house Venus in Āquarius opposing Pluto in Leo fell in love with a much younger man who was from a different cultural background. Their Moons were conjunct and she called him her 'soul friend' because they understood each other so well. There appeared to be an old contact between them but one which raised several issues aligned to her Pluto–Venus. Initially the relationship was wonderful, although it had to be kept secret as they were living in a Muslim country, but she did meet his family (in addition to the secretive Pluto energy, his Neptune sextiled her Venus, her Neptune squared his Mars). She arranged for him to get a job with prospects, which he had been unable to find for himself, but did not at the time realize that this was not acceptable to a proud Muslim man. He had a Grand Cross in his chart which indicated a conflict between his expansive ideas and ambition and his family duty: South Node/Sun opposing North Node/Jupiter, Moon/Pluto/Uranus opposing Chiron/Saturn. Her twelfth house Moon and Saturn conjuncted his Moon/Pluto/Uranus. They had planned to marry and go away to another country together. However, his father said that if he continued the relationship he would be cut off by his family. The young man chose his family, but she would not accept this decision and kept trying to see him and pressure him into seeing her again. Although she said that she understood that he had no cultural acceptance of marrying for romantic love, she still could not understand how the 'soul friend' with whom she had been so close could cut her off and 'become so cold'. She flew home and insisted on an immediate counselling session (Pluto–Venus). I suggested to her that she should practise cutting the ties with him, setting him free to be himself and allowing him to make his own choices. When she tried to image the two circles, with herself in one and him in another, tears rolled down her cheeks. She said that all she wanted to do was to be in the circle holding him. The Pluto–Venus aspect of herself could not let him go.

The Pluto–Venus attuned soul will often find itself in an addictive or co-dependent relationship and its lessons are epitomized in an Al-Anon handout aimed at abrogating the controlling nature of the alcoholic partnership. The lessons are, however, pertinent to all Pluto–Venus contacts:

> To 'Let go' does not mean to stop caring, it means I can't do it for someone else.
> To 'Let go' is not to cut myself off, it's the realisation I cannot control another.
> To 'Let go' is not to enable, but to allow learning from natural consequences.
> To 'Let go' is to admit powerlessness, which means the outcome is not in my hands.
> To 'Let go' is not to care for, but to care about.
> To 'Let go' is not to fix, but to be supportive.
> To 'Let go' is not to be in the middle arranging all the outcomes but to allow others to effect their destinies.
> To 'Let go' is not to be protective, it's to permit another to face reality.
> To 'Let go' is not to adjust everything to my desires, but to take each day as it comes and cherish myself in it.
> To 'Let go' is not to regret the past, but to grow and live for the future.
> To 'Let go' is to fear less and love more.

It is only through the pathway of loving more and loving unconditionally without strings, giving love without expectation or demand of it being returned, that the soul who is attuned to Pluto–Venus can grow beyond its 'black hole' and learn the true power of love.

Neptune

The old relationship pattern for Neptune is to have idealized, idolized, colluded, and sometimes deceived, rarely seeing itself or the person to whom it was relating clearly. The soul attuned to Neptune has a yearning to return to the more spiritually based relationships available in other realms, and can therefore be wide open to deception and disillusionment, both its own and that of another. At the first hint of a possibility of regaining that lost union, it sacrifices its individuality and willingly merges into the other. This is the planet of 'romantic love' based on cultural illusions and stereotypes and unrealistic expectations of eternal fidelity from a one-and-only soulmate. In its highest form Neptune represents a deep soul connection and unconditional love which just *is*, asking and expecting nothing, but unfortunately Neptune is also a master of disguise and all too often subtle control and assimilation of the 'beloved' lie at the heart of the Neptunian masquerade of 'love'.

Neptune–Sun

With the Sun in aspect to Neptune there tends to be idealization of the father, who may be seen as a god, and/or of a significant male, who may be weak and seemingly an inappropriate object of adulation. In such a case it could well be that the relationship is an old one and the attachment goes back to happier times. It may also be that the earlier relationship was a sexual one and that the closeness from that time has manifested in an inappropriate way in the present interaction. This is clearly seen in the child who is sexually 'abused' and yet perceives nothing 'wrong', or in the child who has to enter into collusion with the father to keep the secret of their closeness. This is a different kind of 'abuse' to that based on fear which is linked to Saturn and Pluto. In the case of Neptunian 'abuse' the child longs, on an inner level, for psychic closeness with the father which does not involve physical penetration. The relationship can, however, be emotionally or mentally incestuous and still be damaging in the sense that the child does not develop its own individuality. When the relationship with the father is finally severed, the child will seek the same closeness and merging into any partner, however unsuitable. He or she may fall into a pattern of relationships with 'weak' partners who need to be rescued and saved, and whom he or she believes will then be 'for my very own', with ultimate consequent disillusionment.

Neptune–Sun contact may also project this need for closeness on to a godlike figure and seek to merge into the divine. A woman with first house Neptune in Virgo conjunct South Node (an old pattern) sextile the Sun in Cancer was very aware as a child of having a spiritual vocation. She later entered a contemplative order and made the mystical marriage as a Bride of Christ. She remained in the convent for twenty years, but became conscious that her North Node was demanding she move into a physical relationship rather than spiritual: sacrifice and sublimation were no longer an appropriate life pattern for her. She left the convent and married a man she 'knew' from a past life: 'I recognised him from the back immediately and knew we were destined to marry.' She had a Moon in Virgo and found it difficult to enter fully into her emotional and physical levels of being. Her strong Pisces and Neptune energies still yearned for a more mystical contact and she also entered into a relationship with a guru god-figure who was 'always with her', much to the discomfort of her husband. With her strong Pisces energy she was able to handle with perfect ease the ambiguity of two such partnerships. Perhaps in so doing some of the idealization and unrealistic expectations which might otherwise have been projected on to her husband were channelled into a more constructive, spiritual outlet.

Neptune–Moon–Venus

The idealization for both the Moon and Venus in aspect to Neptune is of the feminine and the mother. The soul incarnates with impossibly high expectations of 'mothering' and 'love', seeking nothing less than perfection. The tendency, particularly for the male, is to place the mother, and later the desired sexual object, on to a pedestal, almost worshipping her: literally idolizing her. Such a 'desired sexual object' may be totally inappropriate. One client expressed this as 'a tendency to put any old slag on to a pedestal and refuse to let her get off no matter what she does'. The women he chose 'to worship' were almost always incapable of a close and loving relationship, a fact which safely prevented him from having to enter into actual relationship and thereby 'soil' the memory of mother and the feminine which his past-life and childhood training had taught him to regard as sacred, non-sexual beings.

Similarly, a young woman was quite happy to have promiscuous relationships with men she did not love (twelfth house Neptune inconjunct seventh house Venus), but not to have sex with the man she loved and married 'because it would spoil everything'. She had been brought up by a mother who herself had an unavailable 'fantasy lover', who she said was her spiritual soulmate, and yet was married to a man with whom she had sex to procreate. The child had absorbed the mother's romantic yearning for a love totally devoid of sexual contact, a yearning which reflected her own old pattern of the inconjunct – particularly in connection with a previous Cathari existence during which she had renounced sex.

The contact may also carry over a memory of a time when it had a particularly blissful relationship with the present-life mother, possibly as lover or beloved. When there is no disillusionment and separation from the mother in childhood, the soul carries this unrealistic expectation of perfection and merging into marriage or other relationships – and is usually deeply disappointed. The soul yearns for the romantic, mystical union which masquerades under the name of 'love'. It is of course very difficult to have a physical relationship with a 'goddess', and great disillusionment is felt whenever the idolized object behaves in any way which is not 'perfect'. Such an unrealistic vision of 'woman' may have been carried over for many incarnations and throughout several different types of experience. Just as the nun became the Bride of Christ, so monks and priests, needing a focus for their sublimated sexual energies, enter into relationship with 'Mary, the Mother of God' or the 'Mother Church', both of whom epitomize perfection.

A soul incarnating into a female body prior to the Christian faith may have experienced 'religious prostitution' in which she would offer her body to any man in order to enter into union with the divine, or may have kept herself chaste as a priestess of the goddess. In some ancient cultures it was obligatory for a woman to seat herself at the temple and wait until a man wished to have sexual union with her. For the young and attractive this presented little problem, but some women may well have waited many years, bringing their consequent sense of rejection and unacceptableness to 'god' forward into the present incarnation (this may also may be reflected through Venus–Saturn aspects).

Romantic, Neptunian notions of love were also present in the Troubadour chivalrous or poetic relationships, expressing 'Courtly Love' in which a woman was 'loved' devotedly but never physically, there being a total divide between 'sacred' – spiritual – and 'profane' – sexual – love. They may manifest in the type of marriage in which the woman is seen as pure and untouchable, and prostitutes are utilized to take care of the partner's physical needs, or in the relationship which is never consummated for one reason or another, and in 'happy-ever-after' fairy stories or Mills and Boon books.

Difficulties may be encountered when the soul has been involved in an ancient mystical marriage and incarnates expecting to be joined in relationship on all the levels of being. Unless the soul consciously and carefully chooses its partner, with full awareness of all the underlying 'shadows' and projections, it is open to disillusionment. However, if the soul does meet its spiritual match then the relationship becomes a way to achieve union with the divine, and as such a valid pathway for spiritual growth.

Uranus

Souls attuned to the vibration of Uranus incarnate with a need for space, a recognition of their own unique individuality, and with lessons to learn concerning commitment. Early relationships may therefore be difficult for the soul with a strong Uranus attunement unless it has specifically chosen Uranian, Aquarian, or Air/Fire parents who are able to tolerate this need for difference.

Aspects to Uranus are often seen in the charts of children who are autistic or who have emotional difficulties caused by a reluctance to fully incarnate on all levels. The lesson the incarnating soul may have to learn is one of individuality and separation, following too many experiences of symbiotic interaction (Uranus in Taurus or Cancer, for example). On the other hand, it may need to learn how to interact with others, taking account of individual difference and yet recognizing the deeper level of interconnectedness (Uranus in Libra or in aspect to Neptune, for example). Its lesson may also involve separation from the father (aspects to the Sun) or mother (aspects to the Moon) or the beloved (aspects to Venus) – which may be linked either to the particular soul who has incarnated as 'parent' or 'beloved', or to the archetypal parental energies.

PARENTAL KARMA AND FAMILY INTERACTION

The Parental Fifth House

Karma with the parents can be ascertained from an examination of the fifth house in the parental charts, which will indicate the expectation the parents have incarnated with regarding their children. For example, a father with fifth house Saturn may either look on the child as a burden, an onerous responsibility, or as a creation to be valued and cherished. The mother with a fifth house Saturn may long for a child for several years before she conceives, or may feel inadequate and fear the responsibility. Much will depend on the aspects and on the sign in which Saturn is placed, the type of parenting received by the parent, and the earlier incarnations. Saturn in Capricorn in aspect to the Sun, for example, may indicate a 'responsible' attitude, but the fear of inadequacy may lead to authoritarian parenting. With Saturn in Cancer the soul may long for a child but experience considerable difficulty in becoming a parent, or lose a child, in order to change an old 'smothering' pattern of mothering.

A woman with Mars in Pisces in the fifth house incarnated with an expectation of conflict with a child, and illusions, instability and restriction around mothering (tenth house Neptune opposing Moon/Uranus in Capricorn. Her daughter (twelfth house Moon conjunct Saturn/Sun/Uranus and a fourth house Pluto) anticipated rejected and separation from the mother as they had past-life karma to resolve. They quarrelled violently (mother's Pluto conjunct daughter's Mars). The mother's Aries Saturn conjoined the daughter's North Node and her Neptune opposition to Moon/Uranus squared the daughter's nodal axis.

Her daughter did not meet her self-centred expectations of how her child should act, and she was totally unforgiving as a result. The daughter had to learn to nurture herself and provide her own emotional sustenance. The past-life contact had also included a violent confrontation and this had been carried forward into the present interaction. Although the daughter very much wanted to resolve the karma between them, all she could do was to practise the spiritual discipline of forgiveness and absolve herself from adding further to the cycle of cause and effect. She could not force her mother to accept or reciprocate the forgiveness, but she could offer her unconditional love and remain open to the possibility of one day healing the wounds between them.

The Sun and Moon

In the child's natal chart, the Sun and Moon will give an indication of the type of karma it will have to face with its parents and show how it will experience them. A Sun–Moon opposition, quincunx or square, for example, will delineate parents, or parental archetypes, fundamentally at odds with each other, whereas the conjunction, trine or sextile will indicate parents who are basically in harmony.

A twelfth house Moon is indicative of strong karma with the mother. The sign on the cusp, and aspects, will give a description of past conditions and of how the karma emerged. Scorpio, for example, has traumatic memories of being mothered and may need to heal old wounds with the mother. Libra or Gemini, on the other hand, may indicate that in the past the mother was a friend and that she has now chosen to undertake a greater closeness and responsibility.

A seventh house Sun or Moon indicates that a father or mother and child were, in a former life, husband and wife. Aspects to the Sun and Moon, and the sign on the seventh house cusp, will clarify the type of karma involved in the relationship and the ease, or otherwise, with which it will be resolved. This past-life sexual interaction between parent and child can cause difficulties such as physically incestuous or abusive behaviour – the father feels it is his 'right' to use the child sexually and to use violence to 'control' the child – or emotional incest between a son and a possessive mother who deeply resents any other woman in his life, particularly on the sexual level. A homosexual man with the Sun in the seventh house, opposing Neptune, was very close to his mother and told her, as a child, that he had been her husband in the past – not that he would marry her when he grew up, which is the fantasy of many little boys. He could not bear the thought of 'loving' any other woman and his mother was extremely jealous of the few girls he dated in his teens. However, they were both happy when he started a sexual relationship with another man.

Synastry between Charts

Synastry between the parental chart and the child's chart will highlight karmic issues, old interaction and plans for the present life. **In assessing these interaspects it is important to bear in mind that either person can 'act out' the role of the outer planet, and that roles may change or reverse as the child matures.**

Jupiter Interaspects

Jupiter aspects between the charts to the personal planets or the angles indicate a basic trust between the souls which comes from a long association and which can mitigate the effect of other, difficult aspects; even if the contact or relationship is onerous, there is still a sense of 'rightness' about it coming from the deeper levels. The interaction will help the incarnating souls to open up and grow in some way. It may be that the parent incarnates with the intention of assisting the growth of the child, or that the child will expand the parent. Jupiter is linked to faith, not religious belief, and knows that it is in exactly the right place, at the right time. It accepts that it is learning the lessons it most needs for its soul growth. This sense of basic rightness can explain why, having experienced a 'deprived' childhood, some souls might not be as severely impaired in emotional functioning as others who have experienced less hardship.

This contact has been particularly noted in the synastry between the charts of handicapped children and their parents in cases where the latter seek understanding of the child's need to incarnate under difficulties, and value the child despite the handicap. They do not grieve for 'the child who might have been', as often happens with Saturn aspects, but rather seek to make the most of what *is*. The Sun or Ascendant of the handicapped child in these cases will almost always fall on the Jupiter of a parent, and the child's Jupiter may well fall on a personal planet in the parent's chart. When exploring the karmic interaction of these souls, it should be remembered that there is always a close spiritual tie and a deep desire to assist in *mutual growth*.

Saturn Interaspects

Saturn aspects to the personal planets between the charts indicate an old debt or sense of duty which is being repaid, either by the parent or the child. The difficulty is that the debt may surface as a deep sense of responsibility which is restrictive and repressive, particularly when an angle of a chart is involved. Issues of control versus self-determination may have to be dealt with. The parent may wish to control the child in order that past mistakes made by either of them may not be repeated. The parent in the Saturn contact is often unable to accept 'failure' or to see that 'mistakes' can be a basis for growth. On the other hand, the parent can guide the child on to a pathway of self-development and self-discipline by applying sufficient discipline and giving the right balance of freedom to choose. The child who feels that it has a debt to repay may well take on the burden of an elderly or chronically sick parent, or accept financial responsibility for the family by way of 'repayment'.

*

A child may experience apparent rejection from the Saturnine parent, a pushing into separation which the child may need but may not feel ready to accept. A woman with fourth house Saturn conjunct her mother's Sun was an unwanted late child – a fact she was always acutely aware of. At the age of fourteen she was sent away from home to work in a hotel. She only saw her parents once a month but sent her wages home each week because she felt she had to. Much later, as she was caring for her infirm mother to whom she had grown very close, she came to recognize that, far from rejecting her, her mother had been offering her what she saw as a 'good' future, a way out of the poverty trap which had dogged her family all her life.

Uranus Interaspects

Uranus contacts to the personal planets indicate a freedom/commitment or control dilemma. It may be that the old contact was one of too much control and that the soul now needs to recognize and acknowledge the other's unique individuality and need for freedom. On the other hand, the parent may in the past have failed to take on responsibility for the child and now have to make a commitment. This was apparent in the contact between a father and the child he had abandoned in a past life. In the present life he felt very strongly, when divorcing the child's mother, that he should be the one with whom the child lived.

Neptune Interaspects

Neptune contacts to the personal planets between the charts indicate an old closeness and a very subtle sense of wanting to care for the other soul to the extent of giving up one's life for it. This contact is very telepathic and can be utilized to 'talk' to the child on the mental level, a technique which can be extremely useful in conveying a sense of reassurance and safety or in ironing out difficulties. Problems can arise with Neptune when individual boundaries are not recognized, as for example, the parent expects the child – or the child the parent – to react as he or she does or has always done 'in the past'. Each person needs to continually check out: 'Am I hearing or understanding correctly?', 'Is my own expectation or ideal getting in the way?', 'Am I falling back into an old pattern which is no longer valid?'. Within these safeguards, there can be a loving communication on a soulmate level between parent and child.

Neptune can also be linked to an old pattern of collusion – entering into another person's distortion of 'reality' – and delusion, as in the case of a mother who felt a very old connection with her sensitive son, whom she always 'protected' from his father. She had a Venus in Pisces opposition to Neptune, squared by the son's Sun. Her Chiron opposed his Moon in Scorpio. The son had Mars conjunct Neptune in Libra in the first house T-squaring the fourth and tenth houses (Capricorn–Cancer) Chiron/North Node opposite Uranus/South Node. His mother's twelfth house Moon conjoined his Neptune/Mars and her Uranus opposed it, her Mercury conjuncted his Chiron/North Node and her Pluto in Cancer his Uranus/South Node. Her karmic Grand Cross contained powerful mothering issues and his interaspect T-square contained both pain (Chiron), escapism (Neptune/Mars) and the possibility for transformation (Uranus). Neptune acted powerfully upon both mother and son. Having found out that her son, then aged thirty, was taking drugs it took her a long time to assimilate the knowledge. Once she had adjusted to the fact that he was smoking heroin she deluded herself for many months that he would not inject – 'he had always fainted at the sight of needles'. Eventually she had to believe the evidence of the marks on his arm. She then colluded with him in his drug-taking, supplying the money and 'controlling' the supply by giving a little less each day. Again it took her a long time to recognize that he was supplementing her 'controlled dose' by buying more and taking sleeping pills. She arranged for him to go to an out-patient clinic and again tried to control his use of methadone by doling it out each day. This time he resorted to a 'chronic cough' and codeine linctus to supplement the dose.

At one point the mother attended a 'Cutting the Ties' weekend group seminar. Half-way through cutting the ties with her son, she 'fell asleep' but told no one. A few days later her navel was raw and bleeding – she had been in the middle of removing an umbilical cord the thickness of a tree trunk which joined her to her son when she had lost awareness. She commented afterwards that she had not felt right about what she was doing as she believed she was cutting off the love he needed rather than the old emotional conditioning between them. It took over two hours of one-to-one work to finish that cutting, and she then slept for fifteen hours. Shortly after that he did enter a clinic as an in-patient but refused to stay as he 'did not need all that head-stuff'. Five years later neither he nor she had yet recognized that he was an addict – now to alcohol – and that she could not 'do it for him'. She found herself unable to use the 'tough love' of Chiron which may just have precipitated him into the crisis he needed in order to find the motivation to deal with his escape from 'reality' – a deep-seated pattern in his chart.

Pluto Interaspects

Pluto aspects to the personal planets in the other chart indicate dependency/independence issues centred around power, manip-ulation and separation. In the past one of the souls has been absorbed by the other, often as a parent/child relationship in which the umbilical cord was never cut (Moon), or the parent had strong power over the child (Sun). A Pluto contact to Venus may indicate old lovers, Pluto to Moon a particularly symbiotic or devouring mothering interaction, and Pluto–Mars an old aggres-sive relationship. The interaction in the present life can include very subtle domination of the child through illness or apparent weakness, a domination which extends far into adulthood and pervades all attempts to have a relationship. It may either cause the incarnating soul to experience such difficulty in separating from the parent that it never enters into an adult relationship, or lead it to try to recreate with its 'adult' partner the patterns of its childhood. The man with Moon–Pluto aspects can, for example, coerce his wife into a mothering role, or the woman with Sun–Pluto aspects can unconsciously manoeuvre her husband into an authoritarian 'father' role. With this interaspect, both souls need to acknowledge each other's right to grow as an independent individual following its own pathway, in charge of its own power and destiny.

THE FOURTH–TENTH HOUSE AXIS

Planets in the natal tenth and fourth houses will show both 'good' and 'bad', positive and negative, contacts with the parents, and the type of parenting the incarnating soul can expect. Either house can equate to a parent, although the tenth house tends to indicate the mother when she is dominant within the family and represents the main source of interaction with the outside world for the child. Planets located in these houses can be linked both to a past-life type of parental interaction, and to the present experience. Once again, the manifestation of karma is subtle and complex and many factors need to be taken into account.

The Sun or Moon

When the Sun or Moon falls in the fourth or tenth house it is likely that the parent represented by that planet has been in the same relationship to the child before, i.e. the Sun indicates that the father has been the father previously, and the Moon that the mother has been the mother before. There is a repeating of the pattern, but the lesson may be to manifest more of the 'positive' energy of the sign in which the planet is situated. For example, if the Sun is in Capricorn then the parent may have been very authoritarian in the past life, and now has the opportunity to encourage the child's autonomy and self-responsibility. It is also possible that the parent may be taking on the opposite sex role to the one it has played before. (The Moon in Capricorn or Sun in Cancer, for example). This can lead to confusion over the role which that parent takes, as when the mother is the dominant parent, or to a 'role-swop' in which the parent takes on a role not usually associated with his or her sex. A baby born with fourth house Sun in Cancer to a Sun in Cancer father and mother was brought up by his father whilst his mother ran a restaurant business. His father gave up a successful career as a concert musician because he wanted to have the experience of nurturing his child. His mother needed a wider experience of nurturing.

*

With the Sun in this placement the incarnating soul may also have to resolve karma carried over from a time when a parent was in a different relationship, but the same kind of issues arose. This was illustrated in the past-life dream of a client with the Sun and Jupiter in the fourth house opposition Mars in the tenth house forming a T-square to the Moon, with the Sun also squaring Pluto, so that there was a projection of her own power on to her father. (The chart is shown under 'Ancestral Karma' later in this chapter.) At the time the dream took place the T-square had been triggered by transiting Pluto, bringing to the surface old emotional trauma. The T-square suggested conflict and difficulties between the archetypal parental energies, but supportive parenting from the fourth house Jupiter:

Having worked with my dreams for five years, I recognised the following as a past life:

Eighteenth-century Europe – I'm married to a man who in this present lifetime is my father [fourth house Sun opposing Mars]. He is a rather weak character [tenth house Neptune] who inherited much wealth. He finds it hard to express his love towards me and I ridicule him [eighth house Pluto trine Mercury]. I'm a vivacious, proud women [South Node, Pluto and the Moon in Leo] who loves high society – I spend his money recklessly [Jupiter in Taurus] and take a string of young lovers which I flaunt in front of him [eighth house Pluto square to tenth house Mars].

A few months after this dream I spend Easter with my family. My father sees me to the bus stop – he has been very withdrawn all weekend which has irritated me [Sun–Mars opposition] and I rather reluctantly say goodbye to him. In return, he gives me a look of misery and hatred [Sun inconjunct Saturn] which touches a chord deep inside and I spend the whole bus journey in total fury. At home, I alternate between floods of tears and fury, and the next morning create a row at my local gym which nearly gets me banned! [Tenth house Mars projecting its rage out to the world.] I realise that I have to sort this out and ring him –

ready to tell him that if he ever looks at me like that again, I'll never see him again. However, I find that he was completely unaware of his actions [tenth house Neptune] and in fact was withdrawn after spending a week in hospital – his first stay in his life.

I realise that I had read meaning into the situation – I had recognised this particular look back to childhood, but now I could see it was beyond this [tenth house Mars opposing Sun]. It wasn't comfortable for me to recognise the pattern of this past life within my present life. I had had affairs with men younger than myself – relationships of little value [Sun inconjunct Saturn] which only lasted a few months [seventh house Uranus] and I have always expected my father to bail me out whenever I got into trouble financially [fourth house Sun square Pluto, eighth house South Node]. When I was able to thank him for all his financial support [fourth house Jupiter] and to share with him my experiences with men, my resentment and my judgemental attitude to his relationships with women disappeared. Acceptance on both sides has brought us closer, but at the same time there is now space between us.

Her karmic lesson, defined by the fourth house Jupiter in Taurus, the Taurean Sun square Pluto and the reversed nodal connection of second house Aquarius North Node, was to contact her own inner resources of security and power. She had been utilizing the personal manipulative power of the eighth house Leo South Node conjunct Pluto to gain support and sustenance from her father; it was now time to move into an era of self-sufficiency and self-responsibility aligned to the nurturing energies of the cosmos. She needed to parent herself, becoming an autonomous, self-supporting member of the extended family of mankind.

Mercury

Mercury in a parental house can indicate that in a previous incarnation the soul interacted with the present-life parent as

friend or sibling, and the sign on the cusp will describe that old
pattern. It may also be linked to intellectual or communication
karma with a parent, perhaps delineating a meeting or a clash of
minds. In Aries, for example, Mercury can be very self-
opinionated, full of its own ideas which may well clash with those
of a parent. If Mercury is in one of the Air signs, it is liable to
function more in accord with parental values and ideals. Mercury
in a Capricorn-attuned soul, particularly with difficult aspects,
may well find itself repeating a conflict with very fixed, old-
fashioned parental ideas. Where Mercury is afflicted, communication with the parents may be, or may have been, difficult or
distorted in some way – through hearing disorders, for example.

Venus

A soul incarnating with Venus in a parental house will, unless
there are difficult aspects, expect to incarnate into a harmonious
environment with people with whom it has experienced pleasant
past incarnations. Such a soul will choose, on the whole, parents
who will enable it to learn through a 'good' early relationship,
although with Venus in Scorpio, Taurus or Cancer it may experience an echo, or re-run of old jealousy and possessiveness. This
can surface in the child or parent who is jealous of the interaction
between other family members and may lead, for example, to an
intense rivalry between mother and daughter for the father's
attention. Such a case may indicate that the souls were old 'lovers',
and that this relationship is very close to the surface in the present
life. This was particularly noticeable in the chart of a child who
had fourth house Venus in Scorpio. Right from the moment of his
birth he would scream in rage whenever his father touched his
mother, whether in his sight or not. The parents' sexual relationship was being seriously disturbed by the child's evident
jealousy. As the mother had her Neptune conjuncting the child's
Venus, it was suggested that she should 'talk' to the child whilst he
was sleeping to assure him that he was much loved, but that their
old interaction as lovers was no longer valid. After a few weeks the
child settled down and accepted the relationship between his
parents.

Mars

Mars in this placement may indicate a violent or aggressive interaction with a parent in the past, and the soul may have issues of self-assertion or courage to work out this time around. There may also be unresolved Will issues coming forward, and the fourth or tenth house Mars may be linked to a past-life pattern in which there was a 'master/slave' type of interaction. Mars can also point to an issue with the masculine energy – possibly to the soul needing to integrate this into its experience – or to a reversal of roles, in that it has formerly been in male interaction with the parent(s) and now is dealing through the female gender or vice versa.

Jupiter

Jupiter in a parental house will expand the incarnating soul in some way, although there may be karma due to previous over-indulgence to overcome, particularly when Jupiter is in Taurus or a Fire sign. There may also be an old pattern of eating food for emotional comfort which has been established. A client with fourth house Jupiter in Taurus was reminded by a cousin of an incident which had occurred when she was still in a high chair. The older cousin had broken off a relationship and had come into the kitchen in a highly emotional state. A small voice had piped up from the high chair: 'Oh dear, she's crying. Give her a biscuit.' When the small child became an adult, she had a weight problem linked to depression and 'comfort eating'.

Jupiter in the parental houses can also indicate a past connection with a teacher or priest who is now a parent, especially if Jupiter falls in Sagittarius, Pisces or one of the Air signs. The parent may also be perceived either as a sage, a fount of all wisdom, or a mage, a worker of magic who is either revered or feared depending on the past experience.

Saturn

Saturn in the fourth or tenth house is indicative of former harsh disciplinarian parenting or of the lack of a father-figure; either way, the soul experiences an emotional coldness and distance which restricts and inhibits its self-development and throws the soul in upon itself. It may well experience being 'deserted' by a parent through death or divorce. For example, a client (fourth house Sun in Leo conjunct Saturn opposing the Moon) experienced the death of both parents in a car crash when he was two. He was brought up in an orphanage – an experience he much enjoyed, however, as it was a stable, extended family situation with disciplined but kindly house-parents.

On the occasions when Saturn is benignly aspected, it indicates an earlier experience of constructive discipline leading to self-control and self-confidence. Saturn can be the authoritarian or authoritative parent, the difference showing up in the aspects and sign energies: Capricorn is an example of the former, and Leo the latter. It can also be indicative of a past experience of, or the present-life need to take up, some kind of family responsibility related to position, inheritance or profession, for example. Such a duty may have been onerous and entailed giving up what one wanted for oneself.

Uranus

With Uranus in a parental house the soul incarnates with the knowledge that life is likely to be chaotic and full of change or that the parent is likely to be unreliable, unstable or unpredictable because that is how it has been in the past and, as always, what is expected is manifested. Mutable signs can cope easily with this and Cardinal signs are pushed into an early independence, but Fixed signs, which require more stability, may find it difficult and will adapt strategies designed to either control life and make it safe, or to stabilize the parent as far as possible. This is one of the placements with which the soul as a child either feels it necessary to always be at home, in order to ward off change or to be aware of it in time to 'cope' (Uranus in Taurus, Cancer or Virgo, for example), or seeks its freedom elsewhere at every opportunity (Uranus in Gemini or Sagittarius, for example).

Neptune

Neptune on the parental axis can indicate a long-standing over-idealization of the mother figure and the feminine or of the father and the masculine. The child may well experience the parent as an elusive figure who, whilst appearing close and loving, cannot be pinned down and never quite meets its emotional needs and expectations. This applies very much to the child who is brought up by a surrogate parent, often in the form of a nanny, or who experiences the mother or father as a rather unreal victim, martyr or saviour figure – one who may need to be saved, pitied or escaped from. It can also apply to the parent who escapes from reality into illness, drink or drugs, or to the image of such a parent brought back from the past, which prevents the child from trusting that it will receive the support and validation it requires for its development.

On the other hand, the Neptunian child may incarnate into a family in which the arts, music, poetry and the imagination are valued and encouraged as a means of self-expression, or in which its spiritual nature is concretized through an innate acceptance of other dimensions of reality.

Pluto

Pluto in this placement delineates a long-standing power struggle with a parent, frequently the mother, who may be dominant and manipulative. She may also be instinctual and deeply frustrated, trying to live out her unfulfilled desires through her family. The father may be strongly authoritarian, particularly when Sun or Saturn aspects are involved. The child can perceive the parent as all-powerful, even when this is not his or her innate nature. For example, a woman who was typically Sagittarian looked on her children as friends and thought she had encouraged them to grow and expand as much as possible. She did not appear, from outside the family, to be in the least dominant. However, all three of her children had Pluto in the fourth and experienced her as the significant parent. Her daughter commented that her mother was so good at 'feminine pursuits' that she found it hard to take them up herself, in case she could not live up to such a high standard. Her mother's response to this was that she 'just did it', it entailed no effort on her part, and she certainly had not realized that her daughter felt intimidated and inadequate. On further exploring the family dynamic it emerged that the mother had been the dominant and significant parent because she had had to be – her husband, a doctor, was away for long periods and they had been in any case divorced when the children were still teenagers. For many incarnating souls who have Pluto in the fourth house, however, this dominance can be experienced as soul-destroying, leaving a deep sense of inadequacy and resentment which is then carried over into the experience of being a parent.

SIBLING KARMA: THE THIRD HOUSE

The third house offers clues as to how the child will fit into the family. It also gives indications of karma with siblings and can illustrate the type of former interaction relating to that karma.

Mention has already been made of the fact that, with Neptune in the third, the soul almost inevitably seems to feel like an outsider in the family. In such a case the elements predominating in the chart are usually incompatible with those of the rest of the family; for example, a child with strong Air and Fire will feel totally alienated from 'Watery' parents and siblings. The third house Neptune may also have issues of deception and delusion with siblings. Compatible elements within the family will make for more harmonious functioning which can help to overcome other difficulties.

Both Uranus and Pluto in this house may, for different reasons, make the soul feel suffocated within the family and experience a need for freedom and space.

The Sun

The Sun in the third house signifies that the soul may well have been, in a previous incarnation, the parent of its present-life parent or sibling. It may be that unresolved authority issues are coming forward from that old interaction, which will create difficulties within the family, or that the incarnating soul may need to recognize itself as separate from the family and claim its individuality.

The Moon

Similarly, with the third house Moon the soul may have been the mother in the past or may find itself mothering its siblings or its parent. It may also have unfinished emotional business with the soul who is now its sibling. This was apparent in the third house Moon of a young woman who found it exceedingly difficult to image cutting the ties with her brother. The ties she perceived were sexual and emotional ones, coming forward from past lives. It was necessary to first explore that old interaction and to recognize what had been unresolved before the present-life 'negative conditioning', in the shape of inappropriate ties with her sibling, could be cut.

Mercury

Mercury in the third house indicates both karma with a sibling who is now repeating the same family interaction, and karma around how the mind and tongue have been used within the family in the past. The two may be linked, in that the sibling may have been 'injured' by unwise gossip or slander in the past, or may have been forced into a career or lifestyle which it did not seek — as in the case of the old family pattern in which one son is destined to inherit the estate, another to join the army, and another to enter the Church, etc.

Venus

Venus on the whole indicates a 'good' prior interaction with siblings which was both loving and harmonious, although this can depend on the sign placement. In Gemini or Libra, for example, the past contact may well have been that of good friends. Whenever Venus is in Scorpio or in aspect to Pluto there is always the possibility of old jealousies. Similarly, emotional games coming forward from the past can pertain to a Leo placement. It should also be remembered that a thwarted Venus can wage a war of attrition for past emotional pain from behind a façade of 'niceness', and that when this happens the old basis of the relationship may need to be explored before a conclusion can be reached.

Mars

Mars in the third house invokes the possibility of violent encounters between the present-life siblings in the past, with karma related to aggression and asserting featuring prominently in the past and present interaction. It is very much the placement of sibling rivalry and may indicate two souls who have previously been 'at war' with one another in some way. The child with this placement may have to learn to assert and 'stand up for' itself within the family as a preparation for interaction with the outside world.

Jupiter

Jupiter can indicate that in the previous interaction the siblings were priests or priestesses, linked in spiritual brotherhood, pupil and teacher or master and apprentice, and that they may have an innate trust in the 'rightness' of the family connection. On the less positive side, there may be karma related to the squandering of an inheritance or assets, as in the case of two business partners reincarnating together again in order to work out unfinished business concerning the misuse of company funds.

Saturn

When Saturn is in the third house there is almost always an issue around one sibling having had control over another. This may be a 'master and slave', prisoner and gaoler or teacher and pupil type of interaction, or an elder and younger brother conflict being re-enacted. The child may experience the family as cold and unwelcoming or unloving, undergoing alienation from, or rejection by, its siblings by virtue of age, its interests, etc. This placement may also indicate a child who becomes, or has been, responsible for its brothers or sisters, as in the case when a parent dies and the elder child brings up the rest of the family; the incarnating soul may carry the burden of, or actually be, a chronically sick sibling. This placement is often connected to a karmic theme of responsibility and self-image which manifests within the family and is then carried over into interaction with the outside world.

Pluto

Pluto in the third house will inevitably involve a power struggle with a sibling which may be overt or covert and which will reflect the past interaction. It may also experience rejection by the family or a symbiotic interaction which must be severed before the incarnating soul can find its own place in life. The roots of Plutonian karma are inevitably deep and difficult to ascertain, going back far into 'the past' and frequently involving death or destruction, domination and manipulation as an underlying theme of the interaction.

Ancestral Karma

There are times when a soul incarnates into a family not only to work on its own karma but also to deal with the ancestral patterns embodied in that family and perhaps to undertake a specific task. Fig. 30 is the chart of the woman whose karma with her father has already been discussed under the fourth house Sun section of this chapter. She found that she had to set free the soul of an ancestor on her mother's side in order to release the family karmic pattern. The planets around the outer rim of the chart are those of that ancestor on the day of her birth into the spiritual world, i.e. the date of her physical death – as it is from this plane of existence that the contact was made. The following is a verbatim account of the events which took place and of the consequent understanding of the family interaction:

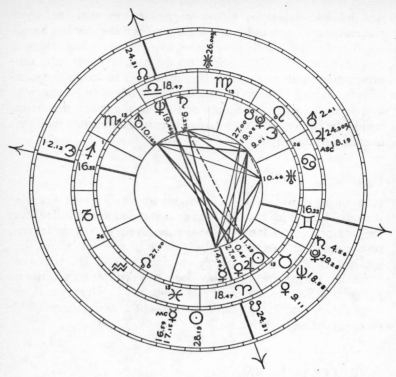

Fig. 30

On March 20th 1983 I arrived in Fermoy for the first time. I was thirty years old and manager of a rock band [Mercury/Venus opposition to Neptune/MC]. I'd been involved with the music business for seven years and was exhausted – inside I felt out of control with panic attacks and depression; within my job I sought to control everything, mainly in an underhand way [transiting Mars opposed eighth house Pluto in January and opposed Saturn and Neptune in March, Saturn is semi-sextile natal Mars] as I didn't have the self-confidence [Saturn inconjunct Sun and sextile Moon] to assert myself and wasn't in touch with my feelings enough [Venus opposing Neptune, Neptune quintile Moon] to know or express [Saturn opposing Mercury] what I really wanted. I had travelled to County Kerry to pick up a guitar and for a short break with a friend, Mary. On the way back to the ferry to England I mentioned I had relatives buried in Fermoy, so we made a detour. I drove straight through the town and parked by a small bridge. We walked into a wood by the river and up a bank to a ruined tower. On returning to England Mary showed me a picture she had painted many years previously of this exact spot. We visited a couple of graveyards but found no evidence of any ancestors, but then, at this point, I wasn't even sure of their name. We left Fermoy because Mary became suddenly giddy and faint, and was ill for the rest of the journey. On my return to England my mother told me this story:

Your great grandmother met and married your great grand-father in Jamaica and he was an Irish man from a Protestant family named Massy in Fermoy. His younger sister was in love with an English soldier and her parents forbade her to see him because he was from a lower, and therefore, unsuit-able, class. In the grief of the enforced separation, she died of pneumonia at the age of 25, after going out horse-riding constantly in her anger to get away from the situation at home.

Meanwhile my own life went from bad to worse and I attempted suicide in June which was rapidly followed by a change of heart [tr. Jupiter trine Moon in Leo] – and with the help of a homoeopathic doctor, Jungian analyst and astrologer, I moved out of the rock business and into the more gentle rhythm of inner exploration – a healing process had started which was to take five years, for I'd lived in such disharmony and turned so much anger inward [Mars in Scorpio opposing Sun, square Moon, semi-sextile Saturn] that I'd damaged most of my internal organs.

   That Christmas, an ageing uncle told Mary of her Irish ancestors – also Protestants from Fermoy, and in the sum-mer of 1985 we journeyed to Kerry for a long stay in a cottage by the sea. We passed through Fermoy and found the only Protestant graveyard. I found one Massy grave and Mary found one of her ancestors but it was only as we were leaving that Mary found another which read:

> *In loving memory of*
> *Elizabeth Susan Cuthbert Massy*
> *who entered on a higher life*
> *18th March 1884 aged 25 years*
> *also her brother*
> *George Alexander Boyle Massy*
> *who followed her Feb 5th 1894 aged 39*
> *both of this parish*
> THEY ARE NOT DEAD BUT SLEEPING

Living in Ireland gave me time to reflect. A hundred years ago, Elizabeth Massy had died a few days after my grandmother, who was named after her, was born. My grandmother died on March 18th 1974, the year my sister had her first child. My sister was also named Elizabeth after her and had been told the story in childhood. She had always felt it reflected in her life as she fell in love with a working-class man and, after tremendous opposition from my family, they married.

I was christened Susan Claire although I have always been called Claire — except for the month before my suicide attempt when close friends started to call me Susan, and I also started to dress in black and white clothes only, which included a nineteenth-century riding costume. My mother was unaware of Elizabeth Massy's full name so my naming was unconscious. In my early twenties I fell in love [Neptune opposing Venus in Aries] with a working-class man and, determined to avoid what my sister had experienced, I dropped out of college and 'ran way' with him. We lived rough in squats, formed a rock band, and in March 1977, when I was 25 years old we had a fight in which I nearly died. At that time I was aware that somehow [Neptune opposing Mercury, eighth house Moon and Pluto] I'd created the part I played, however unconsciously, and it was from this

284

devastating incident that my understanding of the collaboration involved within relationships grew [eighth house South Node drawing on old knowledge] and became the basis of the creativity which followed. This was a black period in my life – and the worst March – but now in Ireland I could trace back to previous Marches as a time when I felt strangely in-between worlds and very low. It was a time that, as a teenager, my relationships with boyfriends had ended.

A few months before leaving for Ireland I met a man whom I instantly remembered from a previous life. We had been young lovers in a Viking incarnation and he'd sailed away and I'd died because he never returned [Pluto and South Node in eighth]. It was a very painful recollection to meet him again – the longing to be with him was intense [Neptune opposing Venus, Venus trine Pluto], but it was not possible for us to be together in this lifetime either, and I knew it was essential that I used this energy constructively, creatively. When I dreamt of him, music followed [Neptune opposing Mercury and Venus] and I started to write songs.

It became clear to me that this was a deep pattern – not only through my family (ancestral line) but also in my own past lives. I began to recognise an ancient wound [first house Chiron opposing seventh house Uranus and inconjunct eighth house Moon, Pluto trine Venus] which had been carried into this lifetime and had brought deep pain into my life and relationships. In embracing this knowledge, in learning to forgive myself and in spending time in the depths of nature in County Kerry, I started to be able to communicate my feelings more harmoniously through music and painting, which was tremendously healing [a constructive expression of the Neptune opposition to Mercury and Venus].

Mary stayed in Ireland and as winter set in, I travelled back alone – stopping in Fermoy to put flowers on the grave and to visit the tower which had now been sprayed with graffiti – the name Claire seven times, Susan once and Claire Buckley once. I happened to be staying in a hotel run by a

Mrs Buckley but she knew nothing of the tower! The next
day I searched for the family home, Woodford, but never
found it. A local historian told me that the last of the Massys
had left for America three weeks previously.

During my recovery March was a very significant time for
me, each year appointments with doctors and healers would
be changed to fall around March 18th. Then, one day, I was
reading a novel and the line 'the sins of our fathers shall be
inherited by the third and fourth generation' stood out, as if
in bold print.

I had the soul of Elizabeth Susan Cuthbert Massy put to
rest on All Souls Day 1987 and on March 18th 1988 my
mother's sister died. I felt that my aunt and grandmother
were helping to free the tormented and trapped soul of
Elizabeth Massy.

It is as if a knot tied impossibly tight within my family has
been unravelled, leaving us freer to be open and loving with
one another, freer to give each other space and freer to take
conscious responsibility for our own lives.

The charts repeat several patterns and planetary aspects, so that
there is empathy between the two souls. Claire acts out Elizabeth's
emotional patterns, including the suicide attempt as Elizabeth's
'illness' can be seen as a passive suicide. For example, Claire has a
wide Jupiter opposition to Mars, Elizabeth has a wide Jupiter
conjunction to Mars; Claire has the Saturn inconjunct the Sun and
sextile the Moon, Elizabeth has Saturn widely sextiling the Sun
and opposing the Moon; Claire has Neptune opposing Venus and
Mercury; Elizabeth has a wide Venus/Neptune conjunction sextile Mercury; Claire has Saturn widely sextile Pluto, Elizabeth a
conjunction.

The synastry between the charts is interesting. Claire's Sun is
conjuncted by Elizabeth's Neptune, giving her a clairvoyant
contact and a very subtle old karmic debt. Claire's own Neptune is
on the Midheaven, leaving her open to 'possession', or at least
impression from a discarnate 'lost' soul. Claire first became
intuitively aware of a spirit being around her, at the age of sixteen,
after her sister's wedding celebration, and this is evident from the

poetry she wrote at that time. In the period leading up to the fight with her boyfriend, she was heavily involved with drugs: 'It was at this point I realised what terrible damage I had done to myself. It was as if I had dug a big pit and jumped into it [Taurus]. The turning point came when I started to change the way I listened.'

Even 'soft' drugs open up a part of the psyche which is normally screened off and protected. Elizabeth was therefore able to make contact with Claire through this link, and through the strong Venus interaspects within the chart, including Claire's to Elizabeth's South Node, another 'old' contact which is very loving. Claire's Jupiter and Venus oppose Elizabeth's North Node conjoined by Claire's Neptune, a very appropriate contact for the releasing into the higher life of this earth-bound soul who died 'for love'. Elizabeth's Saturn/Pluto conjunction squares Claire's Nodes, pulling Claire into a resolution of the paradox of the eighth house Leo South Node and the second house Aquarius North Node, offering her the possibility of rebirthing and restructuring herself through attuning to her own power, and leading to an understanding of the wider pattern involved in the interaction.

During the five years following the fight, she cut her drug and alcohol intake drastically and cleaned out for six months. When she resumed taking drugs, the little she was taking affected her strongly (Neptune is linked into the chemical stored by the 'primitive' part of the brain following alcohol or heroin addiction. This chemical never dissipates, and one drink or one shot of heroin releases it into the bloodstream, putting the addict straight back to the point at which he or she withdrew from the 'drug'). This led to her suicide attempt. It was from the day she had her chart read in 1983 that she was able to stop completely: 'I caught a glimpse of how subtle our energy is, a glimpse of the mystery and beauty we each hold.'

RELATIONSHIP KARMA IN ACTION

Two charts are included here as examples of how the expectation of the incarnating soul will be met by the family into which it incarnates, and to show how family interaction and patterns are carried over into adult relationships. Appendix II contains extracts from a karmic reading for a family.

Figure 31 shows the chart of a man who incarnated into a Jewish family. He has a T-square intimately connected with mothering and relating, first house Venus in Scorpio opposing the Moon, squared by Pluto/Saturn conjunction. Virtually every regression or imaging session he undertook included 'screwing his mother'; it was something that had to be got out of the way before anything

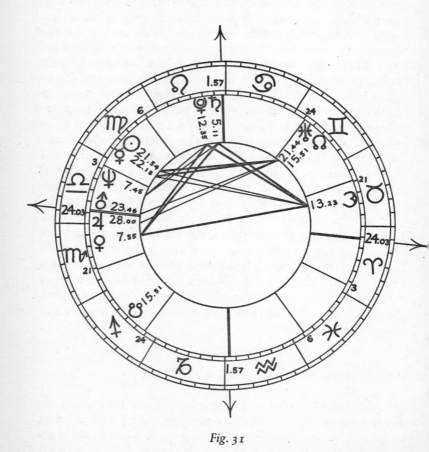

Fig. 31

else was possible. His Pluto square the Moon is a deeply symbiotic conflict symbolized by the archetypal Kali figure of the matriarchal devouring Jewish mother (tenth house Pluto). His mother had been his wife in a past life (Moon in the seventh house) and in the present life she rejected his choice of wife, cutting her off (Pluto/Saturn square Moon), ostensibly because she was non-Jewish and could not continue the matriarchal line of Judaism through her children. He incarnated with an expectation of emotional trauma and rejection bound up within that T-square. In previous lives he had experienced the death of three women directly as a result of their having loved him (Pluto square Venus). He said: 'If people got too close, they would get hurt, I would cause them to suffer. I felt guilty.' In his regression work he also experienced considerable jealousy, trauma and rejection in relationships. In the present life he experienced early rejection and abandonment when his mother went into hospital to give birth to his brother and his father, who was looking after him, was incapacitated by influenza: he was left in his cot, unfed and unchanged, for two days – eternity to a two-year-old. Venus is part of the T-Square and he believed both that he could not be loved (Saturn) and that he could never receive enough loving (Pluto). A bright and intelligent man/child, he said that he felt that he was only ever valued for what he did or achieved, not for who he was. His Moon in Taurus square Saturn subtly emanated an air of doom, gloom and depression, and Pluto brought in an underlying brooding resentment. He carried forward both his pattern of rejection and guilt and an unrealistic pursuit of an unattainable image of 'woman' (Neptune inconjunct, semi-sextile, Venus). After he left his wife in early middle age – an event which engendered more guilt as the marriage had not so much broken down as evolved into a 'good friends' relationship – he relentlessly pursued 'dolly birds' to boost his ego. He spurned more 'mature' women, and retreated in terror when faced with the possibility of a real relationship. He described his relationships as 'gut-wrenching and traumatic'.

As transiting Pluto neared his Venus an astrologer told him to anticipate what he had been searching for all his life, a karmic relationship through a meeting with an 'old soulmate': 'One

where you walk in the room and she's there, you can't escape it.'
He could. The terror generated by Pluto and Saturn was too great.
In the event he spent the transit sharing a house platonically with a
female friend who was undergoing a very karmic relationship
herself. Once again he felt isolated, rejected and abandoned, and
exuded resentment. And, just to complete the picture, his mother
arrived to stay for three months whilst her own home was being
renovated (Pluto/Saturn). He was so much like that line from a
Winnie-the-Pooh song: 'I'm just a little black rain cloud, hovering
over the honey tree.' And, just like poor old Pooh, whenever he
reached for the honey, he got stung.

When I first met him I described him as 'isolated in the ivory
tower of his twelfth house Neptune, cut off from the suffering of
others and totally centred in his own misery'. However, no one
can stay static for ever and when the Pluto transit of the T-square
was well underway he found a relationship based on an old
friendship: 'One which is not in the least gut-wrenching, just
comfortable.' He was able to move out of his total isolation and
self-centred preoccupation and manifest some of the positive
qualities in the chart through teaching and counselling work
(utilizing the Gemini North Node). This brought him into relationship with many people and opened up a new direction to his
life.

Figure 32 is the chart of a woman who was born to a violent
abusive father whom she hated (fourth house Mars opposing
Saturn/Uranus/Sun T-square) and a compliant, collusive mother,
whom she nevertheless idolized. Her mother never gave her any
affection and 'escaped' through an early death (Sun inconjunct
Neptune, Venus/Jupiter Grand Trine with Neptune and Saturn).
She had a Scorpio South Node and manifested a frightening
capacity for rage and revenge, stating that when her father, by
then eighty years old, became senile and helpless she was going to:
'Get him and make him suffer.' She carried her compulsive
patterns of lack of self-worth (Sun square Saturn), acceptance of
abuse (Saturn–Mars), and demand for love (Venus–Pluto) into
her 'adult' relationships. Her first child died at the age of seven
months (wide Pluto/Moon conjunction in Cancer in the fifth). She

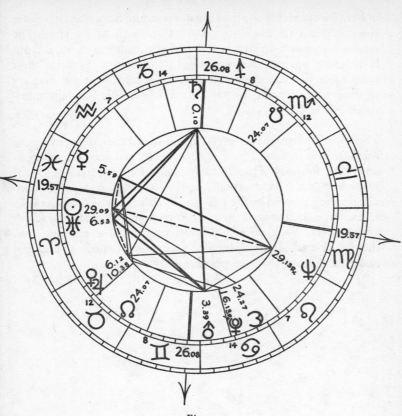

Fig. 32

eventually left her 'too nice' husband and five children and went to live with another 'not so nice' man. She had an abortion despite the fact that he wanted the child – her Cancerian Moon confused being biological with being creative and she unconsciously used her children as a weapon against her men. She said that she felt responsible for her children's pain (Moon in Cancer, Sun in Pisces) and was acutely aware of their rejection of her, and yet she could not connect the 'cause' with the 'effect', feeling herself to be a victim: Pisces colluding with itself to subtly alter and avoid 'reality'. She requested a reading because she was 'unable to let go of her painful childhood and the hurt around her children, whom she could not release to the past' (Cancerian Moon trait). She wondered what the lesson was that she had not learnt, but did not believe the answer she was given. 'Masochists look on their submission to mistreatment as love, whereas in fact it is a necessity in their never-ceasing search for revenge and is basically motivated by hatred.'[11]

The karmic patterns reinforced in childhood are carried over into relationships in adult life. They operate from a deep unconscious level and frequently precipitate totally inappropriate reactions when a trigger is inadvertently activated. Relationships will continue to be coloured by the past until a conscious decision is taken to examine the roots of the present response to, and interaction with others. Such an exploration may involve entering into therapy or analysis, or undertaking regression in order to identify, and release from, the patterns of the past.

Chapter 6

COMPANIONS ALONG THE WAY

When a couple are genuinely related to each other, they are willing to enter into the whole spectrum of human life together.

ROBERT A. JOHNSON, *THE PSYCHOLOGY OF ROMANTIC LOVE*

When examining the concept of karmic relationships it must be borne in mind that relationships can be formed with any and everyone, not just family or 'love' partners. Strong links over many incarnations can bring people together for a specific task, to deal with unfinished business or repay debts and obligations, to act as a catalyst, to meet fleetingly or to spend a lifetime together. Karma may manifest through friendships, business partnerships, teacher and pupil, employer and employee, healer and patient contacts, next-door neighbours, casual meetings or marriage partners, to name but a few possibilities. Karmic ties with lovers are delineated by the fifth house planets, those with friends by the eleventh house, those with enemies by the twelfth house, and those between marriage partners by the seventh house.

Meetings with people from the past can be devastating. Instant antipathy or fear can be traced back to previous interaction, and a chart for the moment of meeting can be illuminating if a chart is not available for the other person. Many years ago, before I had come to consciously believe in past lives, I had an appointment with a local solicitor. As soon as I entered his office I felt cold and could not stop shaking, I was literally terrified of him. I was even affected by his voice on the telephone and always referred to him as 'The Inquisitor'. No one else could understand this as he was a mild, ineffectual little man. Several years later he cropped up in a regression to a former life in which he had appeared in a minor role – as a member of the Inquisition. From that time on he did not affect me at all, I was able to see him as he was in the present incarnation. At the time of our first meeting transiting Saturn was conjunct my natal Mars, activating its difficult position between Uranus and Saturn. The encounter brought out my inner powerlessness and old fear. At the time of the regression transiting Neptune was on my Mercury, opposing Uranus. I was released from the past through the spiritual knowledge and insight offered by Neptune.

Equally difficult to handle can be an irresistible attraction to an 'inappropriate' person. A middle-aged woman was overcome by totally inexplicable but very strong feelings of lust towards the teenage son of one of her friends, a situation which she found extremely embarrassing. In a regression she went back to ancient times when they had made a sacred marriage. The tie had been strongly sexual but he had died at a very young age. She had been left feeling cheated, frustrated and resentful as the sacred marriage had included the vow to be faithful to him for life and she had therefore had to remain celibate. In the present life she had never found the sexual fulfilment she was seeking (Sun/Venus in Pisces opposing Neptune, and Moon/Mars in Aries). The synastry between the charts included his Aries Sun conjuncting her Moon/Mars, signifying a strong sexual attraction, his Pluto conjuncted her Neptune and opposed Sun/Venus, indicating an old symbiotic interaction and the frustrations and resentments (Pluto) from that time together, with the 'desire for what could not be' (Neptune) in the present life.

Viewing the relationship as an old contact coming forward into the present can help the participants to handle this type of attraction constructively. The sacred marriage was a linking together on all the levels of being, but on the physical level it is often the feeling of lust or sexual desire which is most likely to break through from the past. Once this has happened, however, the deeper links are able to manifest, providing an opportunity for unconditional love with spiritual sustenance and support to grow.

The specific purpose of such a contact may be to act as a catalyst for hidden knowledge or abilities. As these emerge from the past they can contribute to the incarnating soul's growth in the present life.

Similarly with contacts which are based on a different type of old interaction, once the soul has learnt to detach itself from the past that past, together with whatever feelings it involved, can be let go of, and a new energy can manifest. Some of the deepest spiritual ties have unpromising beginnings but an examination of the charts will help to clarify the situation and pinpoint the lessons to be learnt from the relationship. A woman was concerned about a teacher with whom she was studying the spiritual aspects of yoga. She said that from time to time, despite her seeming friendliness, she was aware of 'a glint of hatred in her teacher's eyes' and this held her back from fully entrusting herself to her. The woman regressed back to a life in which they had both been sisters. The teacher/sister had been extremely jealous and killed her over a man she had been promised to but whom the sister wanted. Once she had become attuned to this old trauma, the woman was able to forgive. Although she never told her teacher of the regression, the situation between them improved dramatically and they became close friends and spiritual companions. Her Sun/Pluto/Mars conjunction was in the twelfth house of 'enemies' and the aspects between the charts included a Neptune–Mars opposition. Having forgiven her sister/teacher unconditionally, she was able to be receptive to her teaching and to grow spiritually.

The karma embodied in a relationship can be studied through the synastry between the charts of the two partners, and from composite and relationship charts which illustrate how and why the relationship functions. In synastry, the outer planet contacts to the partner's inner planets, angles and Nodes signify the lessons to be worked on, the degree of 'difficulty' being expressed by the type of aspect. These same lessons will be reiterated through several aspects, and by aspects within the relationship and composite charts, and will illuminate the underlying 'karmic theme' of the relationship. Either partner can take on the role of the outer planet within the relationship. For example, if one partner has Uranus in the seventh house conjunct the other partner's Sun, and that partner has Uranus in aspect to Venus which in turn is involved in the synastry through a Venus aspect to the first partner's Uranus, then the underlying theme is freedom versus commitment. At some point in the relationship one of the partners will have to decide whether to stay in the relationship or to move out of it, unless an interaction has evolved which allows for both space and intimacy.

PLANETS IN THE SEVENTH HOUSE

The seventh house delineates the incarnating soul's karma concerning relationships, its expectations, and the type of partner who will bring these issues to the fore. Both the planets in this house and the aspects to them will illustrate the working of the karma.

The Sun

The soul incarnating with the Sun in the seventh house has the need to develop itself through a relationship. The karma may, for example, be one of too much detachment or attachment (often related to Aquarius, Cancer or the Fixed signs), of selfishness or unselfishness (Aries, Libra, Pisces or the Cardinal signs), sensual gratification (Taurus), neurotic fastidiousness (Virgo), jealousy (Scorpio) or infidelity (the Mutable or dual signs). With this placement, the soul can learn about the intimacy which 'derives from authentic contact with another human being who possesses both strengths and limitations'[1]. It can need to learn to share itself in a relationship, whilst maintaining its own integrity and honouring its own needs and those of another. The Self is affirmed in its identity by and through its interaction with another: 'Almost paradoxically, a sense of their own power, purpose and individuality is found through partnership and relationship ... Through the ups and downs and entanglements encountered in the attempt to form vital, honest and life-supporting alliances, the identity is shaped and strengthened.'[2]

The Sun in the seventh house may also indicate that the male partner was the soul's father in a past life, or that the soul has in the past been married to the present-life father. Either way, the incarnating soul may have to deal with incestuous feelings arising either in childhood, when the father was formerly the husband, or in adulthood, when the husband was formerly the father. These feelings may never become conscious but may pervade the under-lying structure of the relationship, causing subtle disharmony and emotional difficulties. Conversely, one of the partners within a seventh house Sun relationship may take on a 'fatherly' role through living out the powerful solar principle on behalf of his or her mate. This is frequently true of both marriages and part-nerships entered into for business reasons. In such cases, one partner will act out the dynamic Sun energy and the other passively allow this. The passive partner may well have to learn to confront and own his or her own power within the relationship.

The working of this type of karma can be subtle and complex. For example, a woman who has a natal seventh house Sun—Pluto contact will most probably have the karmic pattern of an authori-tarian father and project all her power on to men. She may have been aware of her father's incestuous feelings, if not actual behaviour, in childhood. She may subsequently marry a man who imposes his authority on her. Initially, she may be content to be 'the little wife at home', and often the 'power behind the throne' living out all her aspirations through her husband. However, the situation may be further complicated, if she has Mars—Saturn—Pluto aspects in her chart, by her 'addiction' to violence which is compounded by the fact that in her experience pain has become inextricably linked to love and her Will has been sup-pressed. When this woman, under the pressure of transits and resulting inner changes, eventually begins to develop her own inner sense of authority and take back the projection of power, thereby dealing with the karma attached to her Sun—Pluto aspect and her Will issues, violence and conflict may well develop within the relationship – which she may still interpret as 'love' and be unable to release from the situation. She may well face hostility from a husband who has been used to having a compliant wife. Exercising that inner authority in her life may also result in the decision to leave the relationship, or to state clearly that she is going to be autonomous within it. Either way, she will go through a period of isolation and adjustment until a new way of relating which allows her to manifest her own considerable power is developed.

In a different scenario she may enter into an 'inferior role' in a profession traditionally dominated by men. Spurred on perhaps by a need to be 'equal to a man' she may aspire to succeed in that masculine world, being driven by ambition and a need to prove herself. She may also be trying to live out her father's ambitions for her or to emulate him, perhaps compensating for the son he never had. Under the pressure of transits and the need to reclaim her power, her promotion into a traditional male power base may well be opposed and she may have to examine her values and ambitions. The resulting struggle will help her to reclaim her own power and consequently either her career will take off or she will find another way to express herself.

The Moon

The Moon in the seventh house signifies that the incarnating soul is meeting past emotional or mothering karma through its relationships. For many souls with this placement, the past pattern has been to see themselves through the eyes of another, as they are reflected back not as they really are, and conversely to see another as they want them to be, which is coloured by past precedents. Souls for whom this is a deeply ingrained pattern feel naked, uneasy and incomplete when alone. Lacking a sense of Self from which to interact with the inner or outer worlds, they are vulnerable to anyone who appears to offer them a mirror in which to see themselves or who stirs up emotional needs from the past. Consequently they are an ideal hook for the projections of other people and for the false 'identity' to which they are thereby exposed.

The seventh house Moon may also reflect patterns within the incarnating soul through the interaction with another. A man (fig. 33, inner ring) (seventh house Chiron and Moon in Scorpio

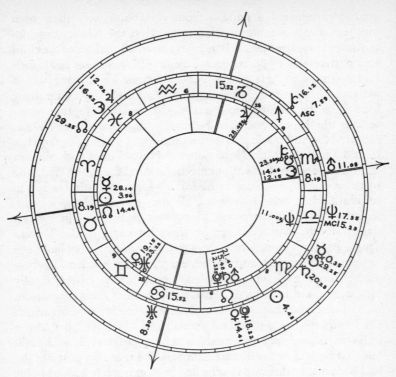

Fig. 33

conjunct the South Node opposing the Sun and Ascendant and widely T-square fourth house Pluto/Saturn/Mars conjunction in Leo) was 'idyllically happy' with his wife (fig. 33, outer ring) until she decided to have a child for which he did not feel ready. She had a Grand Trine of seventh house Uranus to Mars in Scorpio (conjunct his Moon/South Node, so this was an old conflict with him around mothering) and her Jupiter/Moon conjunction in fourth house Pisces, together with a Moon opposition to Saturn/South Node across the parental houses, and an eighth house Pluto/Venus inconjunct to the Moon: they had both incarnated with expectations of emotional difficulty and constriction around mothering and jealousy of others. The 'adult' interaction most probably repeated a pattern from childhood with their own mothers. From the moment of conception the relationship deteriorated rapidly. Her husband was extremely jealous of the child and particularly opposed breast-feeding (Cancer was his fourth house cusp sign). He had a Venus/Uranus conjunction which activated her seventh house and had had difficulty committing himself to the relationship initially, although his Neptune semi-sextile the Moon and her Neptune quincunx to the Moon reflected the 'idolization' in the relationship. His T-square and her Grand Trine and Moon inconjunct to Pluto/Venus had inherent difficulties and conflicts about mothering and the use of Will. The birth brought these issues to the surface for them both. He ceased to idolize her and manifested all the 'thwarted small child' jealousy which his Scorpionic Moon was capable of. There was a Saturn/Pluto/Mars conjunction from his chart to her Venus/Pluto, and his Venus/Uranus squared her Saturn. They had been extremely symbiotic and dependent upon each other. She described them as having been 'each other's best friend, totally inseparable until the birth'. Following on from their separation, he had a nervous breakdown and came to her for support which she interpreted as 'a mothering need', and which with her Moon in Pisces inconjunct Neptune she was happy to provide as she still felt that he was her soulmate. She believed that in a past life she had been his mother and that he had been extremely jealous of his siblings despite the fact that he was her favourite child: a situation which was reactivated and reflected back to her by the birth of their daughter.

The karma of the seventh house Moon may also be one of excessive emotionality within a relationship, the soul having no control over how it reacts to a stimulus and over what past emotional patterns are triggered. In the example above, the Scorpio Moon husband felt deeply rejected and abandoned when his wife brought an 'interloper' into the family. Jealous and unable to accept the child, he reflected the rejection back on to his wife. She did not perceive it as his difficulty but as a reflection on herself as a 'bad mother' and a failure as a wife (fourth house Moon in Pisces opposing Saturn/South Node).

The lesson for the soul with seventh house Moon is to learn to respond rather than react blindly and to recognize a trigger and the feelings it produces. It must become conscious of, rather than identified with, the emotional forces within itself and to step beyond them so that it chooses how to act. The pathway of fully conscious and aware relationship is a difficult one and can entail moving away from long-held beliefs and expectations as to how a relationship 'should' function into an acceptance of how it *is*.

> Human love is so obscured by the inflations and commotions of romance that we almost never look for love in its own right . . . But . . . we can begin to see love within us – revealed in our feelings in the spontaneous flow of warmth that surges toward another person, in the small, unnoticed acts of relatedness that make up the secret fabric of our daily lives.
>
> We can learn that human relationship is inseparable from friendship and commitment. We can learn that the essence of love is not to use the other to make us happy, but to serve and affirm the one we love. And we can discover, to our surprise, that what we have needed more than anything was not so much to be loved, as to love.[3]

The soul incarnating with the Moon in the seventh may also have karma with the mother in the present life arising out of a past life when they were married, or it may have been the mother of the partner to whom it is now married. This tends to result in emotionally incestuous or possessive behaviour, a type of behaviour frequently reflected by a mother who is unable to let go of her son. The unconscious need for a wife to act as 'mother' can be carried over into adult relationships as in the example above. This is reflected in the number of elderly men who seem unable to refer to their wives other than as 'mother' despite the fact that the children have long since left home. The lesson that these souls must learn is to release from the past interaction and to enter into a relationship unfettered by the apron strings of the past.

Mercury

The soul incarnating with Mercury in the seventh house has karma around how the mind or tongue have been used to communicate within a relationship in the past. This can range from the chronic nagger or scold (frequently linked to 'heavy' aspects to Mercury when it is in an Air or Earth sign), to criticism (particularly linked to Virgo or Saturn), over-intellectualization of the feelings (Air signs or Virgo), or intellectual domination by a partner (Pluto aspects). The need in the present incarnation is for open, honest and caring communication and friendship between the partners.

The past-life pattern may also have been that the present-life partner may have been a friend or sibling in a past life. A client had her seventh house Mercury in Gemini conjoined by her husband's Sun. The 'marriage' had not been consummated because they both felt more like brother and sister, with a very deep friendship between them. She said that ever since they had first met she had been convinced that this was a much loved brother from a past life. Although they were devoted to each other, eventually her husband wished to have a sexual relationship and moved out. They remained close friends, however, without engendering any jealousy in the husband's new wife, who recognized and accepted the special platonic link between them.

Venus

On the whole the soul with seventh house Venus incarnates expecting relationships and partners to be a source of content- ment, growth and harmony. However, Venus does have its dark side – particularly when situated in Taurus, Scorpio or Cancer – and there may be past issues of possessiveness, jealousy and revenge to overcome. Much will depend on the aspects to Venus as to the incarnating soul's expectations and past experience, and to the aspects between the charts of the partners. If the charts are compatible with 'easy' aspects, then this placement may indicate a contact coming forward from the past in order that both partners can overcome old difficulties and offer each other the opportunity to grow through a new type of relationship. On the other hand, 'easy' aspects may indicate two very loving souls who have chosen to be together to build upon and further develop their union. Problems can arise, however, if the incarnating soul seeks to grow *through* another instead of by its own efforts, and it will then tend to blame the partner if things go awry, rather than look within itself. The lesson to be learnt from Venus therefore is to be both autonomous and harmonious within a relationship, seeking to share love and bring beauty into the life of another whilst retaining fundamental independence and identity.

Mars

With the seventh house Mars much will depend upon the sign and aspects as to how the karma arose and will manifest. The negative, passive signs may have karma around repressed aggression or difficulties in assertion within a relationship; the soul may need to learn to express its own Will rather than being dominated by that of another. The positive, outgoing signs are more likely to have karma linked with violence and aggression within a past relationship and the soul may have to learn to compromise between its own ego or Will needs and those of another. If Mars has difficult aspects then the soul may seek out an aggressive, dominant partner with whom to work on, or on whom to project, its own Will and assertion energies. Such a partner may be a direct link back to the past, so that there is personal karma between them, or may have been chosen simply because he or she epitomizes the type of brutal or aggressive energies which the soul needs to struggle with in order to manifest the positive side of the energies within itself.

A client (seventh house Mars in Scorpio in Grand Trine to Uranus and Jupiter) who had just split up from her husband responded to her reading:

> I am very familiar with my Will! It can over-ride most obstacles in life. It was, of course, one of the things that first attracted my husband to me but in the end he saw it as a monster. It always carries that danger. I am very assertive but not very aggressive [the Grand Trine is in Water],

although people often cannot tell the difference, I find. At least I don't hate easily as I think my Will would be very damaging under such circumstances . . . I was not approved of as a child, too strong a Will, too clever by half [Saturn conjunct Mercury/South Node in Virgo]. One of the reasons I fell in love with my husband was that he appeared to approve of my cleverness and my success. I found myself opening emotionally when I had sat on my emotions too long from hurt [Saturn square Chiron/Moon in eighth house]. Ironically, this opened up the healer [twelfth house Jupiter] in me and my computer career [Uranus in aspect to Mars] became unimportant . . . Equally ironically and very painfully, it became clear that my husband did not approve of this change and he used to talk of my 'crackpot and loony' friends and activities. I do feel now that I have the freedom to be who I am [Sun in Leo, Aries Ascendant].

I was fascinated by your psychic reading concerning a death in war consumed by fire or an explosion of some kind – by the way, it is almost certainly the First World War as I gave up history at school rather than study it. I have a definite past-death memory prior to that in the Middle Ages with a similar end. I was trying to do some kind of alchemical experiment and caused an explosion in which I was burned to death [another example of Uranus–Mars blowing itself up]. I have always known this and got an awful shock when I realised that most people didn't believe in reincarnation. I have always put my fear of fire and my terror of letting go down to that experience. The letting go bit is a real nuisance. The experiment went wrong because I wasn't paying sufficient attention and now I am very scared of being out of control [Saturn square Chiron/Moon in Sagittarius, Pluto conjunct Venus/North Node]. That means I cannot relax enough to achieve orgasm, which is silly . . . I only hope I work through that sometime.

The seventh house Mars may also indicate the lesson of learning to express anger within a relationship in a clean, non-judgemental or non-blaming manner. It may be a soul who has always suppressed anger in the past, perhaps for fear of being disliked or rejected, or it may have experienced the guilt induced by being told: 'You make me angry', suffered the misplaced anger of another soul who was unable to express it to the source of its anger, or been subjected to the constant rages of an angry partner – it may also have been the angry partner itself. As a result, it may need to recover the energy and vitality of the suppressed emotion rather than suffer the consequences of old rage with constant tiredness, petty irritations or other health problems.

Jupiter

As with all Jupiter placements there is a possibility that over-indulgence and aggrandizement will be part of the soul's karma around relationships, or that partners will be a source of great expansion. Jupiter in this house can certainly help to mitigate other difficult aspects within the chart and the incarnating soul with this placement can begin to positively affirm itself through its contact with another soul. The partner chosen may be benignly expansive, or prone to sensual self-indulgence, and there may be a direct link with a past life in which the karma arose, or a spiritual link to support the soul in its quest to overcome the past. The sign on the cusp and the aspects between the charts will delineate the type of karma involved.

Jupiter has the gift of faith and the power of creative visualiz-ation and this placement can bring into being growth-enhancing experiences of mutual trust and sharing through a deep, spiritual relationship. The sensual joy of Jupiter can be extremely helpful in overcoming past sexual frustrations or frigidity, as can the 'simple' act of learning to trust and open up to another soul – a lifetime's lesson in itself if there are difficult Saturn or Pluto aspects to contend with. However, the expansiveness of Jupiter can accelerate the learning process and attune to the joyous energy immanent throughout the cosmos.

Saturn

Saturn is the Lord of Karma and the soul incarnating with seventh house Saturn has usually encountered difficult relationships on its journey. However, the strength of Saturn only manifests in the face of adversity and hardship overcome, and therefore the soul with this placement has the possibility of entering into a stable, enduring partnership based on mutual love and respect for each other.

The soul with the seventh house Saturn will usually encounter a partner with whom it has direct karma from a past life, old debts and obligations to work on or a promise to be honoured. Although at times the partnership, whatever form it takes, may appear laborious and limiting, through this interaction the soul will become more aware of its own strengths, its inner resilience, discipline and integrity. If it has in the past tended to opt out of relationships as soon as the difficulties began (Air and Fire signs on the cusp or Uranus aspects to the Moon or Venus), then this may be a valuable opportunity to see a relationship through. On the other hand, if the soul has tended to be stuck in a rut (the Earth signs) or tended to immerse itself in some form of sacrifice (the Water signs or Neptune in aspect to the Moon or Venus), then it may be time for it to learn to recognize when it is appropriate to stay in the relationship and when it is better to release from the interaction and let go of the past. The soul may have to learn that there is no value in endlessly repeating an interaction that is on the road to nowhere. The urge of the Self is towards growth, not stagnation.

Uranus

In many traditional astrology teachings Uranus in the seventh house signifies divorce or separation. In karmic astrology Uranus may indicate that in the past the soul has not been committed enough in its relationships, or that the time has now come to be more free in the way it interacts with another. Uranus in this placement is committed to transformation, and if it cannot transform its relationship at the same time as it transforms itself, then it may well have to change partners in order to do so. However, it may also be that a different, perhaps more unconventional, way of relating is needed: one which offers the soul the space it craves to be an individual without excluding the experience of interacting with another which it needs in order to grow. Uranus is the planet of universal love that teaches the soul to recognize and love humanity in its interconnected multifacetedness. With the seventh house Uranus it needs to relate to the organic whole and its individual segments.

The partner represented by the seventh house Uranus may bring the soul a lesson from the past around freedom or commitment; it may be someone to whom the incarnating soul failed to commit itself in the past, or someone from whom it needs to separate to become an individual. The sign on the cusp and the aspects to Uranus from the partner's planets will elucidate the underlying karmic lesson.

Neptune

In Neptune the soul may encounter its previous delusions and projections, or it may meet a spiritual companion from the past for its present stage of the journey. A client with Neptune in Scorpio in the seventh inconjunct the Sun in the twelfth and Venus conjunct Chiron/Mercury in the eleventh had an old soulmate relationship with her husband. He died when she was still young and she refused to accept the 'reality' of his death, insisting on the continuity of the relationship. She became obsessed with the Spiritualist Church, seeking out mediums to contact him, and said that he was still with her constantly and that they would work spiritually together. She wanted to 'work off' all her karma so that they could 'be together for eternity'.

Neptune, perhaps more than any other planet, is capable of extremes and can indicate the potential for both the highest or the lowest to emerge through a relationship. The karma may be that the soul has been deceived in the past and now meets its deceiver or its illusions again; or it may be that it has idealized and romanticized a union and not seen its partner clearly. It may have had unrealized or unrealistic expectations of 'love' which held it back from unconditionally loving another and, therefore, it may have to learn to clearly perceive not only *what* love is but also *who* the partner is:

Love is a force that acts from within, that enables my ego to look outside itself, to see my fellow humans as something to be valued and cherished, rather than used.

Therefore, when I say that 'I love', it is not I who loves, but, in reality, Love who acts through me. Love is not so much something I do as something I am. Love is not a doing but a state of being — relatedness, a connectedness to another mortal, an identification with her or him that simply flows within me, independent of my intentions or my efforts.

Love is the power within us that affirms and values another human being as he or she is . . . rather than the ideal we would like him or her to be or the projection that flows from our minds . . . Love causes us to value that person as a total, individual self, and this means that we accept the negative side as well as the positive, the imperfections as well as the admirable qualities. When one truly loves the human being rather than the projection, one loves the shadow just as one loves the rest. One accepts the other person's totality.[4]

This is the lesson of unconditional love, to love what *is*, not what might be, and it is the karmic purpose of the seventh house Neptune.

Pluto

As with all Pluto contacts the karma behind the seventh house Pluto is deep and devious. It will almost always embody a power struggle, both in the past and in the present interaction, unless the incarnating soul has reached a high level of spiritual evolution and awareness. Pluto has the potential for a creative relationship, one which heals old wounds and releases old resentments. However, for many souls incarnating with such a placement it is those old wounds and resentments which await attention, together with the obsessions relating to relationships which those wounds engender.

Seventh house Pluto offers the opportunity to fully and finally release from the compulsions and karma of the past. This may involve a meeting with a past partner with whom there are power and emotional difficulties to resolve, or it may bring the soul into contact with a powerful force for transformation in the shape of an old 'soulmate' or a new teacher. Pluto offers the soul a companion for its inward journey and can lead to a deep understanding of the interaction between men and women as it is expressed through relationship, with a consequent unlocking of the creative energies of partnership. In the Plutonian union of two individual souls coming together in aware relationship, the energy released is much more than the sum of its parts. It is true transformation and regeneration.

Chiron

Chiron in the seventh house is indicative of a deep wound around relationships and the soul with this placement will meet difficult karma in order to release from suffering in this area. A client with Chiron in Taurus in the seventh also had a Mars/Saturn/Venus/North Node conjunction at the point of a Finger of Fate with tenth house Neptune and eighth house Pluto. She had always found relationships very painful and asked: 'Is it possible that I can find a man with whom I feel secure and safe and with whom I can bodily agree?' She firmly believed that she had been physically tortured in a past life and her main concern was with a friend about whom she asked: 'Why came this friend into my life, who tortures me, how can I recover from these wounds?' In the synastry between the charts the 'friend' had Chiron conjunct the North Node in Leo opposing the client's Mars/Saturn/Venus/North Node — a reversed nodal connection. In addition the friend's Sun, Mercury, Uranus, and Saturn all activated the client's seventh house. The connection to her friend appeared to be an old one with a reactivation of the karmic pattern of 'torture'. Through the relationship she was offered the opportunity to break away from the suffering stemming from her relationships — 'being tortured', and the emotional games and insecurities of the South Node conjunction and the Finger of Fate — and to heal the wounds of the past.

Planets in the Eighth House

The eighth house has links with the cycle of conception, birth, death and rebirth, and with the different levels of consciousness. It describes how the incarnating soul will share itself with others, what the subtle colouring of that interaction is, and how the soul will be connected to the cosmos.

The personal planets in the eighth house bring the soul face to face with the need to give of itself in a very direct experience of the energy of the planet, the planetary energy being a resource to draw on and develop through relationships. The outer planets may incorporate subtle lessons in the encounter with others, widening out the concept of relationship still further, particularly into manifestation of the oneness of life.

Jupiter

With Jupiter in the eighth house the incarnating soul has a resource of creative energy and links to higher levels of consciousness. Attuned to Jupiter, it can share the vision of what may be and transform it through creative visualization and affirmation into what is. The soul attuned to the energy of Jupiter is thereby able, through relationship in the fullest sense of the word, to draw out of another soul its potential to Be.

Saturn

Saturn in the eighth house may represent restriction and limitation on how the soul shares its resources and gives of itself to another. In the past it may have repressed its sexual energies, possibly as a result of a vow of chastity, and it may therefore encounter difficulty in the present incarnation with this area of life. This placement is symbolic of a defensive wall erected between the soul and others in the past, or of a lack of confidence in its ability to give of itself, based on a lack of self-esteem. The soul may well blame other people, however, for its failure to relate rather than recognize that its own inner isolation and restriction are the cause of the problem. The karmic lesson is to transcend the limitations of its inner sense of worthlessness and to find within itself a core of value through which it can respond to another.

Uranus

Uranus in the eighth house indicates an ambivalence and ambiguity concerning sexual orientation and an unconventional approach to relationships. It may be that the incarnating soul found it difficult to make relationships in a past life, being too aware of its separateness and too attached to its freedom. On the other hand, the present ambivalence may be based on past experiences in which the soul was overwhelmed by its own sexuality, withdrawing perhaps into celibacy as an escape from instinctual pressures, or in which its sexual outlet was unusual or considered 'perverted' in some way. This particular placement shows up consistently in the charts of souls with a homosexual or bisexual orientation rather than a heterosexual one. It may indicate that the soul must learn to integrate the masculine and feminine within itself, moving back towards the asexuality of the eternal Self. On the other hand, it may simply be that Uranus insists on being 'perverse' and 'different', in which case the soul is setting up new karma for itself in the future.

One client had a Saturn/Mars/Uranus conjunction in Gemini in the eighth house, forming a Grand Trine with Neptune and the Sun, and the Moon in Capricorn. He said that he suffered from shyness and found it difficult to form personal relationships; he was unwilling to get tied down in one permanent relationship, preferring a variety but not able to achieve that either. His difficulties tied in with both the repressed emotional energy of the Capricornian Moon and the eighth house Saturn. His dual Geminian Uranus was seeking the widest possible range of experiences. It seemed that he might one day surprise himself with his own inventiveness and the number of opportunities to be explored once Uranus had overcome Saturn and he had shed his inhibitions. The eighth house conjunction would never give him tranquillity in the emotional sense, but he could begin to make changes willingly and more smoothly instead of letting them come up with great suddenness. Stephen Arroyo says that the eighth house represents a longing for emotional peace and release from compulsion and he points out that this cannot come through suppression and repression, but will only be attained if the longing is brought out into the clear light of consciousness and if the past is then outgrown.

In the past-life part of the reading the client was told that he had been a very handsome boy, a slave to a wealthy Roman who pampered him and showed him off to his friends, but also used and abused his body in a private sadistic homosexual relationship, giving him much pleasure. However, he was converted to Christianity and welcomed martyrdom, as his sense of having lived contrary to the Will of God was so overwhelming. This also tied in with an earlier incarnation in Babylon in which he was described as 'a pretty painted boy who played the whore' living a very sybaritic life, and to a later life as a religious recluse.

In a follow-up session the client stated that he had felt sexually guilty all his life, but could never pinpoint the reason and he described having had 'curious fantasies' and an attraction towards other men. This had interfered with his forming the kind of relationship with a woman which he desperately wanted. Once he recognized his old pattern and that the 'fantasies' were memories of those times, he was able to transform his relationships and express what he regarded as 'normal' sexuality. This particular client was also very fearful of what else might be lurking in his past. He had been told by a clairvoyant that he had been a Jack-the-Ripper figure who used and abused women and then killed them. Although the feeling of that life 'fitted' the symbolic pattern of his eighth house planets it did not ring true to either of us. He was much relieved to be assured that although the potential for that kind of behaviour could be seen in the chart it did not appear to have manifested. The experience does, however, illustrate the damage which can be inflicted by an unthinking reading of a past life with no further counselling or interpretation available.

Uranus has the potential for truly aware and creative relationships, based on an acknowledgement of, and respect for, individual difference and a recognition of mutual essence. It offers the soul an opportunity to move away from the stultifying patterns of the past into a new and original, mode of relating.

Neptune

With Neptune in the eighth house the lesson is to learn to share the unconditional love and vision it channels down from the higher levels of consciousness through the soul merging itself into another. Or it may be that the soul has to be more realistic about how much it gives of itself as there may have been a past tendency to 'sacrifice all', to immolate and lose itself in a relationship, thereby forsaking its separateness and integration. The sign on the cusp can be helpful here, and so can the aspects to Neptune. Virgo on the cusp or Saturn aspects are more likely to indicate restriction in the past and point to a need to open up to another soul in the present incarnation. The Neptune in Libra soul may well have sacrificed too much of itself in a past relationship and now needs to learn to channel the energy constructively into a mutual sharing rather than self-immolation, in order to discover the true meaning of union and relationship.

Neptune in this house represents the soul's potential to offer to another soul a sharing and merging into a higher level of Being through the spiritual sexual pathway of mutual bliss. It is the pathway of Tantric yoga and Taoist practices, and the soul with this placement can benefit from the study and practical application of these principles to its life.

Pluto

The lesson for Pluto in the eighth house is for the soul to re-attune to its old awareness of the cycle of birth, death and rebirth, the creative energy underlying the universe. It will then have a powerful energy to draw on for healing and transformation which can be shared with other souls on the same journey.

Pluto in this placement may indicate that the soul will be trapped in a pattern of power and exploitation, or that it may be too egotistical and manipulative in how it 'shares' itself: 'Power can easily be misused ... People will be impressed, but not empowered. Dishonesty, a breaking of agreements, subtle bullying, the need to be right at all times, a quick temper, and a misuse of principles are some of the indications of ego involvement.'[5]

A client with Pluto in the eighth (square to Venus in Aries and trine to Mars in Scorpio) was engaged to a man for very many years and eventually married him despite his powerful mother having opposed the union (his Moon in Scorpio conjuncted her Mars). The marriage had sado-masochistic overtones as her husband insisted on dominating her (his Mars trined her Saturn and conjuncted her Pluto, and his Pluto squared her Venus). She tried many times to leave the relationship but never succeeded, as he had considerable power over her through the contact to her Pluto and its reflection of her own inner energies. In many ways it seemed she was addicted to him and to the violence and conflict of the relationship which was based on an old pattern of manipulation and dominance.

When Pluto moves beyond this level into the level of transpersonal power, it is intimately connected with the energy of the cosmos, the eternal creative source, and it can become a channel for healing the earth and all those upon it through its relationship to the whole.

SYNASTRY AND KARMA

The type of karma embodied within a relationship, and the lessons to be learnt from it, can be ascertained from the synastry between the charts and, in particular, from the contacts of the outer planets in one chart to the personal planets in the other chart (the interaspects). Aspects between the personal planets will indicate the degree of superficial or sexual attraction between the partners but it is the outer planet and south nodal (see Chapter 2) contacts to the personal planets which delineate the older and deeper interaction. It should, however, be noted that it is not always the person who has the planet in aspect who acts out the role of that planet. Saturnine contacts, for example, may manifest either through Saturn 'playing the heavy' or through the personal planet taking on the colour of Saturn and acting its role of control or limitation.

Pluto Interaspects

The old interaction with Pluto contacts to the personal planets is symbiotic or parasitic, as in the relationship in which one partner 'feeds' off the other. It can be obsessive or absorbing, one partner being incapable of autonomous functioning within the relationship because it is so wrapped up in the other; or dominant, one partner having total control and power over the other. The type of relationship in the past could have been one between lovers, business partners, arranged marriage partners, master and slave, emasculating mother and son or authoritarian father and daughter. Pluto–Venus contacts in particular signify an old symbiotic 'love' interaction, Pluto–Moon an old mothering issue. Pluto–Mars contacts can include old violence – physical, verbal or emotional, or a festering resentment which may manifest again as an underlying feel to the present relationship, or which may erupt into open aggression.

A Pluto conjunction and a Mars quincunx to the fifth house (love affairs) Moon in Leo, and several Neptune interaspects, featured in the contacts between the charts of two men involved in a violent sexual relationship. The 'Pluto' partner responded to an initial reading of his chart by requesting a follow-up reading on this specific relationship:

> The medieval woman experience is very close to me still and it is agonising and affects any close relationship I enter in-to – and by close I don't mean obviously sexual. It's more of fear – fear I will lose them and that they will betray me – and this fear makes me cling at times which is unhealthy for all concerned . . . the only time I ever loved anyone it ended up with all three of my medieval experiences repeating themselves: 'rape', 'betrayal' and horrific violence.

I know this sounds strange but although he was brutal in many ways I felt he was my child, although he was four years senior in age. When he betrayed me I felt as though an innocent child had been destroyed in front of me.

In the synastry between the charts there was a Sun conjunction to the Midheaven and Stephen Arroyo suggests that this seems to 'correlate with past familial ties wherein one person was the child of another'[6] so that the Pluto–Moon 'mothering' contact was reinforced. The Neptune contacts were strongly idealistic and at first they had both tried to see the relationship as a spiritual one. However, in addition to the Pluto–Mars interaspect, a violent conjunction of Saturn to Mars, a Pluto trine to the Sun and a Pluto–Sun quincunx indicate that old power struggles also featured in the charts erupted into 'rape', also an old karmic pattern. This was followed by six years of domination by the 'Moon' partner of the 'Pluto' partner in a reversal of the previous mother/child relationship. Eventually the 'weaker' partner was able to break free and begin to work on his own inner energies. In time he recognized that the contact had served its purpose, having acted as a catalyst, and it was time for him to move on.

Pluto–Mercury contacts can indicate old mental games and a manipulation of the mind, a psychological pressure which creeps with a subtle yet relentless force into the present contact. A client with this contact found that her husband waged a ceaseless underground 'war of nerves' against her in an attempt to force her out of their joint business and to push her into having a breakdown, so that he could avoid paying her off. When this did not work, he resorted to a slow poisoning of her body and it was only when she had her food analysed that she was able to put a stop to it. But of course, with Pluto involved, she was not able to prove that it was his doing. In the end, she was so manipulated and terrorized by him that she allowed him to divorce her without the settlement to which she was entitled.

In the initial meeting in the present life of souls with a Pluto contact there can be a strong magnetic pull from the Pluto partner and the other partner may therefore be very willing to fall back into the old pattern of relationship. That pattern will almost certainly include being manipulated or dominated and may generate an overt or covert power struggle. With a Pluto contact one of the partners usually feels that he or she can transform the other into something better. The lesson that is needed is to set the other free to be an individual, to put manipulation aside and allow the partner to grow spontaneously according to his or her own life plan. This can at times involve one partner totally removing himself or herself from the relationship in order to live freely, or it may involve a renegotiation of the terms of the interaction in order that both partners may function autonomously.

A client (seventh house Mars in Libra) was married to a man with a Mars/Pluto conjunction in Leo which squared her nodal axis; her Mars squared his nodal axis, his Saturn trined her Mars and his Mercury squared her Pluto. The marriage was full of conflict and her husband, who was a very wealthy man, had all the power in the relationship. When she eventually told him she wanted to separate his response was to cut off all finance. Their old karmic interaction, in which money had been used as a weapon, had been one of business partners and the pattern was being repeated. In the present incarnation, he was more concerned with the convenience of having a wife than with having a loving relationship and he said she could stay on as housekeeper 'with sexual duties'. He also stipulated, however, that she would have to agree to do exactly as he wished in bringing up the children and running the home, including giving up her job. Her response was to withdraw a considerable sum of money from a joint account he had 'forgotten about', secretly buy a house in a different part of the country where she had found a job, and move out. It appeared that she was both dealing with old karmic patterns within the relationship (through her seventh house Mars and his Mars/Pluto conjunction) and being offered the opportunity to totally change the way in which she used her Will. However, the underhanded, devious Plutonian way in which she had intended to deal with the situation indicated that she was moving into the power games associated with the Leo North Node and setting up more karma between them, rather than owning her own power through negotiating for change.

In their constructive manifestation, however, Pluto contacts can bring in immensely creative energies of rebirth and regeneration to heal and transform relationships.

Uranus Interaspects

Uranus contacts are the antithesis of Pluto. Where Pluto indicates that one soul was absorbed, Uranus indicates that the soul never really got committed to the relationship at all. There was sporadic, intensely exciting contact, particularly on the sexual level, alternating with long periods of separation due to war or other manifestation of Uranian chaos. Uranus interaspects to the Sun, Moon, Venus or Mars can indicate a very strong sexual attraction, or if there are Uranus–Mercury aspects, for example, a very deep friendship but no commitment to an even deeper relationship.

In the present life Uranian contacts can be lived very intensely, but the frantic pace cannot continue or the relationship will burn itself out very quickly. The other enemy of the Uranian relationship is boredom. Compromise is needed in order to build into the relationship the freedom to explore other areas of life whilst retaining the secure base of a committed relationship. The karmic lesson is to build a unit consisting of two individuals coming together to form the relationship, to which both are committed, or to set free from the past attraction once and for all.

When the interaspects are between members of a family, this indicates an interaction established in childhood which is then carried over into adult life. A client's Sun/Pluto conjunction in Cancer conjuncted her daughter's Uranus. This was only one facet of an extremely complex chart interaction and network of past relationships, but it was found that the mother had been an all-powerful Mother Superior and the daughter one of her novices. The relationship had been a very old one, stretching back to Egypt and beyond when it involved a very close love bond between two sisters. In the present life the daughter had a conflict between seeking a very close contact with her mother (a natal Pluto—Venus aspect giving her a desperate craving for more and more love) and needing to free herself from her mother's authority (her Uranus conjuncting her mother's Sun/Pluto in Cancer).

This dilemma was reflected in her relationship with her lover, who was anxious to settle down and have a family, and in the Uranus interaspects with his chart. Once she had sorted out her feelings about her mother, finally cutting the psychic 'umbilical cord' in order to obtain her freedom whilst acknowledging the close bond between them, she was able to commit herself to marriage. It was, however, suggested that she should negotiate a 'marriage contract' which would set out and honour both her need for her own space within the relationship and the somewhat unconventional type of interaction she required in order to function freely.

Saturn Interaspects

One of the most common karmic aspects within a marriage or other love relationship is a Saturn contact. Saturn can indicate either a soul who has in the past had authority over its partner, or one to whom there is a sense of debt or responsibility, of having to repay something from the past. The old interaction may have involved one partner saving the life of the other, or having metaphorically done so through an act of kindness or allegiance.

A client with an Aquarian Sun conjunction to his wife's Saturn regressed back to a lifetime during which he had been a gaoler for a group of religious prisoners. He had allowed them to escape as he had not felt they had committed a crime and could not see them die. He had later been executed for this but after the regression he commented that at least he had died with a clear conscience. In passing he noted that his present-life wife was amongst the group, although in that lifetime they had had no other contact. Clearly, however, he had saved her life at that point. Their present relationship was a difficult one, but both partners were very committed to working it out as they felt it was their destiny to come together.

Stephen Arroyo[7] points out that at the commencement of the Saturnine relationship there is a sense of security, of being comfortable and a feeling of each partner having known the other 'for ever'. At that first meeting, however, there may be an initial 'stepping back' from the person, a pause for breath, as though the soul knows instinctively that here is someone with whom a relationship will be serious and growth-inducing. Saturn contacts are rarely entered into lightly, without some forewarning of what is to come. Once the commitment is made, however, then the negative aspects of the interaction start to appear. One of the partners can have a strong sense of duty towards the other, of owing something, 'I cannot leave him, I must see it through' being a usual comment about the relationship. This is a matter-of-fact comment: unlike the Neptunian or Pisces self-sacrificing attitude that the other person cannot live without them, the Saturnine attitude is practical. With this placement the soul feels committed to the relationship and knows that there is a reason for the problems and will try to resolve them.

A Pisces client volunteered to return to her ex-husband to support him in dealing with cancer. They had remained friendly after the divorce and she wanted to be with him 'to repay a debt'. His Sun conjuncted and his Moon opposed her Saturn; his Sun trined, his Moon sextiled, his Venus squared, and his North Node conjuncted her Pluto. She felt that she needed to understand both his and her own behaviour in the past, and knew that his present approach to his condition could not bring about a recovery. She hoped that by being with him at such a difficult time, she could overcome any past karma left in the relationship and perhaps help him change his attitude and therefore the prognosis of the disease.

When the contact is between Saturn and Venus, the relationship may involve one partner – often the male, and not necessarily the Saturn partner – becoming a financial burden on the other, or a chronic illness or other dependency may develop requiring an unusual degree of support. This interaspect is common in the charts of alcoholics or addicts and their partners and may be offering the partner an opportunity to repay something from the past by standing by, and offering support, whilst the addict goes through a karmic lesson.

Saturn in interaspect to Mars can bring in the possibility of old violence resurfacing, lessons around the use of the Will and conflict within the relationship. This can affect both a marriage type of partnership, in which the essence of the interaction is fear and control, or it can surface within a business partnership in which the underlying conflict can make decision-taking a dangerous pathway. With such a contact one soul may very much feel that the other has both power and authority, and that self-assertion is something to be feared as it may cause the underlying violence to explode. However, the issue of assertion and of the 'right' use of the Will within the partnership will be basic to the interaction and will have to be tackled at some stage. This interaspect shows up in the synastry between the Tsar of Russia and Lenin (there is some doubt as to Lenin's correct date of birth but the Mars aspect stands for either date). The Tsar's Mars is trine Lenin's Saturn, and his Pluto is conjunct Lenin's Mercury, indicating the possibility of an old violence and mental manipulation or psychological pressure underlying the current interaction. The Tsar had a Neptune/Moon conjunction in the Aries eighth house, indicating the potential for a sacrifice of himself and a confusion in perceiving the extent of the change and its effect on his life. He may well have believed himself to be infallible and 'immortal' with a divine right to rule. Lenin had Uranus conjunct the North Node in Cancer in the eighth, symbolizing the potential for revolution and the sharing of new ideas of equality and freedom.

Being present at moments of history such as the Russian Revolution can also bring out underlying karma and help a soul recognize its conflicts. A member of the English aristocracy (eleventh house Sun in Cancer opposing Moon in Sagittarius) was welcomed both by the Tsar and later by Lenin. In his chart he had tenth house Venus/Pluto/Saturn/South Node in Gemini opposing Uranus/Neptune/North Node in Sagittarius, with Uranus squared by first house Mars in Virgo. The events at the time strongly activated his own inner conflict regarding ideology, revolution and change versus duty and stability, and his mystic/pragmatist dilemma. The Tsar's Saturn squared his Mars and conjuncted his Uranus, illustrating his helplessness to aid the Tsar in the face of the revolution. Lenin's Saturn conjuncted his Moon, suppressing his emotional response, and Lenin's Mars conjuncted his Saturn, which rendered his aristocratic Will powerless. As a military attaché his role was to stand by in strict neutrality whilst the tragic events took their course, no matter what his feelings as an individual might be.

The lesson to be learnt by the soul who is undertaking a Saturn role within a partnership, whatever the interaspect, is to let go of fear and authority and to accept and encourage the growth of self-sufficiency and the ability to stand alone. The co-dependent partner, for example, therefore has to learn to stand aside placidly and allow the other soul to control its own life, regardless of the mess that may be made of it. Saturn can, even with the best of intentions, be very 'heavy-handed' and be perceived by its partner as critical or nagging, even when it is trying to be constructive and helpful. Lightness of touch has to be developed and humour used to overcome the tendency to moralize. Once some degree of progress has been made, the Saturn soul can experience fear at the loss of control of the other person or of the situation. It therefore has to transcend its own limitations to ensure a complementary, balanced growth within the relationship.

An unusual interaction was signified by a Chiron/Saturn conjunction interaspect to the Sun across the charts of two people who had past-life recall. They were very aware that in another time plane they were simultaneously fighting together in the Vietnam war and that the female partner had died despite her friend's effort to save her. The male partner had Pluto/Uranus/Mars in the seventh house conjuncting the female's Sun and they uncovered many strong past-life links which impinged on the present life. They lived as a partnership which was dedicated to growing together and helping others.

In its positive aspect, Saturn can bring stability and responsibility to a partnership which allows for repayment of karmic debts.

Neptune Interaspects

Neptune represents a very subtle karmic interaction in which there is often an underlying sense of soulmate contact, although unfortunately this does not always turn out to be the case in the present incarnation. Neptune contacts to the Sun, Moon, Venus and Mercury can bring an almost mystical unity or hypnotic quality to the relationship, and telepathic contact can continue even when the partners are physically separated. A client's Neptune was conjuncted by an ex-lover's Moon which in turn sextiled her Pluto/Saturn conjunction. Her Moon was square her ex-lover's Neptune. She described the relationship:

> It is nearly six years since I met this man and three years since we broke up. For six years I have not known a single day without him being 'around' in some way. I don't seem to be able to get rid of him. This was the best and worst relationship I have had – it still hurts. I saw very little of him.

In the past there may have been strong spiritual and psychic bonds forged through early temple training, a contemplative order, or many loving incarnations together in which there were no boundaries or separation, so that the psychic contact and communication on the spiritual level continues despite physical distance.

On the other hand, Neptune interaspects can indicate a high degree of illusion or delusion, or incorporate deep deception, particularly when the soul taking the role of Neptune is deluding or deceiving itself and projects this into the relationship. Although with Neptunian contacts the soul may squirm for a while and try to avoid the truth of the interaction, this truth will be brought up again and again until it does penetrate its consciousness and until its partner is seen clearly for what he or she is *now*.

A client whose Venus was conjuncted by her ex-husband's Neptune said that on first meeting she had been very wary of him, but very soon 'fell under his spell' and believed that 'this was the most wonderful relationship I could ever have. It seemed so perfect . . . I felt as though I had known him for ever, we were meant for each other.' He had a hypnotic effect on her (she was undergoing a transit of Neptune to her Moon at the time and was particularly open to emotional delusion) and when, six months after the marriage, she suddenly realized the extent of her illusions about him she 'felt just as though someone had snapped their fingers and brought her out of a hypnotic trance': the relationship consisted of lies and deception on his part. However, by the time she found out the truth, he had 'conned' her out of a considerable amount of money in the form of 'loans' to get him back on his feet again. She had agreed to lend him the money because she felt a very subtle sense of debt to him and wanted to help – the all-pervasive influence of the Neptunian contact. 'Wanting to help' is very typical of Neptune contacts. Whereas a Saturn contact feels that it has an obligation out of duty, the Neptune contact volunteers out of 'love'.

The deception of Neptune can be apparent in diverse relationships, particularly those which do not have an underlying 'love' bond. A client went to work for a new company. Her boss had promised her the world: a new car, a good salary, travel and excellent promotion prospects. When these failed to materialize, she looked at the aspects between their charts: his Neptune squared her Mutable Sun/Mercury, her Neptune inconjuncted his Mutable Sun which in turn conjuncted her Uranus. She recognized karma-in-the-making, and changed her job rapidly.

Neptune interaspects to Venus or the Sun or the Moon can often indicate an unrealistic idealization of one of the partners involved, based on the soul's past interaction with that partner and expecting the partner to remain the same, leaving no room for change, human frailty or fallibility. This idealization leaves the soul open to disappointment and disillusionment. A Scorpio client with fifth house Venus/Neptune conjuncted by an old friend's Neptune had a past interaction in the present life which was unsatisfactory to say the least:

He's been in and out of my life like a shadow, going away for long periods of time and never making any attempt to get close to me. Recently he contacted me again. After having been a drunken drifter for too long, he's changed his life around – seemingly overnight – and now has a house in the country and a talent for the stock market. He is an extremely complex, secretive, clever individual [Sun/Moon in Capricorn square Neptune reflecting her Scorpionic qualities] and I feel a very deep bond with him. For years I cried lonely tears, only wishing for some receptivity on his part. Am I meant to suffer unrequited love or are we in the fullness of time meant to be together?

His Aquarian Venus conjoined her South Node and she was being pulled back to the past with a yearning for, and illusion of, 'perfection' reflected through the Neptune–Moon interaspect. The reality, however, was more likely to be that his detached Aquarian Venus would never give her the close and fulfilling union she was seeking. It seemed like a classic case of 'unrequited love' and for her own growth she would need to let go of the past, grieve for what could not be, and then move on.

Neptune interaspects to Mercury may have the pattern of having a very deep intuitive insight into the partner's motivation and desires, whilst maintaining secrecy about the soul's own, and therefore needing to learn the value of open and honest communication. On the other hand, they can indicate strongly telepathic qualities and a meeting of minds on the level of spiritual ideals and values. Neptune may also have an understanding of its partner which can be helpful when working on the inner levels, particularly the psychological patterns. Such an aspect always features when a client says: 'He feels that I have a line into his head, that I understand him in a way no one else can, not even himself.' The partner may not always be too happy with this, feeling invaded and lacking in privacy but, if there is an openness to working on him or herself, then this can be an extremely helpful aspect. A meeting between Neptune and Mercury may be the catalyst required to set someone on to the inner transformational or spiritual pathway.

The Neptune-attuned soul is also capable of great personal sacrifice for another, including vicarious suffering. On the other hand, it can play the martyr and delude itself into thinking that others need the sacrifice when it would really be more constructive for them to deal with their own karma. The mother who gives up everything to care for her child is a good illustration of this: her child may have in fact grown more through a mother fulfilled by her own career and/or while, perhaps, struggling with isolation and loneliness. In 'giving up everything' the mother is adding a karmic burden to the child who then feels a guilty obligation to the paragon: an attitude which will colour its subsequent interaction in adult relationships. Then a similar 'sacrifice' on the part of the partner might be expected, or it may prove impossible to find anyone who lives up to the impossibly high and totally unrealistic standard set by mother.

Neptunian contacts can, however, be very healing through the unconditional love and acceptance of frailty which allows the 'weaker' partner to be loved for what he or she is in a non-judgemental way. This can pave the way to self-acceptance and self-love by the other, who thereby gains inner strength.

By accepting and loving others as they presently are, instead of holding back until they meet our idealized images or romantic expectations, they may feel a sense of safety that finally enables them to release the pain of past hurts. These accumulated bodily held hurts and frustrations, which often originate from previous rejection or unreciprocated love, have an opportunity to heal within the context of a relationship characterized by a growing sense of trust. Such a relationship may then become a 'therapeutic' one in that we are resolving conflicts and growing toward a healthier, happier dimension of being.[8]

Jupiter Interaspects

Jupiter interaspects are usually expansive and growth-inducing. Where Jupiter contacts a personal planet, Ascendant, Midheaven or the seventh or twelfth house, the Jupiter soul will help attunement to the highest potential and growth possibilities. This contact is particularly helpful in the teacher and pupil or employer and employee relationship as it can assure success in the chosen field.

The old Jupiter contact is often between teacher and pupil, or priest and priestess, and the partners will be naturally drawn back into a spiritual interaction. When Jupiter is adversely aspected however, or located in Taurus, for example, the karma may be one of intemperance, unrestrained sexuality, or profligacy. Two business partners came together with a Jupiter–Saturn square between their charts, and a trine from the tenth house Sun in one chart to the seventh house Jupiter in the other chart. The partner whose Saturn squared the other's Jupiter stated that he considered his role to be to teach his partner the value of money as this was something he had never learnt. Unfortunately his partner did not see the need for prudence, or budgets, and bankrupted the company twice. Eventually, however, the persistence and faith of the Saturnine partner paid off and they established a successful joint business in which each took equal responsibility, thereby fulfilling the potential of the Jupiter–Sun trine, resolving the dilemma of the Saturn–Jupiter square, and encouraging mutual growth.

Examining the natal chart and its interaction with others can therefore throw light on the underlying processes and evolutionary forces at work both within the individual and those with whom contact is made. Overcoming karmic obligations and outgrown karmic patterns can lead to fulfilment of the purpose of incarnation as manifested through the moment of rebirth, opening the way to reintegration with the divine and a return to the source of Being.

Conclusion

JOURNEY'S END?

With reincarnation man is a dignified immortal being, evolving towards a glorious end, without it, he is a tossing straw on the stream of chance circumstances, irresponsible for his character, his actions, his destiny.

ANNIE BESANT, *THE ANCIENT WISDOM*

Overcoming karmic patterns leads to the fulfilling of potential and to the expression of the highest octave of the chart, moving towards integration and wholeness of the physical, mental, emotional and spiritual states of Being. Within wholeness comes a shift of emphasis to a spiritual perspective, with reclamation of old knowledge and power.

The oldest question known to man must surely be: 'Why are we here?' That question provides the impetus and basis for all religions and all religions attempt to answer it in their own way. The concept of reincarnation, however, is not a religious answer, it is a philosophical, ethical and spiritual one. It teaches that each soul is the sculptor of its life, fashioned on the loom of experience by the power of action and thought, and therefore places the responsibility for the soul's conduct squarely on itself. We cannot blame external forces in the shape of 'fate' or 'nemesis', we can only look within to perceive the cause and manifested effect. When we come to realize that difficulties are the fibre from which inner strength is built, then we face up to problems and get on with the business of living. The doctrine of reincarnation can offer the opportunity for a soul to make recompense for past wrongs, not by undergoing punishment or taking on retaliatory handicaps or events but through service to others which will restore the balance and harmony lacking in the total experience. When life, and in particular the universal problem of suffering, is seen as having a definite purpose then the exercise of choice and free will becomes mandatory for spiritual growth and the birthchart is recognized as the map for the journey to perfection.

However, we do not have to wait until our North Node is in the twelfth house or our Sun is in Pisces to reach a point of release from our karma. We merely have to change our level of awareness and shift our mode of becoming into Being to know that we are cosmic, eternal and therefore already perfect, and free to create our own reality and our destiny. As Richard Bach points out in *Illusions*:

> *You are led*
> *through your lifetime*
> *by the inner learning creature,*
> *the playful spiritual being*
> *that is your real self.*
>
> *Don't turn away*
> *from possible futures*
> *before you're certain you don't have*
> *anything to learn from them.*
>
> *You're always free*
> *to change your mind and*
> *choose a different future, or*
> *a different past.*[1]

To the question: 'Why are we here?', we can reply: 'To learn and expand spiritual awareness through a life of harmony and love and to begin the next stage of the evolution of mankind into a state of higher consciousness.' Just as Freud re-discovered the existence of the unconscious which had remained virtually unrecognized for centuries, so we are now learning that there is a higher consciousness linked to a divine spark buried deep within the soul: the Self. And, just as the unconscious is connected to the collective level, the Self unites with the whole of creation in cosmic selfhood. Attunement to the Self comes about through *listening* in the silence of meditation and spiritual discipline, which are tools for the Aquarian Age. The Self then becomes the guiding star for the soul's journey.

New religions tend to arise at the changeover of the Age

and higher consciousness may form the basis of a new, universal, Aquarian religion as postulated by Jerome Ellison in the Seventies:

> In the beginning it will have two branches, one terrestrial and physical, the other cosmic and psychical . . . The terrestrial . . . is beginning to make itself known under the name of ecology . . . (Man) is rediscovering that the earth is not inert but conscious, with a consciousness comparable to his own. It reacts to him. A mutual dependency exists . . . At the same time as man's ecological consciousness – his awareness of local and outer space – has been expanding, so has his depth – psychological experience – his exploration of inner space. Once this psychic realm is opened, its relationship to the physical realm becomes clear. Man and the living creatures of the earth are seen as products of the cosmic, or divine, imagination. The Great Project of Creation is seen to be evolution – not just of physical shapes . . . but of consciousness . . . These two movements – the broadened awareness of the physical universe through ecology and the deepened comprehension of the psyche by meditation – are not static but growing. For a certainty these outward and inward reachings will become aware of their oneness and for a certainty, this will constitute a new world religion.[2]

When the incarnated soul reaches the point of 'grace' and enlightenment it moves beyond karma. The karmic journey is over. All possibilities are open. It could continue its sojourn on earth as a Master aiding others on their journey. But other planes of being await exploration:

> Beyond the stars are Stars in which there is no combust or sinister aspect.
> Stars moving in other heavens not the Seven Heavens known to all.
> Stars immanent in the radiance of the Light of God, neither joined to each other or separate.
> Who so hath his future from these Stars, his soul drives off and consumes the unbeliever.[3]

Appendix I

CASE STUDY: 'PEOPLE AND PURPOSE'

In the example Karmic Reading given below, the chart for which (fig. 34) has two Fingers of Fate and an Ascendant Pluto–Sun Grand Trine, the client was very succinct about his problem: 'people and purpose'. He was a computer wizard, very withdrawn and introspective and had studied meditation with a sect who insisted that only spiritual experience was real, life in a physical body merely being an illusion. The chart he supplied was tatty, smudged and incomplete, showing only the positive aspects. Excerpts from the Reading are set out below to illustrate the karmic approach to a chart:

I have redrawn the chart as it is a picture of your Self and I did not feel the one supplied helped your self-image. Also I have drawn in the aspects in greater detail as this shows the energy pattern within you, indicating the surface tensions and the deeper disharmonies.

Everything about the birthchart is symbolic and can operate on many levels. It can also operate within your psyche or, if you are not consciously expressing the energies, it can be expressed in the situations which you attract to yourself, and through which you live out the unresolved conflicts. Everything I say needs to be looked at in its widest meaning . . . [so that] you can get to the core. I use examples to illustrate how energies may affect you, but you will need to look at your own life, particularly your child-hood, to see how the energies specifically manifested. The child-hood one builds for oneself in this life is the culmination and reflection of traits/difficulties which have been building up over many lifetimes and which, ultimately, force attention upon these matters.

The elemental pattern shows up the kind of response which you

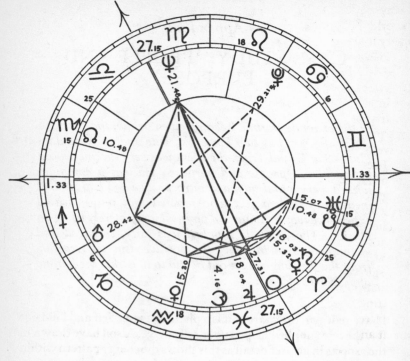

Fig. 34

have brought back with you. The lack of Air often indicates that you have to learn to use the intellect. It can also be that this function was very highly developed throughout several incarnations and now there has to be a balancing up between the intellect and the intuition. You have those four Water planets, including the Sun and Moon, and the Fire Ascendant so that you do have a very strong intuition available for your use. As the Sun and Moon are in the same sign your task is to do what you have done before but in a different way, to utilize more strongly the positive aspects of Pisces. One of your main purposes in incarnating with such a chart is to learn to express that intuition in your life and also to integrate your spirituality into everyday life, so that it becomes a way of life rather than an excuse for withdrawing from the world – which is something which comes forward from your past very intensely.

Pisces has to do with devotion, and the Sun/Jupiter–Neptune opposition indicates great breadth of spiritual vision within you. However, because Pisces also has deep very elusive and unfathomable emotional depths, and can so easily play the part of the martyr who sacrifices all for those visions, I feel that you need to be practical, to learn to keep your feet on the ground, before developing further the spiritual side of your life.

The imbalance of elements, with the emphasis on Water, makes you emotionally very vulnerable. It is as though you cannot bear emotional pain because you have no defences against it. Therefore you need to become more objective and detached and this will be achieved through bringing it up to the surface and facing your own sensitivity. I was watching at the workshop when the tapes [past-life regressions] were being played, particularly the one of the girl who was to be executed. You may be aware that you actually put your hands over your ears to shut it out, it was hurting you because of the extreme Pisces empathy with pain. I also feel that you know deep down inside what it is to hurt like that and are therefore frightened of allowing it to surface again – or to face it in other people. But it is very necessary for you to learn to be in control instead of repressing your responses as you are doing now. It is a question of finding the middle way and of doing something practical to help those in distress, so that you do not feel helpless and useless. All this can only come about through letting go the barriers you have built up and allowing your empathy to flow in a free and unrestricted way, but with the Saturn self-discipline to direct the response into constructive channels.

Pisces has to learn about emotions. It can be like the fishes of its glyph, tugged in conflicting directions by the pull of the water (emotions), and can 'wallow' in emotion or retreat totally. Both responses, paradoxically, continually bring you face to face with what you are running away from. For a Piscean, it is also necessary to face one's illusions and pierce the Neptunian veil to reach the centre of one's being, where one is not swayed by emotions. Ideally, one gets to the stage where one has emotions without being stuck in one's emotions. At this point of evolution the positive links of Pisces to the spiritual realm can manifest.

If you look at the basic pattern of the chart, it is very introspective with only Neptune and Pluto projected above the horizon (that is, out to the external world), and they are transpersonal planets. This is a sign that the qualities which these planets represent (spirituality and healing on their higher vibrations, fantasy illusion and emotional trauma on the lower manifestations) will be what you project out to the world. Obviously if you are still tuned into the lower vibrations of the energies you will find much more difficulty with people and with expressing your own emotions in particular. And yet, by realigning yourself to the higher vibrations a tremendous transformation of your life can be achieved.

The position of the Moon's North Node indicates the areas of life where you most need to grow, and yours falls into the eleventh house. This is the house of group consciousness, of aligning oneself to the wider needs of humanity through working within a group . . .

[Fourth house] . . . is part of the key to the present difficulties. This is the house of parentage, traditionally the mother but also associated with the father. A Mercury/Saturn conjunction in this house immediately implicates your parents as being a particularly relevant influence in the mental and emotional spheres. Saturn in this context is restriction, repressions, fear and inadequacy coming in from the earliest childhood to stunt the development of your self-image. It is often associated with great emotional coldness in the home and with a lack of real love expressed to the child. When Mercury is involved the child may either seem very dull (out of fear and inhibition) or he may be pushed to achieve high intellectual competence whilst other areas of life are pushed aside. He is only valued for what he achieves, not for who he is.

With the Sun–Pluto–Ascendant Grand Trine also affecting this house and the house of learning to share resources with others (eighth house), I feel that the emotional climate of your home may well have been 'tight-fisted' and manipulative. It is obvious that with a birth during the war years there could be a separation from the father, but this occurs even when there is not a war and not just in the physical sense. The quality behind the experience is often an absorption into the mother (an unhealthy expression of 'love' which leaves no room for emotional growth or the development of a sense of self or separateness from the emotional climate of the mother). The Moon–Pluto inconjunct and the position of the Moon in the third house indicate a deep karma with your mother. I had a sense of a previous incarnation together in which she was your sister and there was incestuous contact resulting in guilt. There is also the difficulty (Sun in opposition to Neptune) that your present-life father was 'weak' in some way and was not a good role model for building up your own masculine side. This produces uncertainty and lack of confidence in yourself as a man – which underlies your contact with people and surfaces years later within the confines of a sexual relationship.

As I said, we attract to ourselves the kind of childhood which epitomizes problems encountered in earlier lives and I feel that with the Sun in Pisces there is a lot of emotional drama which has been repressed deep within you and now needs to be gently let up to the surface. With so much Pisces, those watery depths can be a very fearful place, and with the very primitive force behind them which explodes from time to time (Pluto–Moon inconjunct), gentle work is essential for you to avoid being swamped.

The Saturn/Mercury conjunction can often make true communication difficult, holding back the natural Pisces tendency to give of oneself. Mercury is the planet of communication and anything Saturn touches is inhibited. Again this is something I feel can be traced to past lives and to childhood, when you may have felt that you had to be a 'good boy', and never were allowed to express what was within you, so that you became very solitary and unused to sharing your feelings with others. There is also, from the Aries influence, the possibility that you were very centred in upon yourself with little interest in other children. It is as if you have an invisible barrier around: you can see what is taking place 'out there' but feel cut off and isolated from any understanding or interaction.

There is also in your chart a need to explore sexuality and creativity . . . That eighth house Pluto is in its natural house and it has strong connections with the cycle of birth and death; it represents the deeper, darker side of life, together with an ability to penetrate to the depths in search of insight. Being in Cancer it can be hidden away behind the shell of apparent indifference, but ultimately it will surface, and if not directly allowed expression it will become 'subverted' and may appear in many guises – fantasy being one of the least harmful of these, but compulsions and obsessions stemming from a past life are frequent expressions of this energy. Your relationships will have a 'fated' quality about them as they go back into the past.

This is particularly emphasized when we look at the aspects Pluto makes. It is at the head of a Finger of Fate with Mars and the Moon, and this can indicate much violence around sexuality in the past, particularly when you incarnated as a woman. There is no natural outlet for the tremendous creative energy which is bound up within this formation and so, symbolically, it will continue to circle deep within your being at odds with itself until you release it. It is an energy which is best used in nurturing, healing or creative pursuits. As that Pluto also finds itself in a Grand Trine with the Sun and the Ascendant, it seems to me that much of your purpose would become apparent if you went into a healing group.

There is another Finger of Fate in your chart (one is rare, two really needs close looking at). The second Finger of Fate does have a natural outlet. It is formed from Neptune to Saturn/Mercury and Venus, with the outlet through the opposition to Jupiter and the Sun: tied in this one aspect we have your spirituality, your sense of your Self, your mind, your inhibitions and repressions but also your self-discipline, your capacity for relationships (Venus) and the planet of faith and expansion (Jupiter).

Very often Jupiter–Neptune and Saturn–Neptune aspects denote different 'religious' lives – lives guided by innate faith and lives guided by rules and regulations. The natural spirituality and universal love which lie behind religion have to be brought up into consciousness. Venus–Neptune contacts indicate a great idealization of women – a devotion to the Virgin Mary would epitomize the extreme of this, particularly when someone is totally taken up with 'Mother Church' but no physical expression is possible.

There can also be the kind of love which is from 'afar', without hope of consummation. It is a withholding of the physical and emotional Self and is often a substitute for 'real' relating. It is the kind of relationship the Troubadours sang of, great poets wrote about, and many romanticists still dream of. But it is totally impractical, typically Neptunian in being a nebulous, unattainable illusion, and it needs translating into practical expression of the quality of unconditional love which lies behind it.

There is also a great deal of fear and repression built into your relationships from the Saturn aspect; it looks as though you have the traumatic memory of a relationship behind you and have withdrawn from the possibility of being hurt so deeply again. There is an inner sense of vulnerability and defensiveness within your chart, such fear and trepidation, forming a barrier which you have built up around you. But unfortunately there is no magic formula to break through it: only you can do this, and you need to trust (Jupiter), but also to be ready to be hurt a little, to take that risk without guaranteed assurances that a relationship will work without any pain. We learn and we grow by going *through* pain and coming out the other side. It strengthens us and makes us better people, more understanding of others who share our pain. It is not possible to relate to people from inside a glass case, it is necessary to come out and share all the joys and sorrows which are part of the tapestry of life.

You also have a T-square in your chart between the Sun–Neptune opposition and the square to Mars. Looking at this there is a tremendous tension, your sensitivity (Neptune) seems to threaten your maleness so that you withdraw from it. This withdrawal is not a path of growth, however. Mars–Neptune demands that the Will be spiritualized, aligned to the needs of the cosmic Self. You have a very sensitive chart, it has more negative than positive planets and all your Pisces energy is highly psychic and needs to flow up to the surface. Learn to trust and use the intuition and the psychic talents wisely. It seems that you were once totally attuned to that kind of approach to life but that you were then cut off from it through trauma and now need to regain it. The missing leg of the T-square, which is where it would find release, is the house of relationships, and finding a loving, supportive, nurturing and unconditional partner would help you to express all these inner qualities in a positive way.

Jupiter is the ruler of your chart; it is the planet of faith and optimism in the future. If you could just attune to its vibration life would be very much freer for you – I have the sense that you are living out the pessimism of the Mercury/Saturn and lacking all joy in life. I know it sounds corny, but helping others less fortunate than yourself is a good way of doing this. By doing this, you will find inner resources and strengths where previously there was only fear and inadequacy.

You have the ability (Sagittarian Ascendant) to gather in knowledge, process it, and give it out again as wisdom and philosophy to guide others. If you could allow it, a subtle transformation could take place through your own intuition putting together apparently unrelated facts and coming up with a brilliant synthesis to solve a problem or to illumine a mystery. This is something you should be developing, particularly in the sense of trusting what comes into your mind. It would be helpful to keep a record of 'stray' thoughts, little things which will all tie up eventually, particularly in your present search for meaning and purpose. Often we expect a great 'Road to Damascus' revelation when all we need is to tie up all the small ones we have already had!

Your purpose is to regain the lost sense of unity and spirituality which is the heritage of Pisces; to regain your place in the world and to feel at ease once more with the people around you and with your God – both within and without; to find the inner Self and express its wisdom to the world, and to utilize your healing potential to heal both yourself and others. When you begin to experience other people as extensions of the one unity of spirit which the whole universe shares, then your problems with people will naturally fall away and you will be able to express your innate care and concern for others in a constructive way. Allowing Love to flow through you is a beginning, the rest is up to you.

Past lives 'seen' in the psychic part of the reading included the following (astrological indicators have been added for ease of reference):

A forestal . . . something more than a forester, more on the lines of Tolkien . . . you were the guardian of the forest. The trees were revered not as gods but as having a spiritual life . . . someone who was totally at home within that environment, who was a part of it not just living in it. You felt the emanations of the trees, drew sustenance from them. [Astrologically linked to Neptune in Virgo opposing the Sun in Pisces], you were part of the seasonal cycle; you 'died' in winter and were reborn in spring to new life. You were very instinctual and yet very wise; a wholeness is apparent which is lost now . . . having no trouble at all with the concept of infinity and eternity because you were part of the universe and could reach out and touch the outer stars and reach in and touch the tiniest particle . . . sacred groves with earth power, generated through rituals, drawn up from within the earth and utilized to nourish all that was upon it [linked to Pluto].

The Dark Ages: you were very deeply in love with a man, one who was charismatic and magnetic so that you could not help yourself. Much passion and meeting of minds. However, he manipulated you in order to gain power for himself [Pluto–Moon–Mars Finger of Fate]: you were a powerful lady in your own right. It seems to be one of those situations where you had the intelligence to see for yourself what was going on, but you refused to look at it [Venus–Neptune]. There was some kind of 'crusade' (against the king?) [Uranus/South Node conjunction opposing the eleventh house North Node]. The two of you were leading an army and having some success but you were captured and he abandoned you. There is a feeling of tremendous hurt, real physical pain because you knew that he could have saved you but chose to save his own skin. There is a dreadful picture of you being tortured but refusing to betray him and one of a long imprisonment during which you retreated into fantasy as a defence against the surroundings and the rejection and emotional hurt . . . and another life with the same man with a repeat of the betrayal and suicide [Neptune Finger of Fate].

From that point on, you are cut off from intimate relationships — you are a monk, an academic or a recluse, but never in a sexual relationship . . . A monk tending lepers including (with something more syphilitic than leprous) one who had been as a surrogate son to you ... the anguish as you saw him literally falling to pieces under your care until he became so deformed and ugly that no one else could bear to tend him. But you always saw the beauty of his soul and never felt sickened by his condition [Pisces]. There was pain when the disease affected his mind and he raged at you, rejecting your care. You were convinced that it was a just punishment when you in turn contracted leprosy [the Fingers of Fate]. After that, academic lives [Mercury/Saturn conjunction]. A picture of you working in Atlantis with computers [sixth-house Uranus], storing up all the knowledge and technology for those who you believed would come afterwards to inherit it — although there was an interest in the spiritual, technology was really your 'god'.

CASE STUDY: FAMILY INTERACTION

The following (fig. 35) is an extract from a Karmic Reading for a client who requested advice on her life direction and what she could do to encourage and guide her young son. A former nurse, she was drawn to psychotherapy but reported feeling 'strangely reluctant' to commit herself to the training. The client's planets are in the main ring, her husband's on the outer ring, and her son's on the inner:

You have the North Node of the Moon close to the cusp of your Aquarian fourth house. This has a lot to do with childhood and children, with parents and how you develop your Self and take it out to the world. So that I feel you will learn much about your own abilities through having children and being in a family situation. It is obviously an area of experience which you felt you needed to make particular reference to in this life, as is communication which is related to the third house Node.

You also have the Moon (widely conjunct Uranus) in the eighth house, which is connected with learning to share resources with another person and this planet is in Cancer, traditionally seen as the home. The Moon is how we function and it is based very much on our past conditioning. Uranus is an erratic, highly charged energy which wants to bring in change and innovation and which finds commitment to another person difficult. It is very intuitive but you have to learn to distinguish between intuition and negative emotions coming up out of that Cancer–Moon base. Cancer can be very fearful and need a lot of security before it will venture to express emotions, but of course the emotions are always there under the 'shell' which Cancer erects as a defence. Part of your karmic lesson is to let go of that shell, to let yourself trust and relate fully.

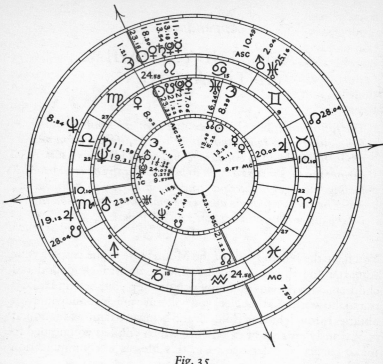

Fig. 35

You have Jupiter in the seventh house, which is a very benefic energy. What you have coming back to you through relationships will be a source of expansion for you. There is a good feel to your relationships from this – not only marriage but friendships benefit from Jupiter. It is in Taurus, a very practical down-to-earth sign which tends to ground things. This can be good for you as it helps you express your feelings in a concrete way and overcome the old karmic pattern of emotional insecurity.

One of the main indications of the inner insecurity brought back from the past comes from the Moon square to Saturn. This can indicate a childhood in which emotional stability and warmth were lacking in some way – often through a parent not being present, being ill, or being emotionally cold – so that an inner sense of being loved, which is essential for inner security of course, is not developed. The Sun/Pluto conjunction also has this connection of having an authoritarian father who has all the power. It then has the effect of making you seek out a strong, authority figure on whom to project your power in male relationships, so that all your husband's Leo planets would hook into this need you have. As you grow and find your own inner authority you will need to take care that it does not conflict too much with his energy. If you are aware of it, then you can work on this together. Two Leos have a very strong energy field and can clash because each wants to be 'king'. A joint rulership has to be agreed upon and established if there is to be harmony.

From that Sun–Pluto aspect (particularly with its connection to Mercury and its point on the T-square involving Mars and Jupiter) you will have a strong urge to remould yourself, to get rid of all your old emotional patterning and find a new, more appropriate way of functioning. You may have already found that you had periodic identity crises during your life and this arises out of this aspect. It usually brings radical alteration in the way you see yourself as you discover new aspects which need expression. These changes are dynamic, often coming out of dramatic moments (Leo) . . . one thing which you may need to avoid is any kind of new religious view which takes you on an ego trip. Leo is prone to this, and the conjunction will make this even more likely. It is karmically necessary to keep a balance between ego strength and humility – a battle which your Saturn–Neptune will continually bring you face to face with.

There is a feeling from the ninth house and the T-square of some kind of fanaticism coming forward from the past. It is not yet clear whether you were victim or perpetrator, but with Mars involved there is some violence involved in this. My feeling is that you were connected with the manipulation of minds and that this is where your hesitancy stems from. You have a deep knowledge of what can be achieved through psychological pressure. I feel that once you can move to the idea of investigation of the mind and its processes being therapeutic rather than the connections which that past experience has, then you will feel more ready to move into therapy work.

. . . Saturn likes boundaries, it needs a wall around the Self but Neptune likes to dissolve this and become one with the whole world. When you have an eleventh house combination like this, you have to be part of the whole, but be an individual as well. It can be a difficult tight-rope to walk. Saturn in the eleventh house can experience intense loneliness until the right kind of group is found. It has to be a kinship of inner essence, external interests are not a sufficient bond . . . Leo needs to be a leader. Therefore you need to be out front, whatever group you are associated with should ultimately be led by you as you will not feel at ease taking a back seat at someone else's direction – although the training leading up to this will help you to keep the balance between power and humility.

Your husband's chart is very much that of the specialist. There could be a difficulty with all the Leo energy, in that he could be totally wrapped up in himself and his needs, not in a consciously self-centred or selfish way but just because they are so important to him and to what he is doing, and because he has been used to being 'in command' and having people attend to his needs rather than having to consider other people. As a result, you may feel a little neglected, especially when your own Leo need to be special comes to the surface. And you may have quite a power struggle when it comes to the manifestation of your joint Sun–Pluto–Mercury energies, which have a strong karmic connection and power issues to work out. He seems to have been very much involved in whatever mental manipulation you were part of. He also has indications from the twelfth-house Uranus/Mars of a very strong Will and assertion skills, but because they are in the twelfth house he may 'lead from behind', being the power behind what is going on, rather than being in the public eye.

The second house is the skills and talents we have brought back to help us in the present incarnation and you can see that half of his planets are in this one house. His Moon is in Virgo and I feel he should seek to put these talents to work for humanity. The Virgo Moon reflects your own difficulties in expressing your emotions . . . He may have difficulty in finding a focus because there are no oppositions in his chart. Another side of no oppositions is having to learn the value of the ability to compromise, so situations may crop up, particularly between you, to teach him this.

Your son will find it difficult to live with two such fiery people, although his Leo Ascendant will modify this to some extent. You will find that your own Water planets will empathize with him as he reflects your own Water/Fire difficulties. Your husband, however, with the lack of Water planets may find it difficult to understand the emotions and sensitivity of both you and your son. The Cancer-Leo conflict is difficult because Leo tends to be extrovert and outgoing and Cancer tends to hide behind its shell. Your son needs drawing out gently to help him find the authority and power within himself which Leo needs to express, but he also needs to be encouraged to be sensitive and caring in accordance with his Cancer Sun . . . He will have a very compassionate and caring nature but may get swamped by all the suffering and pain he encounters (Neptune square to the Moon in Virgo). He needs to learn to set realistic goals, to avoid the search for perfection which would lead him to feel that he had failed and then fall into depression and the lower manifestations of Neptune. You should encourage him to become actively involved in his own learning process and creativity.

Your son has the Mars/Saturn conjunction which indicates some kind of karmic difficulty over expressing his Will and his assertiveness and this links into having two Leo parents, a Uranus/Mars father and a Pluto/Mars mother. You will need to be careful not to blot out his Will but also, with Pluto and Uranus involved, not to let him be totally wilful either. Because he is a Cancer he may hide his needs and his feelings and go along with what happens to him. But this would be disempowering for him and would conflict with his Leo Ascendant which needs a sense of being in control of what happens to him as otherwise the feeling of powerlessness will paralyse him. If his natural aggressive instincts are blocked out by Leo autocracy based on 'I know what's best for you', then he could have great difficulty in later life getting himself established as an adult in his own right.

The Saturn/Mars conjunction connects with Pluto and he has the Finger of Fate involving Venus, Jupiter/Pluto and Neptune with an outlet through Uranus. He has a close connection with the fanaticism in your ninth house, and his chart indicates that in the past, through clashes with authority, he has become frightened to assert himself and comes back with a built-in inhibition. He needs encouragement to go out and face the world as himself. Direct threats or forcing him would be useless as it would activate his old patterns and the double Uranus—Mars contacts between the charts indicate an old battle of Wills. The trines within the chart make me feel he may try to lead through domination and that he should be educated to lead from within, by charisma and ability, rather than seek to impose his Will and way on others. I feel this matter of not thwarting or stifling his Will and his assertion is very important as this has been a feature of the past interaction. Saturn symbolizes limitations and restrictions and although it is a way to grow, too much can be a bad thing in a child who is predisposed to difficulties over expressing and asserting himself. You need to keep a good balance between not spoiling him and yet encouraging him in his endeavours.

. . . Your husband's planets of course activate your own Leo and your ninth house, so that the interaction with him is part of your need to find and own your own power. Your chart is an objective, outgoing one, apart from the Cancer Moon, as it is concentrated at the top half, and you will see that his planets activate this part of you. It does not seem as though you will learn much about your inner qualities through the interaction with your husband; you need to look inside yourself for this, rather than through him.

If we look at the interaction with your husband's Leo planets, there is a strong need to learn to live as two separate individuals who choose to share a life together, particularly as you have the Sun/Venus/Saturn conjunction to the South Node which can pull you back into an old dependent pattern of relating. The Pluto conjunction to the Sun and Venus indicates a previous connection in which one was owned or absorbed by the other, and the Saturn—Mercury connection that one had control over the other's mind at some stage. There is also a Saturn/Neptune conjunction to his chart and this might lead to a situation where you are apparently controlling the way the marriage goes, but your huband will, by his very passivity in going along with this, ultimately be in control – or vice versa. It's a complicated concept. It can also mean that you each act as a 'container' for the other's Neptune energies, perhaps taking it in turn to play the escapist role. You may also find from this conjunction and the Leo planets that there are times when you resent the fact that he has so much to give everyone and you would like a little of it to be concentrated solely on you. You need to programme time into your marriage to be together, but also some space so that each can develop as an individual.

Your son's Saturn/Mars is close to your Saturn/Neptune and so you will have to adapt to his demands which are trying to bind you close when you really want to escape and have freedom (Moon conjunct Uranus). Also there is a Saturn–Moon square between the charts which means that you feel you have an old debt or are duty-bound to him. Loving attention and reassurance will help with this, as when he feels more secure he will be more prepared to give you freedom. The conjunction of his Sun/North Node to your Moon will help you here as you will have that understanding of his emotional needs which arises from your interaction in the past and which will enable you to be patient. However, you should avoid falling back into an older 'sexual' interaction between the Sun and the Moon as it is no longer appropriate. If you are not getting the attention you feel you need from your husband, then you could easily look to your son for this and become the smothering, possessive Cancer mother, whereas his North Node conjunction to your Moon is trying to bring out the nurturing mother in you.

In her feedback the client picked up on the comments with regard to her relationship with her father:

'I must admit my first reaction was to withdraw fearfully into that Cancer shell. I found it quite hard to face the part about my father – he did travel quite a bit when I was a baby – and had a heart attack when I was sixteen which had a deep effect as I felt responsible and also angry with him [Sun–Pluto]. It is very true about my feeling the urge to remould myself [Pluto/Mars/Jupiter T-square].

'The other aspect I found hard was about my son finding it hard to live with 'two such fiery people'. I initially experienced that phrase as a judgement [Saturn] as there's an urge for me to aim for nothing less than perfection, of course destined to fail [Moon square Saturn which conjuncts Neptune has this in-built expectation of failure to be the 'perfect' mother].

'Before he was conceived I cleansed my body using visualization [Neptune inconjunct Jupiter] for a year, and during pregnancy I kept up a constant inner dialogue with him telling him what were my feelings and how when I felt angry etc., these were my feelings and reactions, and not due or related to him [in addition to the Moon/Sun contact, her Neptune squares his nodal axis, indicating that she was able to help him through the trauma of incarnating: he has Venus in the tenth house opposing Uranus in the fourth and in his case, instead of unstable mothering, he is meeting an unconventional but very loving mother who intuitively picked up his need for reassurance]. I imagine myself and those I love lying cupped in God's hands or in the velvet eye of an anemone for protection.

'Going on to the karmic element I was interested in the possibility of having been an Inquisition victim. I feel I may have been threatened with physical damage, amputation of limbs or damage to my eyes, as I have a horror of these things. In fact I thought I might have been physically tortured in these ways [Scorpio Mars opposing Jupiter in Taurus and squaring the Leo/Pluto/Sun/Mercury/MC conjunction indicate that this is a distinct possibility]. I also wonder if I've been ducked as a witch as I had knowledge of herbs and some ability to heal others.'

NOTES

INTRODUCTION

1 Extract from *Echoes of the Orient*, quoted in J. Head and S. L. Cranston (eds.), *Reincarnation: An East–West Anthology*, The Julian Press Inc., New York, NY, 1961, p. 2.

2 Benjamin Walker, *Masks of the Soul: Facts behind Reincarnation*, The Aquarian Press, Wellingborough, Northants, 1981, p. 13.

3 ibid., p. 21.

4 Liz Greene, *The Astrology of Fate*, George Allen & Unwin, London, 1984, p. 10.

5 ibid., p. 10.

6 ibid., p. 11, 6.

7 ibid., p. 8.

8 Origen, quoted in J. Head and S. L. Cranston (eds.), *Reincarnation: An East–West Anthology*, p. 36.

9 St Gregory, ibid., p. 36.

10 St. Augustine, ibid., p. 38.

11 Dr Ian Stevenson, *Twenty Cases Suggestive of Reincarnation*, University Press of Virginia, Charlottesville, VA, 1988.

12 Benjamin Walker, *Masks of the Soul*, p. 8.

13 William James, *Varieties of Religious Experience*, Harvard University Press, Cambridge, MA, 1985.

14 H. Carrington and S. J. Muldoon, *Projection of the Astral Body*, Psychic Book Club, Rider, London, p. 2.

15 Drs Glenn Roberts and John Owen, 'The Near Death Experience'. *British Journal of Psychiatry*, London, 153, 1988, pp. 607–17.

16 ibid.

17 ibid.

18 ibid.

19 Robert Hand, 'The Emergence of an Astrological Discipline', *Astrological Journal*, May/June 1988, p. 117.

20 C. J. Jung, *The Visions Seminars*, Spring Publications, Dallas, TX, 1983.

21 Benjamin Walker, *Masks of the Soul*, p. 127.

22 Rupert Sheldrake, 'Morphic Resonance', *Caduceus*, 4.

23 Alan Jewsbury, 'A New Hypothesis to Explain Astrology', *Astrological Journal*, November/December 1988, p. 298.

24 Robert Hand, 'The Emergence of an Astrological Discipline'.

25 ibid.

26 Alan Jewsbury, 'A New Hypothesis to Explain Astrology'.

27 Tyrell, *The Personality of Man*, Penguin, London, 1947.

28 Joan Grant and Denys Kelsey, *Many Lifetimes*, Corgi, London, 1976.

29 E. H. Whinfield (ed.), *Teachings of Rumi: Mathnawi*, Octagon Press, London, 1979.

CHAPTER 1

1 Thorwald Dethlefsen, *The Challenge of Fate: Ancient Wisdom as the Path to Human Wholeness*, tr. C. McIntosh and E. M. Loewe, Coventure, London, 1984, p. 92.

2 Pauline Stone, *The Astrology of Karma*, The Aquarian Press, Wellingborough, Northants, 1988, p. 20.

3 Commentary extract from *Cities Fit to Live In*, Channel 4, 1988.

4 Christine Hartley, *A Case for Reincarnation*, Robert Hale, London, 1987, p. 109.

5 Liz Greene, *Saturn: A New Look at an Old Devil*, Weiser, York Beach, ME, 1976, p. 121.

6 Roberto Assagioli, *The Act of Will*, Penguin, London, 1974.

7 Anne Parker, *Astrology and Alcoholism: Genetic Key to the Horoscope*, Weiser, York Beach, ME, 1983, p. 34.

8 Richard Bach, *Illusions*, Pan, London, 1979, p. 121.

9 Liz Greene, *Saturn*.

10 Jeff Green, *Pluto, the Evolutionary Journey of the Soul*, Llewellyn Publications, St Paul, MN, 1985, p. 215.

11 Howard Sasportas, *The Twelve Houses*, The Aquarian Press, Wellingborough, Northants, pp. 98ff.

12 Stephen Arroyo, *Astrology, Karma and Transformation*, CRCS, Vancouver, 1978, p. 109.

13 Alan Epstein, *Psychodynamics of Inconjunction*, Weiser, York Beach, ME, 1984, p. 5.

CHAPTER 2

1 Alan Oken, *Complete Astrologer*, Bantam Books, New York, NY, 1980, p. 507.

2 Elisabeth Kubler-Ross, *Death, the Final Stage of Growth*, Spectrum, New Jersey, 1975, p. 165.

3 Phyllis Krystal, *Cutting the Ties that Bind*, Element Books, Shaftesbury, Dorset, 1989, p. 9.

4 Alan Oken, *Complete Astrologer*, p. 499.

5 Debbie Boater, article in *Metamorphosis*, Autumn 1984.

6 Suzanne Lilley-Harvey, 'Thomas Merton: A Study of the Saturn–Uranus Dilemma', *Astrological Journal*, September/October 1987, p. 21.

7 ibid.

8 ibid.

9 Mother Teresa, quoted in *Radio Times*, 1987.

10 Liz Greene, *Saturn*, Weiser, York Beach, ME, 1976, p. 4.

11 Anne Parker, *Alcoholism and Astrology*, Weiser, York Beach, ME, 1988, p. 136.

12 John Lahr, *Prick Up Your Ears*, Penguin, London, 1978.

13 ibid.

14 ibid.

15 ibid.

16 ibid.

17 ibid.

18 ibid.

19 ibid.

20 ibid.

21 ibid.

22 ibid.

23 ibid.

24 ibid.
25 ibid.
26 ibid.
27 ibid.
28 ibid.
29 ibid.
30 Tracy Marks, *The Astrology of Self Discovery*, CRCS, Reno, NV, 1985.
31 ibid., p. 97.
32 ibid.

CHAPTER 3

1 Mary Devlin, *Astrology and Past Lives*, Para Research Inc., Gloucester, MA, 1987.
2 Tracy Marks, *The Astrology of Self Discovery*, CRCS, Reno, NV, pp. 15ff.
3 M. Scott Peck, *The Road Less Travelled*, Rider, London, 1978, p. 119.
4 ibid., p. 116.
5 Paul Wright, *The Literary Zodiac*, Anodyne, Edinburgh, 1988, p. 20.
6 *Concise Oxford Dictionary*.
7 Liz Greene, *Star Signs for Lovers*, Arrow, London, 1980.
8 M. Scott Peck, *The Road Less Travelled*, p. 83.
9 *Concise Oxford Dictionary*.
10 M. Scott Peck, *The Road Less Travelled*, p. 131.
11 Jeff Mayo, *Teach Yourself Astrology*, Hodder & Stoughton, London, 1980.
12 Liz Greene, *Star Signs for Lovers*.
13 Debbie Boater, article in *Metamorphosis*, Autumn 1984.
14 Liz Greene, *Relating: Astrological Guide to Living with Others on a Small Planet*, Coventure, London, 1986.
15 Howard Sasportas, *The Twelve Houses*, The Aquarian Press, Wellingborough, Northants, 1985.
16 Liz Greene, *Relating*.
17 Quoted from Martin Luther King's famous speech, 'I Have a Dream', made at an anti-racist rally on 28 August 1968.

18 ibid.
19 ibid.
20 ibid.
21 M. Scott Peck, *The Road Less Travelled*, p. 302.
22 Christine Hartley, *A Case for Reincarnation*, Robert Hale, London, 1987, p. 62.
23 Melanie Reinhart, *Chiron and the Healing Journey*, Arkana, London, 1989.
24 Howard Sasportas, *The Twelve Houses*.
25 Christine Hartley, *A Case for Reincarnation*, p. 121.
26 Jonathan Cott, *The Search for Omm Sety*, Doubleday, New York, NY, 1987.
27 ibid.

CHAPTER 4

1 Emma Jung, *Anima and Animus*, Spring Publications, Dallas, TX, 1983.
2 Talat Sait et al., Dost Yayinlan, *Celaleddin Rumi & the Whirling Dervishes*.
3 Extract from untitled American newspaper cutting in the author's collection, undated.
4 ibid.
5 Glen Williston and Judith Johnstone, *Discovering Your Past Lives*, The Aquarian Press, Wellingborough, Northants, 1988, p. 86.
6 Stephen Arroyo, *Astrology, Karma and Transformation*, CRCS, Vancouver, 1978, p. 79.
7 Stephen Arroyo, *Astrology, Psychology and the Four Elements*, CRCS, Reno, NV, 1975, p. 75.
8 ibid., p. 120.

CHAPTER 5

1 Robin Skynner and John Cleese, *Families and How to Survive Them*, Methuen, London, 1983.
2 Dr Susan Forward, *Men Who Hate Women and the Women Who Love Them*, Bantam Books, New York, NY, 1989, p. 43.

3   Liz Greene, *Saturn*, Weiser, York Beach, ME, 1976.
4   Richard Bach. *Illusions*, Pan, London, 1979, p. 65.
5   Dr Susan Forward, *Men Who Hate Women*, p. 113.
6   Nor Hall, *The Moon and the Virgin*, The Women's Press, London, 1980.
7   ibid.
8   Dr Susan Forward, *Men Who Hate Women*, p. 111.
9   Stephen Arroyo, *Astrology, Karma and Transformation*, CRCS, Vancouver, 1978, p. 139.
10 ibid. p. 140.
11 Susan Forward, *Men Who Hate Women*.

CHAPTER 6

1   John and Kris Amodeo, *Being Intimate*, Methuen, New York, NY, 1986, p. 15.
2   Howard Sasportas, *The Twelve Houses*, The Aquarian Press, Wellingborough, Northants, 1985.
3   Robert A. Johnson, *The Psychology of Romantic Love*, Arkana, 1990.
4   ibid.
5   Debbie Boater, article in *Metamorphosis*, Autumn 1984.
6   Stephen Arroyo, *Astrology, Karma and Transformation*, CRCS, Vancouver, 1978, p. 154.
7   ibid., p. 226.
8   John and Kris Amodeo, *Being Intimate*, p. 108.

CONCLUSION

1   Richard Bach, *Illusions*, Pan, London, 1979, p. 51.
2   Arthur Ford and Jerome Ellison, *The Life Before Death*, Abacus., London, 1971.
3   E. H. Whinfield (ed.), *Teachings of Rumi: Mathnawi*, Octagon Press, London, 1979.

GLOSSARY

Akashic Record   Esoteric record in which each individual soul's experience is chronicled, and which can be read by those trained to access it.

Angles   The Ascendant, Descendant, MC (Midheaven) and IC.

Ascendant   The degree of the zodiac rising over the eastern horizon at the moment of birth, forming the cusp of the first house. The opposite point, forming the cusp of the seventh house, is known as the Descendant.

Aspect   The distance between two planets measured around the zodiac. The major aspects are the conjunction (0°), sextile (60°), square (90°), trine (120°), quincunx (150°) and opposition (180°).

Being   A state in which the incarnating soul is totally attuned to the Self and simply *is*.

Cardinal   The initiating Cardinal signs are Aries, Cancer, Libra, Capricorn.

Cusp   The division point dividing the zodiac into houses.

Ecliptic   The circle *apparently* traversed by the Sun in a year.

Elements   The astrological elements are the active and intuitive Fire (Aries, Leo, Sagittarius), the communicative Air (Gemini, Libra, Aquarius), the practical Earth (Taurus, Virgo, Capricorn), and the emotional Water (Cancer, Scorpio, Pisces) energies.

Finger of Fate   An aspect pattern formed from two quincunxes radiating out from a planet to two other planets, themselves joined by a sextile.

Fixed   The constant Fixed signs are Taurus, Leo, Scorpio, Aquarius.

Free Will   The ability to choose one's actions and destiny.

Grand Cross   An aspect pattern formed by four squares and two oppositions linked together.

Grand Trine   An aspect pattern formed by three trines linked together.

House   The zodiac is divided into twelve houses each representing a sphere of experience.

Interaspect   A planet in one natal chart aspecting a planet in another natal chart.

Karma   The law of cause and effect, according to which for every action there is a reaction. Karma is the causal factor behind fate or destiny.

Kite   An aspect pattern formed from a Grand Trine with an opposition to a fourth planet which is sextile to two of the planets forming the Grand Trine.

M C (Midheaven)   The highest degree reached by the ecliptic at a particular time and place, the tenth house cusp in the Placidus house system. The opposite point, the IC, forms the cusp of the fourth house.

Moon's Nodes   Points indicating the intersection of the Moon with the ecliptic of the earth as it passes from North to South. The nodal axis is an exact opposition aspect.

Mutable   The adaptable Mutable signs are Gemini, Virgo, Sagittarius, Pisces.

Natal chart   A map of the planets at the moment of birth.

Natal planet   The position of a planet at the moment of birth.

Negative signs   The Negative astrological signs (Taurus, Cancer, Virgo, Scorpio, Capricorn, Pisces) are self-repressive, passive and receptive.

Nodal return   The conjunction of the transiting Node to its natal placement. The Node takes eighteen and a half years to travel around the zodiac.

Personal planets   Sun, Moon, Mercury, Venus, Mars.

Placidus   System of house division.

Positive signs   The Positive astrological signs (Aries, Gemini, Leo, Libra, Sagittarius, Aquarius) are self-expressive, active and outgoing.

Psychic   1 Pertaining to the Psyche. 2 Able to utilize extra-sensory perception and expanded states of consciousness to interact with other levels of being.

Orb   The number of degrees allowed for an aspect between planets.

Reincarnation   The successive taking on of a physical incarnation, following a previous death.

Self   The eternal, divine, essence of Man.

Soul   The portion of the Self which takes on a physical body at incarnation.

Synastry   The interaction between two natal charts, depicting the relationship between two people.

Transit   When a planet in the heavens at a given moment, crosses or aspects a natal planet.

T-square   Two planets forming an opposition with a third planet squaring them both.

CHART SOURCES

BAKER, DOUGLAS: Private source

DEBUSSY, CLAUDE: Astrological Association

DU PRÉ, JACQUELINE: Her mother

DYLAN, BOB: Jeff Green

FELIX, JULIE: Herself

GARBO, GRETA: Alan Oken

GELDOF, BOB: *Prediction*

HALLIWELL, KENNETH: John Lahr

HARTLEY, CHRISTINE: Herself

HIGGS, DR MARIETTA: Stuart Bell

KENNEDY, JACQUELINE: Jeff Green

KENNEDY, JOHN F.: Alan Oken

KENNEDY, ROBERT: Jeff Green

KING, MARTIN LUTHER: Alan Oken

KUBLER-ROSS, ELISABETH: Herself

LENIN, VLADIMIR ILYICH: Astrological Association

MERTON, THOMAS: Suzanne Lilley-Harvey

MONROE, MARILYN: Alan Oken

MOZART, WOLFGANG AMADEUS: Jeff Green

OMM SETY: Jonathan Cott

ORTON, JOE: John Lahr

WATERS, ROGER: Private source

TSAR OF RUSSIA (NICOLAS II): Astrological Association

BIBLIOGRAPHY

ASTROLOGY

ARROYO, S., *Astrology, Karma and Transformation*, CRCS, Vancouver, Canada, 1978.

CUNNINGHAM, D., *Healing Pluto Problems*, Weiser, York Beach, ME, 1986.

DEVLIN, M., *Astrology and Past Lives*, Para Research Inc., Gloucester, MA, 1987.

GREEN, J., *Pluto, the Evolutionary Journey of the Soul*, Llewellyn Publications, St Paul, MN, 1985.

GREENE, L., *Astrology of Fate*, George Allen & Unwin, London, 1984.

GREENE, L., *Saturn: A New Look at an Old Devil*, Arkana, London, 1990.

MARKS, T., *The Astrology of Self Discovery*, CRCS, Reno, NV, 1985.

SASPORTAS, H., *The Twelve Houses*, The Aquarian Press, Wellingborough, Northants, 1985.

STONE, P., *The Astrology of Karma*, The Aquarian Press, Wellingborough, Northants, 1988.

REINCARNATION, ETC

CARRINGTON, H., and MULDOON, S. J., *The Projection of the Astral Body*, Rider, London, 1929.

CERMINERA, G., *Many Mansions*, New American Library, New York, NY, 1988.

CERMINERA, G., *Many Lives, Many Loves*, De Vorss, Marina del Rey, CA, 1981.

CHALLONER, H. K., *The Wheel of Rebirth*, Theosophical Publications House, Wheaton, IL, 1976.

CROOKALL, R., *The Study and Practice of Astral Projection*, Citadel Books, Secausus, NJ, 1987.

DEVLIN, B. L. *I am Mary Shelley*, Condor, Souvenir Press, London.

EBON, M., *Reincarnation in the Twentieth Century*, Signet, New American Library.

FISHER, J., *The Case for Reincarnation*, Grafton Books, London, 1986.

GAMMON, M., (ed.), *Astrology and The Edgar Cayce Readings*, ARE Press, Virginia Beach, VA, 1973.

GLASKIN, G. M., *Windows of the Mind*, Wildwood House, Aldershot, Hants.

GRANT, J., *Eyes of Horus*, Ariel OH, Columbus, OH, 1988.

GRANT, J., *Far Memory*, Corgi, London, 1975.

GRANT, J., *Lord of the Horizon*, Ariel OH, Columbus, OH, 1988.

GRANT, J., and KELSEY, D., *Many Lifetimes*, Corgi, London, 1976.

GREEN, C., *Lucid Dreams*, Institute of Psychophysical Research, London, 1968.

GREEN, C., *Out of the Body Experiences*, Institute of Psychophysical Research, London, 1968.

GREEN, C., and MCCREERY, C., *Apparitions*, Institute of Psychophysical Research, London, 1977.

GREY, M., *Return from Death, an Exploration of the Near Death Experience*, Penguin Books, Harmondsworth, 1985.

GUIRDHAM, A., *A Foot in Both Worlds*, Neville Spearman, Saffron Walden, Essex, 1990.

GUIRDHAM, A., *We are One Another*, Newcastle Publications, North Hollywood, CA, 1985.

GUIRDHAM, A., *The Cathars and Reincarnation: The Record of a Past Life in Thirteenth-Century France*, Neville Spearman, Saffron Walden, Essex, 1990.

HAICH, E., *Initiations*, tr. J. P. Robertson, Unwin Paperbacks, London, 1979.

HARTLEY, C., *A Case for Reincarnation*, Robert Hale, London, 1987.

HEAD, J. and CRANSTON S. L., (eds.), *Reincarnation: An East–West Anthology*, The Julian Press Inc., New York, NY, 1961.

IVERSON, J., *More Lives Than One*, Pan, London, 1977.

LANGLEY, N., *Edgar Cayce on Reincarnation*, Warner Books, New York, NY, 1967.

LUNDAHL, C., *A Collection of Near Death Research Readings*, Nelson-Hall, Chicago, IL, 1982.

MONROE, R., Journeys out of the Body, Doubleday, New York, NY, 1977.

MOODY, R., Life After Life, Bantam Books, New York, NY, 1983.

REINHART, M., Chiron and the Healing Journey, Arkana, London, 1989.

RICHARDSON, A., Dancers to the Gods: The Magical Records of James Seymour and Christine Hartley, The Aquarian Press, Wellingborough, Northants, 1985.

RICHARDSON, A., Gate of the Moon: Mythical and Magical Doorways, The Aquarian Press, Wellingborough, Northants, 1984.

ROGO, S. D., Life after Death: A Case for the Survival of Bodily Death, The Aquarian Press, Wellingborough, Northants, 1986.

RUSSELL, E., Design for Destiny, Neville Spearman, Saffron Walden, Essex 1973.

RYALL, E., Second Time Around, Macdonald Optima, London, 1989.

SHELDRAKE, R., A New Science of Life, Paladin Books, London, 1987.

SHELDRAKE, R., The Presence of the Past, William Collins, London, 1988.

STEVENSON, I., Twenty Cases Suggestive of Reincarnation, University Press of Virgina, Charlottesville, VA, 1988.

STEWART, A., Died 1513, Born 1929, Macmillan, London, 1978.

TOYNBEE, A., Life after Death, Weidenfeld & Nicolson, London, 1976.

UNDERWOOD, P. and WILDER, L., Lives to Remember, Robert Hale, London, 1975.

WALKER-MCCLAIN, F., Past Life Regression, Llewellyn Publications, St Paul, MN, 1986.

WALKER, J., Masks of the Soul, The Aquarian Press, Wellingborough, Northants, 1981.

WAMBACH, H., Reliving Past Lives, Century Hutchinson, London, 1979.

WAMBACH, H., Life Before Life, Bantam Books, New York, NY, 1979.

WATSON, L., The Romeo Error, Coronet, London, 1979.

WILLISTON, G., and JOHNSTONE, J., Discovering your Past Lives, The Aquarian Press, Wellingborough, Northants, 1988.

WILSON, C., C. G. Jung, Lord of the Underworld, The Aquarian Press, Wellingborough, Northants, 1988.

WILSON, I., All in the Mind, Doubleday, New York, NY, 1978.

WOOLGER, R. J., Other Lives, Other Selves, Crucible, Chatham, 1990.

Cassettes: The Wrekin Trust, Runnings Park, West Malvern, Worcs. WR14 4BP, UK, have available an excellent selection of cassette tapes on Death and Dying, Mysticism and Spirituality, Reincarnation, The New Scientific Paradigm and Spiritual Development.

COPYRIGHT PERMISSIONS

Element Books Ltd, for *Cutting the Ties that Bind* by Phyllis Krystal (new edition, Element Books of Longmead, Shaftesbury, Dorset, England).

Thorsons Publishing Group Ltd for *Relating* by Liz Greene; *Masks of the Soul* by Benjamin Walker, *Jungian Birthcharts* by Arthur Dione; *The Astrology of Karma* by Pauline Stone; *The Twelve Houses* by Howard Sasportas; and *Discovering Your Past Lives* by Glen Williston and Judith Johnstone.

The late Maurice Barbanell, for permission to quote from Psychic Press and Psychic Book Club books.

The Society of Authors, as the literary representative of the Estate of John Masefield, for 'A Creed'.

The extract from 'Healing', by D. H. Lawrence, is included by kind permission of Laurence Pollinger Limited and the Estate of Mrs Frieda Lawrence Rowagh.

The extract taken from *The Astrology of Fate* by Liz Greene, reproduced by kind permission of Unwin Hyman, © Liz Greene, 1984.

Samuel Weiser, Inc., for *Saturn: A New Look at an Old Devil* by Liz Greene, © 1976, Liz Greene (York Beach, ME, Samuel Weiser, Inc., 1976). Used by permission. Published in the UK by Arkana. Also, for *Astrology and Alcoholism: Genetic Key to the Horoscope* by Anne E. Parker, © 1982, Anne E. Parker (York Beach, ME, Samuel Weiser, Inc., 1982). Used by permission. See Chapter Notes for pages details of each work.

NOTE Every effort has been made to trace the copyright holders of works quoted from in this book, but in some cases this has not proved possible. The author and publishers therefore wish to thank the authors or copyright holders of any material which is included without acknowledgement above.

INDEX

NOTE: Aspects are shown as outer planet to personal.

Addiction/alcoholism, 48, 114, 189,
    230, 269
AIDS, 204–9
Allergies, 193, 198
Ancestral karma, 281–7
Anima/animus, 203–4
Anorgasmia, 199
Aquarian Age, 36, 54
Aries South Node, 87
Ascendant, 136–8, 238ff.
    through the signs, 136–45
Aspects, 37, 76
    difficult, 37; easy, 37; conjunction,
    37; opposition, 37; squares, 37, 76;
    Grand Cross, 77; trine and sextile,
    37, 78; Grand Trine and Kite, 80;
    inconjunct, 37; quintile, 37, 80;
    Finger of Fate, 82
    to the Nodes, 113
Astrological twins, 127ff.
Atlantis, 48, 61, 70, 193
Attitudinal karma, 189
Autistic children, 38, 264

Baker, Douglas, 80
Blindness, 190
Body image, 191
Bodily karma, 61
Borgias, 42

Caesar, Julius, 18
Cancer–Leo conflict, 345
Capricorn South Node, 51
Capricorn Moon, 178
Career possibilities, 61
Carrot meditation, 228
Cayce, Edgar, 98
Cause and effect, 14
Child abuse, 200, 242, 266
Chiron, 160–74
    in aspect and houses, 161
    first house, 167, 285; second, 168;
    third, 170; fourth, 51, 54, 171;
    fifth, 171; sixth, 168; seventh, 171,
    298, 308; eighth, 21, 128, 168,
    172, 208, 230; ninth, 173; tenth
    and eleventh, 173; eleventh, 162;
    twelfth, 173

in aspect to Sun, 167, 174, 248;
    Moon, 171; Mercury, 161, 174;
    Venus, 171, 183, 223; Mars, 164,
    208; Pluto/Chiron/Mars, 165;
    Moon/South Node in seventh, 298;
    MC, 204
    in Sagittarius, 24; in Virgo, 181
    conjunct Moon in synastry, 129
Chronic illness, 193
Collective karma, 54, 57
Communication karma, 60
Conception experience, 242
Creative karma, 60

Deafness, 189
Déjà vu, 26
Debussy, 48–86
Devouring mother, 256ff.
Disassociate planets, 212
Dual signs, 66, 143, 144, 214, 296
Dylan, Bob, 86

Eating disorders, 191, 275
Egypt, 69, 129, 168
Eighth house, 310–15
Elements, 216–25
    Air, 218; Earth, 223; Fire, 217;
    Water, 219
    Grand Trine in, 80
    planets in, 83
    imbalance of, 181, 183, 197, 225,
    226, 332
Emotional expectations, 245ff.
Enlightenment, 36

Family karma, 236ff.
Fate, 16
Fate v. free will, 37
Felix, Julie, 86, 148
Finger of Fate, 21–4, 82, 204, 210, 224,
    230, 234, 309, 331, 345
Fifth house, 264ff.
    Saturn/Neptune, 24
First hosue, 214, 238
Fourth–tenth house axis, 271ff.
Freedom v. commitment, 318

Garbo, Greta, 104
Geldof, Bob, 111

Gender difficulties, 201ff.
Ghosts, 26
Grand Cross, 77–8, 177, 222, 258, 269
    out of element and orb in synastry,
    130
Grand Trine, 51, 80, 224, 251, 299,
    303, 311, 331
Greed, 42
Griffin, Lawrence, 119

Halliwell, Kenneth, 77, 116ff.
Handicapped children, 267
Hartley, Christine, 42, 128, 159, 168
Health karma, 61
Higgs, Dr Marietta, 200
House cusps, 38
Houses and planets in houses
    First, 58, 167, 214, 238–45
    Second, 58, 59, 168
    Third, 59, 60, 280, 161, 278–81
    Fourth, 51, 54, 171, 332
    Fourth/tenth axis, 271–8
    Fifth, 60, 171, 265
    Sixth, 61, 168, 184–99
    Seventh, 61, 63, 171, 266, 296–309
    Eighth, 21, 63, 168, 172, 310–15
    Ninth, 173, 214
    Tenth, 173, 271–8
    Eleventh, 63
    Twelfth, 65–75, 173, 265
Huntington's chorea, 193

Idiopathic Thrombocytopenic Purpura,
    187
Imbalance of positive/negative, 202ff.
Impotence, 183, 199
Inconjunct, 80–81
Inquisition, 64, 293

Jung, 28
Jupiter
    in aspect to Sun, 332; Moon, 196,
        204, 299; Venus, 189, 196; Mars,
        45, 189, 303; Saturn, 40, 43, 69,
        85, 184, 189; Uranus, 44;
        Mars/Pluto, 49; Neptune, 189;
        Neptune/Chiron, 196; Nodes, 116
    interaspects, 266, 327
    in first house, 58, 244; second, 58;
        third, 280; fourth/tenth, 275; fifth,
        60; sixth, 191; seventh, 43, 305,
        342; eighth, 310; twelfth, 69, 169
    in Capricorn, 40, 189; Sagittarius, 44;
        Taurus, 189
    in Air, 189; Earth, 189; Water, 189
    Jupiter transiting, 189
Justinian, 18

Karma, 14
Karma of health, 180–4
Karmic causes of disease, 212–13
Karmic dilemmas, 40
Karmic houses, 57
    planets in, 58–65
Karma in the making, 184
Karmic justice, 35
Karmic patterns, 36–7
Karmic potential, 82–4
Karmic relationships, 293
Kennedy family, 41–2
Kite, 56, 79–80, 196
King, Martin Luther, 157ff.
Krystal, Phyllis, 102
Kubler-Ross, Elisabeth, 100, 168

Lahr, John, 117
Lenin, synastry with tsar, 321
Leo North Node, 209
Letting go, 259
Level of evolution, 56

Mars
    ruler of twelfth house, 21
    aspect to Nodes, 116, 204
    in first house, 58; second, 58; third,
        280; fourth, 290; fourth/tenth, 275;
        fifth, 60, 264; sixth, 188; seventh,
        208, 303; twelfth, 68
    in Cancer in twelfth, 69; in Scorpio in
        seventh, 303; in Sagittarius, 189; in
        Taurus, 189; in Fire signs, 189; in
        Capricorn, 190
Mars square Mars in synastry, 220
ME, 181
Mental states, 32
Mercury
    in aspect to Pluto, 119;
        Saturn/Neptune, 22; Neptune/South
        Node, 114; North Node in Cancer,
        120
    in first house, 58; second, 58; third,
        279; fourth/tenth, 273; fifth,
        60; seventh, 302; twelfth, 66,
        189
Merton, Thomas, 106
Monroe, Marilyn, 111
Monty Python team, 119
Moon, 135, 265;
    through the signs, 138–45
    in aspect to Mercury, 196; Pluto,
        253ff; Moon/Pluto/Mars, 186;
        Nodes, 113, 116, 196
    in first house, 58, 194, 244; second,
        58; third, 59, 194, 279, 332;
        fourth/tenth, 271; fourth, 249;

fifth, 265; sixth, 187, 224; seventh, 266, 298; twelfth, 66, 265
in Cancer, 196, 291; in Scorpio, 223, 300, 225; in Sagittarius, 251; in Taurus, 289
Morphic resonance, 29
Mother Teresa, 107
Muldoon, Sylvan, 20
Munro, Robert, 20
Mystic/pragmatist dilemma, 40, 133, 322

Natal chart, 35
Nature v. nurture, 237
NDE, 21–5, 72
Neptune, 23, 287;
in aspect to Sun, 260, 290; Sun/Mars, 182; Moon, 72, 177, 183, 186, 232, 282, 332; Moon/Venus, 261; Mercury, 65, 194, 201, 212, 234, 282; Venus, 130, 133, 248, 252, 289, 290, 322, 336; Venus/Mercury/Moon, 84ff.; Mars, 48, 51, 123, 175, 194, 202, 208, 220, 227, 234, 269, 336; Saturn, 24, 40, 51, 194, 204, 208, 220, 227, 234, 269, 336; Uranus, 194; Pluto, 194; Chiron, 194; to Nodes, 86, 116, 261; on angles, 215; MC, 282
interaspects, 268, 315, 323
in first house, 58, 239; third, 59; fourth/tenth, 252, 277; fifth, 61; sixth, 193ff., 220; seventh, 188, 307; eighth, 313; ninth, 214; tenth, 248; eleventh, 208; twelfth, 65, 71, 289
in Virgo, 40; in Capricorn, 40; in Leo (ninth), 41; in Libra, 72
'New' souls, 33
Ninth house, 214
Nodes, 87–110
North Node in Aries, 90; Taurus, 93; Gemini, 96; Cancer, 99; Leo, 103; Virgo, 107; Libra, 91; Scorpio, 94; Sagittarius, 97; Capricorn, 101; Aquarius, 105; Pisces, 110
reversed nodal placement, 112
aspects to nodes, 113ff.; in Grand Cross, 177; conjunction to South Node, 113; to North Node, 124; Venus/Saturn, 123; Jupiter/Neptune, 103; Moon, 123, 125; Mars, 124; Sun/Venus, 124; North Node/Neptune to Sun, 125
planets squaring the nodal axis, 126
in relationships, 122; North Node to

North Node synastry, 127; synastry case study, 130ff.; Venus square Nodes, 117; Mars square Nodes, 317
reversed nodal connection, 128, 273
resolution of nodal dilemma, 134
third/fourth house cusp, 341
Nymphomania, 200

Omm Sety, 174–9
OOBEs, 20
Origen, 18
Orbs, 38
Optimist/pessimist, 43
Orton, Joe, 77, 116ff.

Parental karma, 264
Patterns of dis-ease, 210–13
People pleaser, 132
Personal planets in first house, 244
Phobias, 74, 169
Pisces Sun–Moon, 333
Pisces North Node eleventh house, 23
Plato, 81, 21
Pluto, 23, 237;
in Cancer, 65; in Scorpio, 54; in Leo, 55, 74
on MC, 169
interaspects, 270, 315
in aspect to Sun, 55, 65, 79, 80, 81, 132, 195, 250, 273, 332, 341; Moon, 74, 81, 178, 194, 204, 220, 253, 289, 290, 299, 315, 332; Moon–Mars, 186; Mercury, 119; Venus, 81, 130, 172, 225, 257, 285, 289, 299, 314; Mars, 21, 49, 81, 199, 200, 201, 209, 226, 299, 314, 317, 332; Uranus/Moon, 188; Pluto/Saturn/Mars, 50, 57, 75; Nodes, 115, 120
in first house, 242; third, 281; fourth/tenth, 277; fourth, 299; sixth, 184, 198; seventh, 308; eighth, 299, 313, 332; ninth, 214; tenth, 289, 346; eleventh, 63; twelfth, 65, 74
Power issues, 81, 183, 242
Pré, Jacqueline du, 194–8
Premature ejaculation, 200
Psychosomatic illness, 183, 187, 197

Quincunx, 81
Quintile, 37

Reincarnation (definition), 17
Relationship karma, 63, 67, 287–92
Retributive karma, 180, 189

Reversed nodal placement, 115
Rumi, 206

Saboteur, 182
Saturn, 237
    in aspect to Sun, 194, 246, 282;
        Moon, 72, 81, 194, 228, 247, 251,
        282, 289, 299, 341; Mercury, 81,
        195, 249, 283, 332, 341; Venus,
        43, 123, 178, 199, 249, 309; Mars,
        46, 79, 181, 184, 186, 199, 234,
        250, 290, 299, 309, 341; Jupiter,
        40, 43, 227; Neptune, 40ff., 209,
        341; Uranus, 55, 56; Nodes, 85,
        113; Chiron, 322; Moon/South
        Node, 247; Uranus/Mars in eighth,
        311
    in Capricorn, 83; in Virgo, 44, 182
    interaspects, 267, 319
    in first house, 43, 58, 214, 240;
        second, 59; third, 60, 280; fourth,
        299, 332; fourth/tenth, 275; fifth,
        60, 265; sixth, 181, 185, 192;
        seventh, 61, 305; eighth, 209, 310;
        ninth, 214; eleventh, 63; twelfth,
        69
    in Sagittarius, 40; in Pisces, 40; in
        Cancer, 41, 195; in Scorpio, 41
Schizophrenia, 211
Scoliosis, 193
Scorpio Ascendant, 43
Scorpio South Node, 43, 290
Scorpio intercepted in sixth, 21
Self, 17
Semi-sextiles, 81
Seventh House, 296ff.
Sextiles, 78
Sexual malfunctioning, 199–201
Shadow, the, 241
Sheldrake, Rupert, 29
Sibling karma, 59, 278
Sins of omission, 35, 213–15
Sixth house, planets in, 184–99
Skynner, Robin, 241
Split charts, 211
Soulmates, 122, 130
Squares: Fixed, 76; Cardinal and
    Mutable, 76
St Augustine, 18
St Gregory, 18
Stillbirth and suicide, 226–35
Sufis, 206

Sunrise charts, 38
Sun, 135, 265;
    and Moon in same sign, 134, 332
    through the signs, 145–60
    Pluto/Mars, 24; conjunct Mars in
        Taurus, 181; conjunct Pluto
        twelfth, 65
    to MC in synastry, 316
    in first house, 58; second, 58; third,
        59, 278; fourth, 272; fourth/tenth,
        271; fifth, 60, 265; seventh, 266,
        296; tenth, 194; twelfth, 65
Synastry and karma, 314ff.
    Mars trine Saturn, 119; Mercury
        contacts, 119; Chiron conjunct
        Venus, 120; Jupiter conjunct
        Jupiter, 129

Thera, 48
Third house, 278
Times of birth, 38
Transits, 23
Trine, 33, 78
Tsar, 321

Unaspected Saturn, 118
Unaspected Venus in Aquarius, 51ff.
Uranus, 263
    in aspect to Sun, 81, 224; Moon, 204,
        341; Mercury, 24, 85; Venus, 133,
        191, 208, 220, 300; Mars, 47, 198;
        Nodes, 85, 86, 115; conjunct
        Ascendant, 70
    interaspects, 248, 268, 318
    in first house, 58, 243; second, 59;
        third, 53; fourth/tenth, 276; fifth,
        61; sixth, 61, 193; seventh, 273,
        285, 306; eighth, 208, 311, 341;
        eleventh, 63; twelfth, 70, 344

Venerable Bede, 21
Venus
    in aspect to Saturn, 43; conjunct
        South Node, 65; square Nodes, 117
    in first house, 58; second, 58; third,
        279; fourth/tenth, 274; fifth, 60;
        twelfth, 67
    in Sagittarius, 117; in Scorpio, 288; in
        Aquarius, 51

Will, 45, 68, 183
Will–love–power, 51